W9-BUO-647

THE
STRENGTHS PERSPECTIVE
IN
SOCIAL WORK
PRACTICE

THE STRENGTHS PERSPECTIVE IN SOCIAL WORK PRACTICE

Edited by:

DENNIS SALEEBEY
University of Kansas

Longman

New York & London

Copyright © 1992 by Longman Publishing Group.
All rights reserved.
No part of this publication may be reproduced,
stored in a retrieval system, or transmitted
in any form or by any means, electronic, mechanical,
photocopying, recording, or otherwise,
without the prior permission of the publisher.

Longman, 95 Church Street, White Plains, N.Y. 10601

Associated companies:
Longman Group Ltd., London
Longman Cheshire Pty., Melbourne
Longman Paul Pty., Auckland
Copp Clark Pitman, Toronto

Senior editor: David Estrin
Development editor: Virginia Blanford
Production editor: Dee Josephson and New Day Production Company
Cover design: Anthony Alberts
Text art: Circa 86, Inc.
Production supervisor: Richard Bretan

Library of Congress Cataloging in Publication Data

The Strengths perspective in social work practice/edited by Dennis
    Saleebey.
        p.   cm.
    Includes bibliographical references.
    ISBN 0-8013-0549-7
        1. Social service—United States—Psychological aspects—
Congresses.   I. Saleebey, Dennis.
HV41.S827 1991
361.3′2′0973—dc20   91-14056
                                                                CIP

1 2 3 4 5 6 7 8 9 10-MA-9594939291

DEDICATION

To my parents, and to my children who have, in their individual ways, exemplified strength and resourcefulness, and especially to Ann whose entrance into my life renewed my belief in the restorative powers of love.

In memoriam: Bette A. Saleebey

"Keep away from people who try to belittle your ambitions. Small people always do that, but the really great make you feel that you, too, can become great."
—Mark Twain

Contents

List of Figures and Tables

Foreword

I first learned about the strengths perspective in the mid-1970s when Robert Scott, PhD, from Hershey, Pennsylvania, was hired to train the professional staff of a Kansas state psychiatric hospital in goal setting. We were headed for major problems with the Joint Commission for the Accreditation of Hospitals if we did not quickly master the art of converting our psychodynamic formulations into measurable treatment goals and objectives.

Unfortunately, this task was not as simple as it might seem, for it is difficult to transform psychodynamic principles into goals. We had to view clients differently if we were to write goals that would meet JCAH standards for treatment plans. Dr. Scott presented the how-to's of a strengths assessment that lent itself nicely to measurable goals. While I'm sure Dr. Scott was aware that the strengths perspective represented a radical departure from traditional approaches, we were not. Our staff accorded this novel approach mixed reviews; among the more enthusiastic was our team psychologist and myself, the team social worker.

Following the training, the next client to be staffed grimly entered the room in which our team was assembled. Being a veteran inpatient, he appeared to have steeled himself for the traditional recitation of his problems and treatment plans designed to correct them. When he received, instead, a lengthy listing of all the positive characteristics, interests, ambitions, aspirations, and abilities that he possessed and a treatment plan built on putting these strengths to use, the expression that we characteristically read as apathetic, resistant, or amotivational disappeared, and was replaced by something resembling excitement. Since excitement was a rare commodity among the client population, the staff got excited, too.

In the ensuing months, we diligently experimented with the strengths approach. Jack, a lovable guy with more hospitalizations than anyone could count, wanted to work but had no job skills. He was quite adept at group therapy, however, having had more experience than even the clinical staff. In fact, he was wonderful at supporting other clients, helping to assuage their anxiety. With a lot of help he ultimately landed a job as a work crew supervisor in a vocational training program for people with psychiatric disabilities. There he spent his days helping people through their anxiety and symptoms so that they could accomplish their tasks. He stopped using the hospital. When that program lost its funding, he went on to a different job and eventually got married.

And there was Jeff, who, at 19, was on his fifth involuntary hospitalization. In spite of treatment, Jeff's symptoms evidenced a severe departure from reality such that he was shunned by other clients and frustrated the staff enormously. The only thing Jeff wanted to do in life was invent an "energy bed" so that he would not feel so lethargic. He spent his days writing formulas that made sense only to him. With a lot of fancy talking and promises on the part of staff, Jeff was accepted into an electronics training program. He completed the program although he often could not hear or see the teacher because of his hallucinations. During this process, he gradually gave up the "energy bed," his other delusions, and the state hospital. He went to work, built friendships, and lived independently. Now 33, he continues to work part-time and live in his own apartment where he often entertains his friends.

For both Jack and Jeff, we first represented just one more treatment team in a long list that had failed to be of much assistance to either. I believe that they, as well as many others, were able to escape the trap of chronic symptoms and treatment and move on to more satisfying lives because we stumbled upon a different way of helping them.

Within months, I had become a strengths perspective zealot. Wanting to experiment further, I introduced this concept in a class I was teaching. One student was managing a substantial day program for the elderly. It was by reputation a humane program of good quality offering structured time, socialization opportunities, and mental stimulation, among other things. In response to an assignment, the student surveyed the elderly clients and was astonished by the wide range of talents and experience that existed among them. Equally surprising was that most of the clients placed a high priority on feeling that they were contributing to each other and the community as a whole. The program was restructured. Many games, hobbies, and social events were replaced by community service and education activities and opportunities for clients to help one another more. Attendance and level of involvement increased for program participants. Clients and staff reported high levels of satisfaction with the program.

I don't know how a strengths perspective works, I only know that it does. I believe that a focus on enhancing strengths provides the opportunity for success defined in very personal terms. Perhaps it also assists the individual in developing the confidence to pursue success. Problems that act as obstacles to meaningful pursuit sometimes spontaneously disappear, or at least come to have relevance to the client who is expected to solve them.

It is very exciting to see that others are investigating a strengths approach and coming to similar conclusions.

Ronna Chamberlain, MSW, PhD
Director of Community Support Services
Johnson County, Kansas Mental Health Center

Preface

Interest in the strengths orientation at the School of Social Welfare, University of Kansas has emerged as several community-based research/service/education projects in mental health have unfolded. To the participants in those projects, who were working with people with long-term mental illness and youth with emotional disabilities, it seemed increasingly clear that one avenue out of the morass of services and institutions for clients was for them to learn to appreciate and develop their own capacities, talents, skills, and interests, and to give voice to their needs. The early success of this approach encouraged those who ran the projects to begin to look around the country for people who had similar interests.

This text represents the work of some of those individuals—from the University of Kansas and from other institutions. The following people contributed to this book:

Howard Goldstein, DSW, is Professor Emeritus at the Mandell School of Applied Social Science, Case Western Reserve University. Professor Goldstein now lives in Maine and continues a most distinguished career as a scholar, educator, and practitioner. In 1991, he won the Richard Lodge Memorial Prize given to outstanding social work scholars.

Eloise Rathbone-McCuan, PhD, formerly of the University of Vermont, is now a Research Associate at the Veterans Administration Medical Center in Topeka and an adjunct faculty member at the University of Kansas. Professor Rathbone-McCuan has an international reputation for her research and writing in various areas of gerontology.

Julian Rappaport, PhD, is Professor of Psychology at the University of Illinois at Urbana. He is the author of several books and a nationally recognized expert in the field of community psychology, where his focus has been on the empowerment of vulnerable populations.

Charles Cowger, PhD, is Associate Professor at the School of Social Work, University of Illinois at Urbana-Champaign. He has written several articles on the role and direction of social work research and has an abiding interest in developing alternatives to social control models of social work practice and research.

Mary Bricker-Jenkins, DSW, is Associate Professor at the University of Western Kentucky, Department of Social Work and Women's Studies Program, and has devoted much of her practice and research to conceptualizing a feminist model of social work practice, as well as developing a competency-based model of practice for individuals who receive public welfare benefits.

William Patrick Sullivan, PhD, is Assistant Professor of Social Work at Southwest Missouri State University. Professor Sullivan has devoted much of his practice, research, and writing to the development of empowering case management programs for persons with long-term mental illness.

John Ronnau, PhD, is Assistant Professor of Social Work at New Mexico State University, Las Cruces. Professor Ronnau has considerable practical experience and has been actively involved in several research projects aimed at empowering youth with emotional disabilities and their families.

Ann Weick, PhD, is Dean and Professor at the School of Social Welfare, University of Kansas. She is well-known and highly regarded for her work in reexamining and reconceptualizing traditional notions of practice and inquiry in the helping professions. Much of her work is focused on developing more generative and transforming conceptions of helping so that individuals' inner and outer regenerative and healing resources are tapped.

Charles A. Rapp, PhD, is Associate Dean and Professor at the School of Social Welfare, University of Kansas. He has worked to develop programs for people with chronic mental illness that are innovative in both conceptualization and practice. Research and training emanating from these programs has fortified the strengths perspective. The National Alliance for the Mentally Ill honored Professor Rapp and his coworkers in 1988 with the "Exemplary Program Award."

John Poertner, DSW, is Professor at the School of Social Welfare, University of Kansas. His research and writing in the field of child welfare and in the client-centered approach to administration (with Charles Rapp) has brought him national acclaim. Professor Poertner has directed a number of research projects—with youth with emotional disabilities, with caregivers, and about child welfare issues—and his writing evidences his abiding interest in these populations and the development of the strengths perspectives.

Dennis Saleebey, DSW, is Professor and Chair of the PhD program in Social Welfare at the University of Kansas. Much of his writing has critiqued conventional social work wisdom and explored alternative approaches to knowledge-building, inquiry, and practice.

Walter Kisthardt is a PhD candidate at the University of Kansas School of Social Welfare, and is nationally known among mental health professionals for his training and development of educational materials for case management based on a strengths perspective.

Gary E. Holmes, MLS, MS, teaches at Emporia State University in Kansas. Mr. Holmes has been a prolific writer in the field of vocational rehabilitation. Central to much of his writing is the conviction that we must capitalize on the inherent powers possessed by those who have a disability (or who are differently abled) if we are ever to develop effective rehabilitation programs.

Chapter 7 was co-written by Julian Rappaport and two colleagues, Thomas M.

Reischl and Marc A. Zimmerman. **Dr. Reischl** is an Assistant Professor in the Psychology Department at Michigan State University, and **Dr. Zimmerman** is Assistant Professor in the School of Public Health, Department of Health Behavior and Health Education, at the University of Michigan.

PLAN OF THE BOOK

The book is divided into three sections. Part I, The Philosophy of the Strengths Perspective, introduces readers to the underlying philosophical principles, as well as the basic vocabulary, of the strengths perspective, Dennis Saleebey critiques the disease model of social work and outlines the strengths perspective. Ann Weick and Howard Goldstein explore the roots of the two perspectives, lay out the unique philosophical commitments and appreciations of the strengths perspective, and introduce elements of the strengths lexicon. Chapters 2 and 3 emphasize how clients are viewed differently in the two perspectives.

In Part II, Practice Ideology, Principles, and Methods in the Strengths Perspective, the chapters begin to articulate the shapes and contours of social work practice guided by the twin commitments to building on client strengths and empowering client groups. Charles Rapp, a leader in conceptualizing and applying the strengths perspective in work with the persistently mentally ill, opens this section laying out, with precision and direction, the principles gleaned from nine years of research and practice with a strengths orientation, as well as some durable insights on the effects (and effectiveness) of the approach. Walter Kisthardt presents a small compendium of principles and methods employed in the strengths approach to case management with persons with long-term mental illness. His discussion is lavish with anecdotes about the approach from his own experience and that of other case managers. Julian Rappaport, Thomas Reischl, and Marc Zimmerman describe a successful mutual help program (GROW), and from that develop a set of principles that enhance the empowerment mechanisms inherent in such groups. Each of the principles is illustrated with the stories of individuals struggling with a variety of personal and interpersonal problems and possibilities. Eloise Rathbone-McCuan focuses her attention on a group that is typically thought of in terms of deficits and problems, the elderly, especially those older persons who *seem* unable to care for themselves. Like individuals in other categories of "official" pathological conditions, these individuals show an amazing capacity to care for themselves if some basic principles, developed by Rathbone-McCuan, are honored. At the other end of the developmental continuum, John Poertner and John Ronnau challenge the conventional wisdom that has accumulated around the diagnosis and treatment of youth with emotional disorders. Employing a disability/strengths orientation, Poertner and Ronnau demonstrate that loyalty to such a perspective can overcome many of the self-limiting and client-defeating principles of other approaches to practice with these youth. Finally, Mary Bricker-Jenkins provides a detailed critique of the competency-based approach to practice in public welfare and demonstrates how a strengths approach is more essential and effective. We hope that after reading these chapters, as a practitioner or student, you will have a strong sense of the ideas, principles, and methods that might flow from this practice orientation.

Part III, The Strengths Approach to Assessment and Research, begins with an exploration by Charles Cowger of an instrument he has developed for assessing client strengths, individual and social, as well as for gaining an understanding of barriers to the realization of clients' strengths and resources. Pat Sullivan's chapter is intended to be a guide for those who would also like to find sources of strength, support, and growth in the environment. Rejecting the idea of the environment as either toxic or sorely limited, Sullivan presents the case for any environment as a complex ecology of resources. Gary Holmes lays out an argument that our understanding of research is necessarily going to have to change if we come to embrace the strengths perspective in the helping professions. Research we do under a strengths aegis will be compatible with the values of the social work profession, will be compelled to empower those whom we study who can only be understood as stakeholders and collaborators in our research, will probably employ more qualitative, participative methodologies, and will probably develop a language that is founded on phenomenological conceptions of inter-subjectivity. In conclusion, Dennis Saleebey attempts to draw out some of the persistent themes in all of these chapters, as well as answer some of the questions that inevitably arise from practitioners who learn of the strengths perspective for the first time.

SOME PREFATORY DIRECTIONS AND CAUTIONS

Most of the chapters in this book begin with a critique of what the author(s) consider the traditional wisdom in a given field of practice. While they might seem repetitive, we think it is important to mount the critique from as many angles as we can because most practitioners have been weaned on the conventional wisdom. We also believe that critique provides reasons for people to change their minds about the world of concern to them.

Although many of the chapters are directed toward the field of mental health, the authors are convinced these ideas transcend fields of practice and are generalizable. The work of Bricker-Jenkins and Rathbone-McCuan in different arenas of practice are meant to illustrate the transferability of some of these ideas and methods.

A major difference among the authors, and one that has been left for the reader to see, is the role and relevance of the more traditional pathology or problem-focused models. This is an extremely important issue, one that will probably be decided by each individual practitioner. The range of opinions herein extends from the idea that we would be best served by ignoring the language, methods, and social uses of the older model to the proposition that we would do well to regard the disease (problem, deficit, disorder) as one part, but certainly not the most important part, of the individual's makeup, and although attending to it as we must (e.g., monitoring medication), throw the bulk of our efforts into constructing an enduring edifice of resources, interests, and strengths.

At the very least, the contributors hope that this volume provokes a serious discussion about the assumptions and directions of more conventional models of practice, and a consideration of others' ways of imagining about, and thinking through, the kind of work that we do, work that historically and morally begins with a belief in the dignity and possibility of every human being.

ACKNOWLEDGMENTS

The most obvious declaration of appreciation goes to the authors who have contributed to this book. I have learned from each of them, and benefited from their advice and continuing discourse about the nature of the strengths perspective. All of the authors not only preach the virtues of the strengths orientation, but, as practitioners, demonstrate their fealty to empowerment in their day-to-day contacts with clients and students.

I suppose I have always, at some level of consciousness, believed that most individuals have powers within them, some of which are beyond their own awareness, but it wasn't until I joined the faculty at the School of Social Welfare at the University of Kansas that the possibilities and realities and shape of such a notion came to life. Ann Weick and Charles Rapp, in particular, gave the idea resonance philosophically and practically, and made its importance and its promise clear. John Poertner and a host of doctoral students including, among others, Pat Sullivan, John Ronnau, Chris Petr (all are now faculty members at various universities), and Wally Kisthardt extended the idea and exemplified it in their approach to clients and students. The major lesson I think I learned, and it was welcome, was that idealistic conceptions do not have to be inane, and can be forged into real programs and practices.

Finally, I want to thank Marian Abegg for her help in getting the manuscript together, an extremely complex task. Marian's skills, her keen eye, and her unfailing good humor, however, made the job much easier. David Estrin at Longman and his assistant, Victoria Mifsud, made the doing of this book rewarding. Their enthusiasm for the project and their steady support have been appreciated by the author.

I have taken, at various places, some editorial liberties for which I accept full responsibility. But, in the end, the quality and usefulness of this book comes directly from the contributors.

PART I

The Philosophy of the Strengths Perspective

CHAPTER 1

Introduction:
Power in the People

Dennis Saleebey

The idea of building on clients' strengths has achieved the status of adage in the lore of professional social work. Authors of textbooks, social work educators, and practitioners all acknowledge the importance of this principle (Hepworth and Larsen, 1990; Compton and Galaway, 1989). In truth, however, most such nods to building on strengths are little more than lip service; the idea of centering practice on eliciting and articulating clients' internal and external resources has not been reasonably explicated as either an idea or a practice. Social work, like so many other helping professions, has constructed much of its theory and practice around the supposition that clients become clients because they have deficits, problems, pathologies, and diseases; that they are, in some critical way, flawed or weak. This orientation is rooted in a past where certainties and conceptions about the moral defects of the poor, the despised, and the deviant held thrall. More sophisticated terms prevail today, but the metaphors and narratives that guide our thinking about our clients are essentially negative constructions that are fateful for their future. The diction and symbolism of weakness or deficit shape how others regard clients, how clients regard themselves, and how resources are allocated to groups of clients; in the extreme, they may lead to punitive sanctions.

The language of pathology and deficit gives voice to particular assumptions and leads to certain ends.

The person *is* the problem or pathology named. Diagnostic labels of all kinds tend to become "master statuses" (Becker, 1963), designations and roles that subsume all others under their mantle. A person suffering from schizophrenia becomes a "schizophrenic," an appellation that obscures or displaces other, perhaps more important, facets of the person's character, experiences, knowledge, and aspirations. Inevitably, discourse about the individual becomes dominated by the imagery of disease, ineptitude, and failure, and relationships form or re-form around such interchanges. To the extent

Copyright ©1992 by Longman Publishing Group.

that the status takes hold, the individual, through a process of surrender, transforms the self to conform to the once alien designation (Scheff, 1984; Goffman, 1961).

The problem/deficit orientation speaks with the compelling voice of "base rhetoric," a way of persuasively referring to individuals that debases, belittles, or discounts them. Thomas Szasz (1978), citing the work of R. M. Weaver, suggests that a base rhetorician is an individual who, regardless of appearance, is "always trying to keep individuals from the support which personal courage, noble associations, and divine philosophy provide a man [sic]" (p. 20). There is nothing that a practitioner of base rhetoric fears more than a genuine dialogue that begins on an egalitarian plane and extends from that point. Noble rhetoric, on the other hand, persuades individuals that they have the tools to be their own masters, weakens their need and inclination to depend on the evaluations of authority, and salvages self-esteem (Szasz, 1978). Much of the language and the discourse in the helping professions does not ennoble, or is unremittingly base.

Accentuating the problems of clients creates, in a variety of subtle as well as ham-handed ways, a web of negative expectations about the client, the client's environment, and the client's capacity to deal with the demands of that environment (Rosenhan, 1973; Scheff, 1984). Whatever else their impact (socially and politically, for example), these pejorative expectations, repeated over time, have the insidious capacity to alter the way individuals see themselves and how others see them, and in the long run shape patterns of behavior and relationship. As Norman Cousins (1989) suggests, people *do* ride the wave of their expectations. Paulo Freire (1973) has maintained for many years that the views and expectations of oppressors have an uncanny and implacable impact on the oppressed, so that oppressed individuals and groups come to live and rationalize these tainted designations, subjugating their own knowledge and understanding to those of the oppressors (Foucault, 1980).

Given the above, it could not be otherwise that the relationship between helper and client is almost always going to be marked by distance, power inequality, control, and manipulation. Goldstein argues (see chapter 3) that the "posture of detached objectivity required to construct a 'case history' and diagnose another person's condition poses the risk of creating an aura of separateness. Such an approach becomes even more elitist should I intimate that I have the special knowledge of the professional, which grants me the authority to define your problems and, out of this definition, determine the plan that should produce the desired results." The surest route, then, to detachment is the building of a "case," a process supposedly requiring not only expertise but objectivity. And the language of case construction, be it DSM-IIIR or the penal code, is thoroughly negative. Furthermore, the legal and political mandates of many agencies, the elements of social control embodied in both the institution and ethos of the agency, may strike a further blow to the possibility of partnership and collaboration between client and helper. The search for professional respectability, a drive within the profession since Abraham Flexner scolded the profession in 1915, drives the profession further down the path of what Donald Schön (1983) designates as "Technical/Rationality"; a conception of professional thinking and doing smitten with the notion of professional as applied technologist (or technical expert) and of client as naive and passive recipient of professional technique and ministration.

Problem-based assessments encourage individualistic rather than ecological (social, political, and cultural, as well as individual) accounts of human predicaments and possibilities. Curiously, such a focus does not genuinely individualize since, as indicated above, the purpose of the assessment is to find an appropriate diagnostic niche for the individual, thus transforming the client into a "case"—one among many. Such a categorical imperative operates by selectively destroying or ignoring information that, although not salient to the assessment scheme, might reveal to us the abiding uniqueness of the individual in this particular context. We amass a variety of pointed and relevant data so that we can safely categorize the individual as "Bipolar II," ADHD— findings that may ultimately deface she who sits across from us.

The active seeking of a problem or disease (so clearly based on the assumptions and predilections of medicine) proceeds, in part, from the assertion that there exists in the world a concrete, definable, and, hopefully, available solution to "this particular problem." Naming the poison leads us to the antidote. But in the world of human activity, human nature, and the human condition, such linear thinking ignores the steamy morass of uncertainty and complexity that typify human affairs.

> In the varied topography of professional practice, there is a high hard ground where practitioners can make effective use of research-based theory and technique, and there is a swampy lowland where situations are confusing "messes" incapable of technical solution. The difficulty is that the problems of the high ground, however great their technical interest, are often relatively unimportant to clients or to the larger society, while in the swamp are the problems of greatest concern (Schön, 1983, p. 42).

Remedies in the "lowland" usually begin with reinterpretations, resettings of the problem that emerge out of continuing dialogue with the situation and client. They are mutually crafted constructs that may only be good for this client, at this time, under these conditions. They are tentative (though they may have considerable power to transform clients' understandings, choices, and actions) and provisional. The capacity to "frame" such responses depends, not on a strict relationship between problem and solution that is known by the professional, but on intuition, tacit knowing, hunches, and conceptual risk-taking (Saleebey, 1989). Schön (1983) has characterized the tension between the usual conception of professional knowing and doing and the more "reflective" one as that between rigor and relevance. Relevance does not simply refer to society's investment in, or concern about, the problem, but to the individual client's investment as well. To what extent are clients consulted about matters relevant to them? What do they want? What do they need? How do they think they can get it? How do they see their situation—its troubles as well as its possibilities? What do they see as resources from within and in the environment? What values do they want to maximize? How have they managed to survive so far? These and similar questions, as they are answered, allow us to move toward a relevant appreciation of the client's unique attributes, abilities, and knowledge.

THE STRENGTHS PERSPECTIVE: A PREVIEW

The obsession with problems, pathologies, and defects, while productive of an impressive lode of technical and theoretical writing, may be less productive when it comes to actually helping clients grow, develop, change directions, or revise their personal meanings, accounts, and narratives. While the strengths perspective, at this point, is nascent and has conceptual gaps and practical uncertainties, it is founded on a clearly different set of prerequisites and assumptions.

Respecting Client Strengths

Social work practice is guided first *and* foremost by a profound awareness of, and respect for, clients' positive attributes and abilities, talents and resources, desires and aspirations. Furthermore, the practitioner must be genuinely interested in, and respectful of, clients' accounts and narratives, the interpretive slants they take on their own lives. These are the most important "theories" that guide practice (Goldstein, 1986). The discovery of who clients are does not unfold as the result of a litany of troubles, snares, embarrassments, lacks, and barriers. The client is best known as someone who knows something, who has learned lessons from experience, who has ideas, who has energies of all kinds, and who can do some things quite well. These may be immanent as the client begins the process of transformation or regeneration, and may be obscured or suppressed by the stresses and confusions of the moment.

Clients want to know if you actually care about them, that how they do makes a real difference to you, that you will listen to them, that you will respect them no matter what their history, that you believe that they can build something of value on the resources they have within and around them, and that you believe they can surmount the assault on their functioning (Cousins, 1989).

Clients Have Many Strengths

Individuals and groups have vast, often untapped and frequently unappreciated reservoirs of physical, emotional, cognitive, interpersonal, social, and spiritual energies, resources, and competencies. These are invaluable in constructing the possibility of change, transformation, and hope. It is clear that individuals sometimes do not define some of their attributes or experiences as resources. It is likewise true that individuals sometimes are unaware of some of their own strengths, that some of their knowledge, talents, and experience can be used in the service of recovery and development—their own and that of others (Saleebey and Larson, 1980; Weick et al., 1989).

Client Motivation Is Based on Fostering Client Strengths

Individuals and groups are more likely to continue autonomous development and growth when it is funded by the coin of their capacities, knowledge, and skills. There may be many reasons for that, but some theories of motivation offer some suggestive ideas about why this is so. McClelland (1987), after decades of research on achievement, affiliative, and power needs—motivational domains—argues that for any increase in these motives to occur the individual has to be assured that they are grounded in the daily reality of life and her system of meanings (and values). If such a connection is perceived by the individual, then the network of imagery, language, emotion, and goals that make up each of these domains persists and grows without much external prodding or reinforcement. Similarly, Alderfer (1969), revising the work of Maslow, has demonstrated that once an individual's needs for survival and relationship have been reasonably secured, then growth needs become prepotent; these needs are almost always pursued autonomously. The strengths perspective is powered by a similar faith: you can build little of lasting value on pathology and problem, but you may build an enduring edifice out of strength and possibility inherent in each individual.

The Social Worker Is a Collaborator with the Client

The role of "expert" or "professional" may not provide the best vantage point from which to appreciate client strengths. A helper may be best defined as collaborator or consultant; an individual presumed because of some specialized education, training, and experience to know some things, but definitely not the only one in the situation to have relevant, important, even esoteric knowledge. Clients are usually the experts on their own situation (see chapter 10) and we make a serious mistake when we subjugate their knowledge to official views. There is something liberating about genuinely connecting with clients and their hopes, fears, stories; much more liberating, perhaps, than trying to stuff them into the narrow confines of a diagnosis or assessment category. As we have said, to appreciate the strengths of the individual is to begin to understand the uniqueness of that individual.

Avoiding the Victim Mindset

Emphasizing and orienting the work of helping around clients' strengths can help to avoid "blaming the victim" (Ryan, 1976). Victim blaming assumes many guises, but the "art of savage discovery" is its enduring face and is supported by an unwavering, destructive logic: discover a social problem; set about (as researcher or practitioner, agency or academy) to determine how those who suffer from the problem differ from those who do not; and then demonstrate how these differences actually cause or perpetuate the problem (Ryan, 1976). Ultimately, we find the problem within the individual and ignore two critical factors: how elements of the environment eventually pervade individual identity and energy, and how the individual has managed to survive, perhaps thrive in, an oppressive, even catastrophic environment. In the strengths orientation we want to understand as best we can the first factor, but our work with the client begins with an appreciation and investigation of the second.

Any Environment Is Full of Resources

No matter how a harsh environment tests the mettle of inhabitants, it can also be understood as a lush topography of resources and possibilities. This seems to run counter to conventional social work wisdom (and public policy). However, in every environment there are individuals and institutions who have something to give, something that others may desperately need: knowledge, succor, an actual resource, or simply time and place. Usually these individuals and institutions exist outside the usual panoply of social and public services. And for the most part, they are untapped and unsolicited (Saleebey and Larson, 1980; also see chapter 12). Such a view of the environment does not abrogate the responsibility for working, as citizens and social workers, toward social justice, but recognizes that while we await the Godot of political transformation, there are reservoirs of energy, ideas, and tools out there we can draw on. To regard the environment as persistently and totally inimical moves us to ignore these resources or mistakenly to regard them as disreputable.

Key Concepts in the Strengths Perspective

The strengths perspective rests upon a core of ideas and themes that will be pressed throughout this volume: empowerment, membership, regeneration, synergy, dialogue, and suspension of disbelief.

Empowerment.   In danger of becoming a buzz word, the reality behind the necessity for an empowering agenda in practice and politics has probably never been so urgent. "To be committed to an empowerment agenda," suggests Julian Rappaport (1990), "is to be committed to identify, facilitate, or create contexts in which heretofore silent and isolated people, those who are 'outsiders' in various settings, organizations, and communities gain understanding, voice and influence over decisions that affect their lives." Inevitably, the need for empowerment is often critical in those vulnerable and excluded populations we serve. However, the empowerment agenda is not based on returning power to the people, but on discovering the power within the people (individually and collectively). To discover that power, we must subvert and abjure pejorative labels; provide opportunities for connection to family, institution, and community; assail the victim mindset; forswear paternalism (even in its most benign guises); and trust people's intuitions, accounts, perspectives, and energies. Empowerment is aimed not only at reducing the sense and reality of individual and community powerlessness, but also at helping people discover the considerable power within themselves, their families, and their neighborhoods.

Pursuing an empowerment agenda requires a deep belief in the necessity of democracy and the contingent capacity of people to participate in the decisions and actions that define their world. The antithesis of empowerment, argues Carolyn Swift (1984), is paternalism. Regrettably, the helping professions, with admirable intent and sometimes beneficent impact, have proceeded, under a variety of banners, to tell people (and communities) what is good for them and to make sure that they "do the right thing." The empowerment or strengths program requires a different attitude and set of commitments. Rappaport (1981) says it well:

> On the one hand it (the empowerment agenda) demands that we look to many diverse settings where people are already handling their own problems in living, in order to learn more about how they do it. . . . On the other hand, it demands that we find ways to take what we learn from these diverse settings and solutions and make it more public, so as to help foster social policies and programs and make it more rather than less likely that others not now handling their own problems in living or shut out from current solutions, gain control over their lives (p. 15).

The fact is that the strengths of individuals and communities are renewable and expandable resources; as they are used they fuel and power other resources and opportunities

(Katz, 1984). It is likewise the case that strengths and power, even those of the individual, almost always lie embedded in a community of interest and involvement. Western stereotypes notwithstanding, an individual rarely discovers and employs strengths and gains a perceived sense of power in isolation. That is why the ideas of community (or neighborhood) and membership are central to our emerging perspective.

Membership.   Michael Walzer (1983) instructs that a communal place and identity is an absolute requisite for the realization of distributive justice. Individuals without membership (who are perceived as strangers or, in fact, have been torn from their natural and geographical roots) are extraordinarily vulnerable. To be without membership, Walzer writes, is a "condition of infinite danger" (p. 32). The strengths orientation proceeds from a profound recognition that all of those whom we serve are, like ourselves, members of a species, entitled to the dignity, respect, and responsibility that comes with such membership. However, in more specific terms, those who seek our help are often alienated in reality, or in spirit, with either no place to be (or be comfortable) or no sense of belonging. Once individuals become estranged (or are thought of as strangers) the circumscription of their rights and their access to resources often becomes legitimized. The loss or absence of membership makes the discovery or restoration of strengths, the empowerment program, more difficult. So, as helpers, certain things are required of us at the outset:

- Instigating a collaborative (mutual, consultative) stance
- Helping give voice to, and acknowledging the authenticity of the individual's story, values, and beliefs
- Recognizing the individual's efforts and successes in surviving despite rootlessness
- Giving attention and making links to possible communities of interest where the individual's strengths are respected and can begin to flourish

The sigh of relief of those who come to understand their membership and its attendant rights and responsibilities and securities, to those who have experienced it, is unmistakable—the first breath of empowerment.

Regeneration and Healing from Within.   Disease and pathology are realities, but not the only ones, nor even the most important ones. In fact, their presence may not even be a definitive statement of the wellness of the individual. Likewise, understanding disease does not necessarily mean understanding the individual. Finally, the deficit and disease model of helping, as we have suggested, is rife with assumptions and practices that may be inimical to the strengths and resources of clients or patients. Not the least of these practices is the "giving over" of one's self (mind, body, and spirit) to a caregiver in order to get well (Weick, 1983).

For this reason and others, Ivan Illich (1976) calls the professions "disabling." The professionalization of a variety of social tasks and transitions has left the laity unprepared to make sense out of their own suffering and pain, their own life transformations (often transformed under the deft hand of professionals into problems—death, birth, adolescence, old age), and their own resources (inner and outer) for healing. Yet there is a small, vocal band of rebels in medicine and related professions who are reclaiming and proclaiming the transformative powers of individuals which are often fueled by a caring community and rituals of connectedness and expiation (Dossey, 1989). Neuroscientists probing the curious and complex relationship between brain, mind, body, and social structure have provided some interesting and suggestive ideas about the nature of self-healing and the sense of being well. Michael Gazzaniga (1988) who, along with Roger Sperry, conducted the pioneering split-brain research, contends that the mind plays a powerful role in healing:

> The mental state of the patient affects brain states which in turn affect somatic response. Hope, positive mental attitude, and depression-free states of mind are all supposed to help tremendously in ridding the body of disease and the pain that accompanies disease and injury (p. 212).

Ornstein and Sobel (1987) characterize the brain as a health maintenance organization: modules of discrete neural pathways that function to maintain health without our conscious interposition. And the sense of wellness that we have is strongly related to the sense of meaning and comprehensibility that we have about life. The role of interpretation in health is probably hard to overestimate. Neither should we forget the fact that institutions play a powerful role in the availability of resources and the possibility of transformation: the relationship between structure and experience cannot be abrogated.

Norman Cousins' (1979) now-fabled recovery from a chronic degenerative collagen illness, ankylosing spondylitis, was attributed (by him) to his assuming control over his illness, his refusal to give in to pessimism, his determination to create a positive emotional atmosphere (prominently featuring laughter), and using his own experience and self-knowledge in developing a treatment regimen.

In his latest book, *Head First: The Biology of Hope,* Cousins (1989) chronicles the process and lists the findings of his ten-year odyssey at UCLA Medical Center searching for some of the keys to understanding how people respond positively and remarkably to serious, catastrophic, and often terminal illness, as well as improve the quality of life during the illness. While the neurohormonal and neurophysiological mechanisms are not well understood, the conditions of their activation seem to be the following:

> Positive expectations of recovery and transformation (all realistically defined within terms of the illness)
>
> A caring community
>
> Maintaining a sense of autonomy and control over the disease and recovery process
>
> Using humor, fun, laughter, and a sense of pleasure to trigger immune system responsiveness and fight stress

These findings are clearly preliminary, but they have dramatic implications. At the least, they challenge the assumption of the deficit model that experts know what's best for clients and that curing, healing, or transformation comes exclusively from outside sources. In like fashion, community development theorists (Kieffer, 1984) are now turning to the proposition that neighborhoods, for example, may have within them powers of transformation, powers that may be undercut or ignored by social institutions and public policies. It is to this phenomenon that we now turn our attention.

Synergy.   Richard Katz (1984) writes: "Resources created by *human activity and intentions,* such as helping and healing, are intrinsically expanding and renewable, and need not be [subsumed] under a scarcity paradigm" (p. 202).

The scarcity paradigm that Katz thinks dominates Western thought includes the idea that natural and human resources as well as power are in short supply, and the dominant act of public policy is distributing these limited resources, often inequitably. The synergistic perspective assumes that when phenomena (including people) are brought into interrelationship, they create new and often unexpected patterns and resources that typically exceed the complexity of their individual constituents. Furthermore, the definition of what constitutes a resource varies between the synergistic and scarcity paradigms, the latter being more restricted. Though we might quibble about the definition of community (and its consciousness of itself) in any given case, Katz (1984) and Freire (1973), using different language, argue that every community, no matter how seemingly in disarray, has the possibility of synergy. To realize such a possibility requires educating people, elevating their consciousness of local resources, extending control and autonomy to members of the community in matters that concern them, and developing concrete skills to enhance day-to-day living.

A synergistic community over time, and in varying degrees, will develop certain kinds of qualities, including a practical sense and accounting of actual generative (renewable and expandable) resources within the community, a sense that any individual or family is a part of the larger community, structures intended to ensure equitable sharing of resources, a greater interest in establishing stronger relationships with institutions outside the community; and a greater resistance to those agencies and groups regarded as noxious or hostile to community interests and health (Katz, 1984; Kieffer, 1984).

What constituencies actually make up a community, and to what extent there is even a beginning sense of community in a geographical area is problematic. But one might take a heuristic approach and begin by drawing the line between the system (community) and environment where it seems most useful and resonant with members' perceptions (Heineman-Pieper, 1989).

Dialogue and Collaboration.   Humans can only come into being through a creative and emergent relationship with the external world (with others). Without such a transaction there can be no discovery and testing of one's own powers, no knowledge, no heightening of one's awareness and internal strengths (Becker, 1968). Martin Buber (1955) wrote:

> Human life touches on absoluteness in virtue of its dialogical character, for in spite of his uniqueness man can never find, when he plunges to the depth of his life, a being that is whole in itself and as such touches on the absolute. Man can become whole not in virtue of a relationship to himself but only in virtue of a relationship to another self (pp. 167–168).

It is only in dialogue that we confirm the importance of the other; it is only in dialogue and subsequent confirmation that we begin to heal the rift between self, other, and institution. Ronald Laing (1971), in commenting on the importance of a nurse giving a cup of tea to a schizophrenic patient, put it this way:

> It is the simplest and most difficult thing in the world for *one person,* genuinely being his or her self, *to give* in fact and not just appearance, *another* person, realized in his or her own being by the giver, *a cup of tea,* really, and not in appearance (p. 106f).

Dialogue, argues Maurice Friedman (1985), includes empathy, identification with, and inclusion of the other person. Paulo Freire (1973) is convinced from his years of work with oppressed peoples that it is only in humble and loving dialogue with another that we can begin to surmount the barriers of distrust, paternalism, oppressor–oppressed dynamics, and rampant subjugation of the knowledge of the oppressed. His formula for dialogue, disarmingly simple, requires of us several things: "Founding itself upon love, humility, and faith, dialogue becomes a horizontal relationship of which mutual trust between the dialoguers is the logical consequence" (pp. 79–80).

A caring community, one in which synergy is possible, is a community that confirms otherness; giving each person a ground of his own, affirmed through encounters that are egalitarian and dedicated to healing and empowerment (Friedman, 1985).

The idea of collaboration has a more specific focus. When we collaborate with clients we become their agents, their consultants, stakeholders with them in whatever projects we undertake. This requires helpers to be open to negotiation, to appreciate the authenticity of the views and aspirations of those with whom they collaborate, and to be willing to subdue their own voices in the interest of bespeaking those of their clients (Rappaport, 1990). The "expert" role may have to be forsworn if one presumes to become collaborator. Weick et al. (1989) say this about starting a collaborative relationship:

> In making [a strengths] assessment, both client and the social worker seek to discover the individual and communal resources from which the client can draw in shaping an agenda. The question is not what kind of life has one had, but what kind of a life one wants, and then bringing to bear all the personal and social resources available to accomplish this goal (p. 353).

Suspension of Disbelief.   It would be hard to exaggerate the extent of disbelief of clients' words in the culture of professionalism. While social work, because of its enduring values, may fancy itself less culpable in this regard than other professions, a little circumspection is warranted. As just one example (and probably somewhat unfair because this is from a text on social work practice that generally assumes a positive view of clients), Hepworth and Larsen (1990) wrote:

> Though it is the primary source of information, verbal report is vulnerable to error because of possible faulty recall, distorted perceptions, biases, and limited self-awareness on the part of clients. It is thus vital to avoid the tendency to accept clients'

views, descriptions, and reports as valid representations of reality. Similarly, it is important to recognize that feelings expressed by clients may emanate from faulty perceptions or may be altogether irrational (p. 197).

Suspension of belief may have resulted from the suffusion of scientific thinking throughout our culture and into the professions. The ideal of the scientific investigator as objective and dispassionate observer has been transmuted into a certain skepticism about, and distancing from, clients as the professional practitioner becomes applied technologist. The rise of professions (and the ideology of professionalism) was part of the extension and reinforcement of the institutions of socialization and social control during the Victorian era, which seemed to require detachment and the reserving of confirmation of "clients' " views of their situation (Bledstein, 1978). Professionals typically reserve affirmation in a number of ways:

By imposing their theories over the theories, stories, and accounts of the client

By using in assessment an interrogative style (however benign) designed to assert certain diagnostic hypotheses (or one of several competing hypotheses), thus confirming their suspicions

By self-protective maneuvers (like skepticism) designed to prevent the embarrassment of being lied to, or fooled by, a "wily" client

To protect self-esteem, non-normative lifestyles, and/or self-interests, clients may have a vested interest in not telling the truth. But we must consider the possibility that avoiding truth may be a function of context and manner in which truth is sought, and may be a matter of whose truth is being sought. Rooney (1988) wrote an excellent exposition on the role of the reactance we inadvertently create in involuntary clients; one of the ways that clients may reduce the arousal of reactance (a reaction to implied or threatened loss of free behaviors) is to lie.

Proponents of the strengths perspective believe that the suspension of disbelief has far more advantages than the self-protective and sometimes defensive operations spurred by suspension of belief. At best, it encourages the emergence of the client's truth and interpretive slant far more often than it promotes dissimulation.

In summary, the conceptual core of the strengths perspective urges us toward a different attitude about our work and those with whom we work. In essence, the shift is away from professional work as the exertion of the power of knowledge and/or institution to professional work as collaborating with the power within the individual (or community) toward a life that is palpably better, and better in the client's own terms.

The Strengths Perspective in Social Work: A Brief Critique and Appreciation

Mary Richmond (1922) asserted, "Individuals have wills and purposes of their own, and are not fitted to play a passive part in the world" (p. 258). Bertha Capen Reynolds (1951) looked at the issue in terms of the workers' obligations (italics added):

> The real choice before us as social workers is whether *we* are to be passive or active. . . . Shall we be content to give with one hand and withhold with the other, to build up or tear down at the same time the strength of a person's life? Or shall we become conscious of our own part in making a profession which will stand forthrightly for human well-being, *including the right to be an active citizen*? (p. 175).

The historical tension between the need, on one hand to become more professional, to focus on "function" rather than "cause" (Lee, 1929), to elevate casework method and technique to a new respectability, and on the other hand, the interest in social action and the addressing of inequities, seems to have been resolved, to date, in favor of increasing professionalization, technical deftness, and individualization of problems. It is clear that the writing, perspective, and diction of activism and casework (or, now, clinical social work) are different, and maybe at odds. It is in this difference that we see the focus, anecdotally and tentatively, on client deficits override the language of resilience and the appreciation of the hardiness of those who suffer vulnerability, disease, and/or oppression.

There is no necessary or implacable conflict between the interests of social action and the concerns of social work practice, as Clark Chambers (1962) has argued. But as Bisno (1956) pointed out, the infusion of psychoanalytic thinking, the status anxiety of social workers, and the insistence on strengthening method and technique led to an inevitable individualizing of, and focus on, client problems. Since World War II— although the conflict has existed since the first stirrings of the social welfare profession (Chambers, 1962; Bisno, 1956; Bruno, 1957)—the tension between reformist impulses and the development of a professionally respectable body of theory and technique underlying the treatment of individuals and families has been resolved in favor of the latter. And the theories that define the arena of social work treatment are extruded from a philosophy of professional practice that emphasizes the assessment of, and intervention into, individual (or family) problems and dysfunctions. Despite sentiments (or perhaps, protests) to the contrary, it is not the resources and positive attributes of clients that draw our attention and define our efforts; rather, it is the pathologies that have become our obsession.

Today, social work practice texts, as we have said, typically give a nod to the idea of client strengths but little guidance to the student or worker about what the obligations and methods of such an orientation might be. Anthony Maluccio (1979) is one of the few social work educators and writers who gives more than lip service. In his study of the perceptions of workers and clients about the treatment process, outcome, and client functioning, he discovered that clients were much closer to the strengths orientation than their social workers.

> In general, clients presented themselves as *pro-active*, autonomous human beings who are able to enhance their functioning and competence through the use of counseling service along with the resources operant within themselves and their social networks. Workers, on the other hand, tended to view clients as *reactive* organisms with continuing problems, weakness, and limited potentialities (p. 399).

But even Maluccio assumes that, for the most part, competencies and skills have to be developed; for, were they extant, clients would not be stuck in their attempts to adapt to life tasks and life transitions.

The strengths perspective also seeks to develop abilities and capacities in clients. However, it assumes that clients already have a number of competencies and resources that may be used to improve their situation. Steve de Shazer, one of the developers of focused solution development, claims that, in almost every case (he usually sees families), individuals and families are already doing something about the situation and it is the obligation of the therapist to build on that, to collaborate with those efforts, extend them, maybe augment them. Ordinarily, the family has to make only a slight shift in what they are doing. An excerpt from the end of a first session with a family illustrates the orientation (de Shazer et al., 1986).

> We are impressed that, in spite of the many difficulties (in this case, much of the difficulty centered on the hostility and violent behaviors of one of the sons) you've told us about, there is success going on. The children are doing well in school and are not in trouble of any kind; the marriage has survived 15 difficult years; both father and mother's careers are going well. This means to us that you all are doing something awfully right, and we'd like to know more about this. Therefore, between now and next session, we'd like each of you, separately, to observe what happens in the family that you'd like to see continue to happen (p. 212).

The therapist, says de Shazer (1988), builds her interventions on what the clients are already doing that works. A side benefit of this approach is that the struggles between clients and therapist over power and resistance fade into the background.

Conclusion

This book of readings touches on a subject that has been part of social work lore (building on strengths) for decades, but that has rarely been extended and articulated in terms of philosophy, principle, and practice. This book is intended to be a start in that direction. The strengths perspective is not a model or a "paradigm" or a theory at this point. It is a collation of principles, ideas, and techniques, some of which are contradictory, others of which are still developing. But taken together, these provide enough nutriment for the practitioner interested in moving away from a deficit approach to one emphasizing the resources and resourcefulness of clients.

You will notice as you read that many of the chapters contain, in a variety of ways, critiques of the problem or disease approach. We believe that awareness of the elements and inherent dangers of the deficit model is an absolute prerequisite for beginning to embrace a different way of regarding clients and their environments. We also try to make it clear that any approach to practice is based on the interpretation of the experiences of practitioners and clients and is composed of assumptions, rhetoric, ethics, and a discipline. The importance and usefulness of any interpretation lies not in some independent measure of its truth, but in how well it serves us in our work with people, how it sustains our values, and how it generates opportunities for clients (and their environments) to change positively. We hope you will see that the strengths perspective may be prolific in generating such opportunities for workers and clients.

REFERENCES

Alderfer, C. P. (1969). An empirical test of a new theory of human needs. *Organizational Behavior and Human Performance, 4*, 142–175.

Becker, E. (1968). *The structure of evil*. New York: George Braziller.

Becker, H. (1963). *Outsiders: Studies in the sociology of deviance*. New York: Free Press.

Bisno, H. (1956). How social will social work be? *Social Work, 1*(2), 12–18.

Bledstein, B. (1978). *The culture of professionalism*. New York: W. W. Norton.

Bruno, F. J. (1957). *Trends in social work 1874–1956*. New York: Columbia University Press.

Buber, M. (1955). *Between man and man*. Boston: Beacon Press.

Chambers, C. A. (1962). An historical perspective on political action vs. individualized treatment. In *Current issues in social work seen in historical perspective* (pp. 51–64). New York: Council on Social Work Education.

Compton, B., and Galaway, B. (1989). *Social work processes* (4th ed.). Chicago: Dorsey Press.

Cousins, N. (1989). *Anatomy of an illness*. New York: W. W. Norton.

Cousins, N. (1989). *Head first: The biology of hope*. New York: E. P. Dutton.

de Shazer, S. (Summer, 1988). A requiem for power. *Contemporary Family Therapy, 10*, 69–76.

de Shazer, S., Berg, I. K., Lipchik, E., et al. (1986). Brief therapy: Focused solution development. *Family Process, 25*, 207–221.

Flexner, A. (1915). Is social work a profession? *Proceedings of the National Conference on Charities and Corrections* (pp. 576–590). Chicago.

Foucault, M. (1980). *Power/knowledge*. New York: Pantheon.

Friedman, M. (1985). *The healing dialogue in psychotherapy*. Northvale, NJ: Jason Aronson.

Freire, P. (1973). *Pedagogy of the oppressed*. New York: Seabury.

Gazzaniga, M. (1988). *Mind matters*. Boston: Houghton Mifflin.

Goffman, E. (1961). *Asylums: Essays on the situation of mental patients and other inmates*. Garden City, NY: Anchor/Doubleday.

Goldstein, H. (September/October, 1986). Toward the integration of theory and practice. *Social Work, 31*, 352–357.

Heineman-Pieper, M. (November, 1989). The heuristic paradigm: A unifying and comprehensive approach to social work research. *Smith College Studies in Social Work, 60*, 8–33.

Hepworth, D. H. and Larsen, J. (1990). *Direct social work practice: Theory and skills* (3rd ed.). Chicago: Dorsey Press.

Illich, I. (1976). *Medical nemesis: The expropriation of health*. New York: Pantheon.

Katz, R. (1984). Empowerment and synergy: Expanding the community's healing resources. In J. Rappaport, C. Swift, and R. Hess, eds., *Studies in empowerment: Steps toward understanding and action*. New York: Haworth Press.

Kieffer, C. H. (1984). Citizen empowerment: A developmental perspective. In J. Rappaport, C. Swift, and R. Hess, eds., *Studies in empowerment: Steps toward understanding and action*. New York: Haworth Press.

Laing, R. (1971). *Self and others*. New York: Penguin Books.

Lee, P. R. (1929). Social work: Cause and function. *Proceedings of the National Conference of Social Work*, pp. 3–20.

Maluccio, A. (1979). *Learning from clients: Interpersonal helping as viewed by clients and social workers*. New York: Free Press.

McClelland, D. (1987). *Human motivation*. Cambridge: Cambridge University Press.

Ornstein, R. and Sobel, D. (1987). *The healing brain*. New York: Touchstone/Simon and Schuster.

Rappaport, J. (1981). In praise of paradox: A social policy of empowerment over prevention. *American Journal of Community Psychology, 9*, 1–25.

Rappaport, J. (1990). Research methods and the empowerment agenda. In P. Tolan, C. Keys, F. Chertak, and L. Jason, eds., *Researching community psychology*. Washington, DC: American Psychological Association.

Reynolds, B. C. (1951). *Social work and social living: Explorations in philosophy and practice*. Silver Spring, MD: National Association of Social Workers.

Richmond, M. (1922). *What is social casework?* New York: Russell Sage Foundation.

Rooney, R. (March, 1988). Socialization strategies for involuntary clients. *Social Casework, 69*, 131–140.

Rosenhan, D. L. (January, 1973). On being sane in insane places. *Science, 179*, 250–258.

Ryan, W. (1976). *Blaming the victim* (revised). New York: Vintage Books.

Saleebey, D. (1989). Professions in crisis: The estrangement of knowing and doing. *Social Casework, 70*, 556–563.

Saleebey, D. and Larson, S. (1980). Resource development networks: Theory and practice. Unpublished manuscript. Fort Worth, TX: Bridge Association.

Scheff, T. J. (1984). *Being mentally ill: A sociological theory* (2nd ed.). New York: Aldine.

Schön, D. A. (1983). *The reflective practitioner*. New York: Basic Books.

Swift, C. (1984). Empowerment: An antidote for folly. In J. Rappaport, C. Swift, and R. Hess eds., *Studies in empowerment: Steps toward understanding and action*. New York: Haworth Press.

Szasz, T. (1978). *The myth of psychotherapy*. Garden City, NY: Anchor/Doubleday.

Walzer, M. (1983). *Spheres of justice*. New York: Basic Books.

Weick, A. (November–December, 1983). Issues in overturning a medical model of social work practice. *Social Work, 28*, 467–471.

Weick, A., Rapp, C., Sullivan, W. P., and Kisthardt, W. (July, 1989). A strengths perspective for social work practice. *Social Work, 37*, 350–354.

CHAPTER 2

Building a Strengths Perspective for Social Work

Ann Weick

Throughout the long history of humankind, there has been a theme occupying a persistent place in our collective attention. It takes many forms, from metaphysical categories of the nature of evil to a mundane concern with mistakes and errors in everyday actions. Whatever its expression, we see consistent evidence of a profound tilt toward the negative or shadow side of human life. Our preoccupation is so intense and so ingrained that it seems ill-advised to question its legitimacy. And yet, it is just such commonplace beliefs that merit full-scale scrutiny.

Because this chapter tends toward developing a perspective based on a different set of assumptions, a close examination of the predominant orientation toward what can be called a problem-solving model allows us to both understand and offer a critique. The argument will be made that a problem-solving model fails as a perspective for social work practice on both philosophic and practical grounds. Through a systematic examination of the limitations of this perspective, space is created for considering an alternate orientation, one based on the strengths and positive resources each person possesses.

HISTORICAL ROOTS

From an historical perspective, it is apparent that moral frailty has been a central concern of Judeo-Christian cultures. In the metaphoric renderings of the creation story, the "fall from grace" depicts the wayward impulses of our species and the unending drama of the struggle between good and evil. In discussing these religious underpinnings of American welfare institutions, Leiby (1978) underscores the pessimistic tone of the Protestant and Catholic creeds, which characterize life as "a vale of suffering and

Copyright ©1992 by Longman Publishing Group.

tears," where "frustration, pain, and ultimately death are inevitable" (p. 13). Human fallibility is a central belief in this construction of moral reality. Much of Christianity has been devoted to the need for a "miraculous transformation" (Randall, 1926, p. 48) of this fallibility.

Although the Christian struggle for redemption has laid a strong thematic base for the Western world view, contemporary life has also been shaped by a companion theme; namely, the possibility of secular redemption through the aid of reason. As Randall (1926) put it, the Copernican and Cartesian revolutions in the fifteenth and sixteenth centuries "broke the bonds of the medieval world. . . . Purposes gave way to mathematics, human will and foresight to immutable and inflexible mechanical order" (p. 227). Underlying the scientific method was a belief in reason as a "guarantee of truth" (Randall, 1926, p. 254) and the ability of enlightened people to explore the far reaches of the physical and social worlds through the method reason provided.

While the Age of Enlightenment signaled a new optimism about human progress, it also produced a crucial decentering. Unlike the integrated conception of the medieval world view, where human beings were linked to God and creation in a grand and purposeful design, the Copernican revolution and the ensuing scientific view made humans "puny, irrelevant spectator(s)" (Burtt, 1931, p. 236) in a mathematically designed universe. Rather than having a central place in their world, they were cut adrift and consigned to the role of observers of rather than participants in their own experience. The power of reason, as expressed in scientific method, gave humans a new sense of power and control, but the cost was alienation and a demoralizing skepticism.

To a large degree, social work has been influenced by contemporary scientific ideology. The connection has been indirectly but powerfully made. The first step was the assimilation of the "newly invented social sciences . . . to the physical sciences" (Randall, 1926, p. 255). Just as it was believed that the secrets of the physical world could be revealed through scientific investigation, so was it thought that human beings and their social world could be understood by the same method. As fledgling professions began to develop in the late nineteenth century, the lure of scientific practice began to take shape. In social work the rational, logical method espoused by Mary Richmond (1917) in *Social Diagnosis* was gradually embellished by the introduction of social science methodology that promised a more rigorous and predictable approach to social work practice.

The connection with both science and religion is essential for understanding social work's preoccupation with human problems and its longstanding orientation toward problem-solving. Social work, unlike many other professions, draws from both traditions in shaping its practice: Religious tradition has contributed to a sense of its moral failure, and scientific roots have created concerns about its technical insignificance. The different guises of the same message help to account for the profession's preoccupation with the negative aspects of human situations.

As a grounding for understanding the religious strain in social work, Leiby (1978) discusses the relationship between salvation and charity. Although Protestants and Catholics developed different expressions of the value of work, both saw that aspect of their lives as a vehicle for salvation. The monastic tradition in Catholicism and the valorizing of work in the world through the Protestant ethic gave work a vocational attribute. One could reach salvation through work, but at the same time, the failure to work was viewed as a personal, moral failure. As Leiby (1978) notes, the "Christian tradition . . . furnished a cosmic drama . . . in which suffering had a meaning and so did efforts to relieve and correct it" (p. 21). The helping relationship was thus bound up in the larger story of creation and redemption.

The scientific tradition offered a secular version of this same drama. Instead of sin and moral insufficiency, the scientific method devoted itself to problem-solving. Through an optimism inspired by a belief in mathematically based method, problems in the natural and human worlds were sought out for repair. In what Schön (1983) terms the myth of technical rationality, the rise of science produced a belief in the human capacity to make and fix things—any problem was thought to be susceptible to a solution if the appropriate technology were applied. The application of scientific method became the litmus test for determining whether human rationality could win against the constant anomalies presented in the natural and human realms. The drive of scientific research can be seen as a grand project to reincorporate human beings into the world from which the scientific world view drove them.

PROBLEM-SOLVING IN SOCIAL WORK

Although the scientific paradigm was not accepted by social work in a wholesale fashion, the assumptions underlying that approach have permeated social work thinking. In broad terms, its earliest influence could be seen in Mary Richmond's (1917) work, in which an emphasis on a logical strategy for determining need was established. Decision-making based on empirical evidence was to replace moralistic judgments. Gathering and weighing facts became the foundation for the process of determining human need. The lean toward rationality became a hallmark of scientific practice as social work developed. Even though Freudian theory introduced the powerful realm of the unconscious and the irrational in human behavior, the attempt to systematize and catalog human failings and their treatments continued apace.

This trend culminated in the late 1950s with the formation of the problem-solving school of social casework. As advanced by Helen Harris Perlman (1957) and developed within social casework, this approach assumed that "although clients come to social workers with specific concerns, their fundamental difficulty is in their manner of solving problems" (Scott and Miller, 1971, p. 28). The fundamental goal is to "restore the clients' problem-solving capacities" (Scott and Miller, 1971, p. 28) within an educational approach defined as "exquisitely rational" (Scott and Miller, 1971, p. 29).

While a shift from a focus on deep-seated intrapsychic problems to problems in daily living seemed to offer a refreshing new direction for social work, the persistent attention to individual difficulties has continued to pervade social work practice. The language of diagnosis varies dramatically within various approaches, from the medical labels of DSM-IIIR to the analysis of family problems across generations. However, the underlying rationale repeats a similar theme: name the problem and the treatment follows. Thus, an implicit, longstanding axiom of social work is that practitioners must understand what is wrong before taking any action. The fact that it is the professional who makes the assessment virtually ensures that the problem definition will achieve sophisticated and elaborate dimensions during its examination.

As we understand the entrenchment in a problem-focused orientation to practice, it may seem strange to consider an alternative. The push of history and past practice seems to suggest that problems in human life deserve the care and attention we have devoted to them. When one considers the elaboration of theory and the extent of research devoted to analysis of problems and their solutions, taking another tack appears to be sheer effrontery.

First, it seems dangerous to ignore the existence of social ills and human difficulties. By doing so, it appears that we are condoning the presence of circumstances that could and should be eradicated. Second, a shift away from problems appears Pollyanna-like. It seems that we are not serious about the pain and suffering associated with problem situations. Third, there is a deep unease about consciously choosing to ignore what seem to be incontrovertible facts about human life. We know that human beings have a shocking capacity to wreak harm on their earth and its inhabitants. Unless there is constant vigilance to keep this evil strain in check, we fear that even more problems could occur. Fourth, there is a collective fascination with the shadow side of human life. Newspapers and texts alike call our attention to the lurid, the pathological, and the obscene, rather than to the good and uplifting. All of these factors point to an intense preoccupation with problems and their extensive roots.

REWORKING BASIC ASSUMPTIONS

In order to form a perspective that runs counter to the problem-solving approach, one needs to create a base of assumptions that has some philosophic heft. It is not enough to claim that people have strengths, although that is an important assertion. In order to develop an alternative to the dominant model, it is necessary to consider what the notion of "strengths" might mean. There are at least three lines of thinking that can be helpful. One involves a reconception of the nature of human problems themselves. The second focuses on the metaphor of healing as representing the inner force for growth and change. And the third rests on a reconception of knowledge and its attendant power.

The strategy of reframing is a familiar one in professional practice. It flows from social science theory through the sociology of knowledge and cognitive psychology. In essence, this position holds that human interaction is based on socially and personally constructed views of reality (Berger and Luckmann, 1967; Geertz, 1973). In contrast to a positivist, scientific perspective, it is assumed that all perceptions are mediated by culture, language, and meaning and that human experience reflects a dynamic interplay between events and the meanings we attach to them. We constantly shape our reality and negotiate its meaning as a social process. What is "real" is what we believe to be so and what others may choose to agree with (Gergen, 1981).

This stance is opposed to a scientific model of knowledge, which rests on the assumption, among others, that reality can be measured, tested, and objectively verified. It is this model that has created the belief that problems are identifiable, measurable entities susceptible to investigation and solution. If, however, the notion of problem is viewed from the "constructed" perspective, we see that the identification of a human situation as problem reflects not what we are looking at but who is doing the looking. In other words, we can upend the problem-focus by treating problems as creations that we have designed and by analyzing not the problem itself but the process of creating and defining something as a problem.

Unlocking our vision from the endproduct by accepting our collective role in constructing things we consider problematic achieves two important objectives. It creates new angles from which embedded assumptions can be examined. For example, we can stop treating poverty and poor people as a problem and instead focus on the social processes that create and maintain systemic inequality. This vantage point allows a larger set of factors to be considered and addressed. It also allows us to be more playful and more creative about our thought and action. If what we see is not decreed by some force outside ourselves but is of our own making, then we can remake it. We can, in the popular lingo, "reframe" our situations to allow for more humanely creative responses.

What reframing allows us to do, then, is to write a very different scenario for human situations. Rather than accepting our self-imposed definitions of human problems, we can radically shift our perspective from the negative to the positive pole. Instead of asking questions that direct our attention to the deficiencies and limitations in human situations, we can choose to ask questions with positive loading. For example, instead of asking, "What's wrong with this individual?" we can ask, "What are the strengths that have helped this person survive? What are her aspirations, talents, and abilities? What social, emotional, and physical resources are needed to support her growth and well-being?" This shift in focus is a matter of conscious intent. Doing so recognizes and honors our capacity to see in a new way that challenges traditional assumptions about the nature of problems and human behavior and that sets forth a constructive and active orientation for our practice. Gergen (1981) calls such alternative, critical views generative theories, which are absolutely essential for social progress.

In order to take this stance, traditional beliefs about human growth and change need to be examined, because a strengths perspective is based on different ground. A typical view of human growth, promulgated in social science and professional texts, suggests that there is a normative process governing human development. A preponderance of research has been devoted to investigating the predictable phases of this development and has, even with the recent work on adult change, focused on discovering patterns that apply across the life span (Levinson et al., 1978; Vaillant, 1977).

The notion of normal development can be criticized from many angles, not the least of which is its close connection with a physical science paradigm that searches for law-like occurrences in the natural world. The belief that human behavior conforms to the assumptions of the scientific paradigm is a matter of serious consequence for professional practice. However, the more telling criticism for our purposes is that the acceptance of normalcy as a standard for human behavior immediately creates an astonishing array of problems. Every profession has been commissioned to deal with people who do not fit the norm: the poor, the mentally ill, the disabled, the learning impaired, the sick. Adopting a construction of human behavior that assumes normalcy as its base consigns us to caring for an endless supply of people who do not fit the accepted definitions.

If our theories of human behavior create this destructive consequence, then we can, in the fashion previously discussed, reframe our perspective. In order to ground a strengths perspective, we must develop a more fluid and expansive sense of how human beings grow and change. Central to this view is a belief in people's inherent capacity to transform themselves by getting in touch with their own natural resources. Ruth Smalley (1967) spoke of this as "the human power in individuals for personal fulfillment and social good . . ." (p. 1). It is the life force, present in all living things, that pushes for expression.

One metaphor for capturing this energy is that of healing (Weick, 1986). Our physical bodies have astounding powers to heal us as, minute by minute, the hundreds of biological processes work within to keep us alive and well (Cousins, 1989; Ornstein and Sobel, 1987). In a similar way, our energy force expresses itself as an emotional resilience that helps us absorb and reflect on the hundreds of interactions present in our daily lives. Healing suggests that there is a push for wholeness, for becoming more of who we are capable of being in all aspects of our lives.

If a belief in the transformational capacity of this life force is central to our thinking, then the path of human growth is far less predictable and far more illusory than we have chosen to think. Studying the rich patterning of human development across the life span creates the broad outlines of what human development might entail, but cannot represent or accurately capture the tremendous nuances or contingencies of growth that individuals actually experience. Theory about human growth and change needs to be unhinged from the lockstep view of what is considered "normal" development and turned instead to fluid models built on assumptions that recognize the creative and powerful energy underlying all human growth (Weick, 1983). The aleatory (contingency-based) approaches to life-span development, just now surfacing, are testimony to these assumptions (Gergen, 1981).

As an important companion to the inner strengths propelling us toward growth is a different view of knowledge. In much the same way that traditional theories of human development place the fulcrum for development outside the individual's control, models of knowledge-building, borrowing heavily from an empiricist paradigm, maintain an objectified view of human knowing. Both the manufacture and the transmission of legitimate knowledge is handled by experts, carefully trained in the proper procedure for testing theory. In this model, knowledge is a precious commodity over which there is a carefully constituted monopoly. Academicians and professionals form the honor guard to ensure its privileged status.

In the growing critique of empiricist approaches to knowing, this privileged status of professional knowledge is increasingly called into question. Logic, rationalism, and hypothetic-deductive method are being seen not as ultimate strategies for mediating truth claims but as oppressive standards that primarily serve to maintain the power status of the truthsayers. By maintaining scientific method as the supreme vehicle for gaining legitimate knowledge, a broad category of knowledge is inevitably discounted. What Wilhelm Dilthey (Rickman, 1979) called "lived experience" sinks under the weight of the scientific superstructure.

Recapturing the category of disqualified knowledge is a fitting task for a strengths perspective. Foucault (in Gordon, 1980, p. 85) has spoken eloquently about the need to reactivate "local knowledges" that have been subjugated by such overarching theories as Marxism and psychoanalysis. In part, his strategy involves a genealogical study of the historical context of human drama; seen, for example, in his work on psychiatric patients and prisoners. Understanding how their experience has been reshaped and suppressed by both theory and methodology reveals the power inherent in professional knowledge and suggests the need for approaches that consciously incorporate and honor people's own experience.

In taking this tack, people's own knowledge of their lives is treated as a natural resource. The imposition of a hierarchical knowledge structure in which professional knowledge is unquestionably superior to lay knowledge is overturned. In its place is the recognition of a multiplicity of knowledges, each deserving an honorable position. In keeping with a framework of socially constructed knowledge, every knowledge position is seen as an expression of meaning that must ultimately be negotiated. Lived experience and intuitive knowledge take their rightful place alongside systems based on logic and analysis. Thus, human experience as understood by those living it can be seen as a source of strength that is individually energizing and collectively empowering.

A STRENGTHS PERSPECTIVE

Given the broader conceptual perspective that is formed by a critical examination of the nature of human problems, the nature of human development, and the nature of knowledge, the stage is set for a closer examination of what it means to say that people have strengths. There are three essential assumptions that give this statement its meaning. First, it is assumed that every person has an inherent power that may be characterized as life force, transformational capacity, life energy, spirituality, regenerative potential, and healing power. These and other terms point to an inexplicable, probably biologically grounded, but vibrant quality that is an irrevocable aspect of being human (Cousins, 1989). The act of empowering reawakens or stimulates someone's own natural power.

Second, a strengths perspective assumes that the power just described is a potent form of knowledge that can guide personal and social transformation. Accepting one's own experience as a valid form of knowledge while, at the same time, honoring the experience of others, creates a communal basis for knowledge exchange. Dialogue among equals replaces hierarchical knowledge structures, so no individual or group has a monopoly on knowledge or its attendant power.

Third, there is a crucial pragmatic presumption about the nature of change. A strengths perspective assumes that when people's positive capacities are supported, they are more likely to act on their strengths. Thus, a belief in people's inherent capacity for growth and well-being requires an intense attention to people's own resources: their talents, experiences, and aspirations. Through this active attention, the probability for positive growth is significantly enhanced.

These three assumptions form the core of a strengths perspective. They may seem innocuous, but they point in a direction that runs directly counter to major cultural, political, and moral assumptions of Western thinking. Instead of the current epistemology of power, which assumes that knowledge is a scarce and esoteric resource, the strengths perspective supports a vision of knowledge universally shared, creatively developed, and capable of enhancing individual and communal growth. There is no question that this view challenges institutionalized authority structures, whether the government, the academy, or the professions; it is this challenge that creates the major obstacle to its acceptance. At the same time, it offers a revitalized view of a core belief of social work and opens the way for a thoughtful reexamination of current practice.

The strengths perspective consciously creates a new agenda for practice. It draws attention away from increasingly technique-laden approaches to human situations and reminds us of a simple truth: that each person already carries the seeds for his or her own transformation. A steadfast belief in that potential is one of the most powerful gifts a social worker can offer. By understanding in a deep, reflective way what it means to say that people have strengths, it is possible to recast what has been, for much of social work, a glibly stated maxim. Rather than viewing it as an ancillary and easily expendable belief, it becomes the measure against which all practice is judged.

It may be tempting to diminish the force of this claim by asserting that social work has always practiced from a strengths perspective. But it is a precarious position to maintain in the face of the themes of pathology, problems, and human deficiency that lace social work texts, journals, and professional workshops. The commitment to working with people's strengths has an admirable tradition in social work. But putting it at the center of practice will require an effort that consciously challenges both cultural and professional shibboleths. Until we can come to a point where it is strengths rather than problems that most significantly identify who an individual is, we will know that we have not overcome the seduction of pathology.

Social work is ideally suited to the task of developing a more explicit and sophisticated strengths perspective for its practice. It has the philosophical stance to support this exploration. It has a rich practice wisdom that recognizes the power of human resilience, and it has the ability to challenge prevailing models of pathology by offering a value-based alternative. Encouraging this alternative view to flourish would allow the profession to move from its own strengths and bring to full light the deep wisdom of one of its most cherished values.

REFERENCES

Berger, P. L. and Luckmann, T. (1967). *The social construction of reality.* Garden City, NY: Anchor/Doubleday.

Burtt, E. A. (1931). *The metaphysical foundation of modern science.* London: Routledge and Kegan Paul.

Cousins, N. (1989). *Head first: The biology of hope.* New York: E. P. Dutton.

Geertz, C. (1973). *The interpretation of cultures.* New York: Basic Books.

Gergen, K. (1981). *Towards transformation in social knowledge.* New York: Springer-Verlag.

Gordon, C., ed. (1980). *Michel Foucault—Power/knowledge.* New York: Pantheon.

Leiby, J. (1978). *A history of social welfare and social work.* New York: Columbia University Press.

Levinson, D. J., Darrow, C. N., Klein, E. B., Levinson, M. H., and McKee, B. (1978). *The seasons of a man's life.* New York: Alfred Knopf.

Ornstein, R. and Sobel, D. (1987). *The healing brain.* New York: Simon and Schuster.

Perlman, Helen Harris. (1957). *Social casework: A problem-solving process.* Chicago: University of Chicago Press.

Randall, J. H., Jr. (1926). *The making of the modern mind.* New York: Columbia University Press.

Richmond, M. (1917). *Social diagnosis*. New York: Russell Sage Foundation.

Rickman, H. P. (1979). *Wilhelm Dilthey: Pioneer of the human studies*. Berkeley: University of California Press.

Schön, D. (1983). *The reflective practitioner*. New York: Basic Books.

Scott, B. and Miller, H. (1971). *Problems and issues in social casework*. New York: Columbia University Press.

Smalley, R. E. (1967). *Theory for social work practice*. New York: Columbia University Press.

Vaillant, G. (1977). *Adaptation to life*. Boston: Little, Brown.

Weick, A. (March 1983). A growth-task model of human development. *Social Casework, 64*(3).

Weick, A. (November 1986). The philosophical context of a health model of social work. *Social Casework, 67*, 551–559.

CHAPTER **3**

Victors or Victims:
Contrasting Views of Clients in Social Work Practice

Howard Goldstein

Ordinarily, we pay little attention to the language we use. We assume that the words and sentences we express convey what we intend them to mean. And when we resort to scientific terminology, we are even more convinced that what we intend to communicate is precise and specific.

We cling to this illusion even though the events of everyday living prove otherwise: More often than not, we are reminded that our words either do not reveal exactly what we want to say or that our listener doesn't understand them. Language, after all, can only symbolize what we think about, what we feel, or even the concrete things we want to describe. At the same time, the frailties of human communication add spice and richness to living; they press for a constant search for meaning and understanding of the nuances and subtleties that symbolize our relationships with others. Indeed, there would be no poetry, art, literature or biography—and perhaps no science—if words were literal and transparent representations of reality. The eminent physicist, Werner Heisenberg, observed over thirty years ago (1958) that even the concepts, axioms, and laws represented by a mathematical scheme are actually idealizations that can be compared with the development of an artistic style. In both art and science, language is a product of the interplay between self and world that enables us to speculate about the remote parts of reality.

All this is by way of introducing the central theme of this paper: Tied to the ethical, humanistic, and professional issues that arise when we enter the lives of our clients are questions of the language that we employ (expressed in theories, concepts, and frameworks) to describe, explain, and as a consequence, deal with our clients' problems of living. Depending on culture, region, and other factors, ordinary people might use a wide variety of terms and images to account for their own or others' unusual actions or

Copyright © 1992 by Longman Publishing Group.

feelings. In the helping professions, descriptive/explanatory schemes typically express two contrasting points of view: one, a humanistic perspective that is concerned with processes of strength and survival; the other, a medico-scientific model that centers on classifications of pathology and disability. Clearly, each perspective poses critical implications for our work with people.

Given the polarities that each perspective represents, controversies about the strengths and weaknesses of either position have flourished in the literature over the past many years. In these pages, the argument (or perhaps more accurately, the polemic) will focus more on the rhetoric, the ethics, and to some extent, the politics of each position. The basic assumption is that each frame of reference persists not because either can claim any real evidence of essential "goodness," "truth," or "effectiveness," but rather because each stands for a disparate set of assumptions about the nature of the human state that are expressed in language forms that, typically, are unquestioned and ingrained in our lexicon.

Consider, first, that the term *psychopathology* is a misnomer. Its literal meaning is "illness of the mind" (or if we use Freud's definition of *psyche,* "illness of spirit or soul"). Since "mind" is an elusive and fuzzy concept that, in one definition, refers to the emergent properties of the brain (Gazzaniga, 1988), it would seem that the more precise term *neuropathology* should be used. However, this term is equally inappropriate since it refers only to the physical properties of the brain.

Yet for political and other reasons that will be discussed, the term persists. We find the doctrine of the pathological model inscribed in the DSM-III, chapter and verse expressing the finely wrought elements that characterize human frailties and flaws. In turn, the resulting taxonomies become even more persuasive and respectable expressed as they are in the medical idiom. For example, in section 301.82, the classification of Avoidant Personality Disorder commands more regard than more commonly used descriptions, such as self-conscious, fearful, or shy. There are other nonmedical attributions that pretend to be less pathological in scope; yet ascriptions such as "defense mechanisms," "denial," "resistance," and "dysfunction" equally convey a quality of morbidity and defect on the part of the client.

On the other hand, *strength* and its many synonyms—*competency, wellness, effectiveness,* for example—is a more modest term that owns little of the authority of the tenets of pathology. As an approach to practice, it is not systematized or standardized by a handbook comparable to the DSM-III. Its vocabulary, relatively free of jargon, sounds much like the language most people use every day.

Despite these sharp differences, the two perspectives do have something in common: Neither one is securely anchored in fact, whether it be scientific proof, empirical evidence, or conformity with some established truth. As will be shown, *strength* or *pathology* are terms that more accurately fall into the linguistic class of metaphor— terms that allow us to relieve confusion and say something meaningful and intelligent about otherwise baffling human conditions that, themselves, are typically expressed in metaphorical terms. Rather than a presentation of objective facts, the client offers an account, a story, that is often peppered with all sorts of figurative statements, such as similes ("I feel like a lost dog"), symbols ("my mind is just a blob of nothingness"), irony ("my husband is such a sweet bastard"), euphemisms ("I'd call it social drinking"), and metaphors in all shapes and sizes. These terms, in turn, may camouflage something as elusive as a state of mind, a puzzled feeling, or a forbidden impulse—all in themselves metaphors.

Such vague and obscure statements require interpretation by the caring listener. It is when we ask how they are interpreted that the differences between the pathological and strength orientations again come into sharp relief. And the "how" of interpretation is directly related to the "what for." If the intent is to achieve the illusion of neutral and scientific objectivity—based on the assumption that the human state can, in fact, be rationally ordered—then the medico-scientific psychopathological framework will suffice. If, however, the listener's purpose is to gain some grasp of the meanings and themes contained in the client's message—based on the assumption that understanding or *verstehen* is inevitably subjective and tentative—then the humanistic strength orientation is called for.

The point of this preliminary overview is to suggest that our professional activities are not, as we would prefer to believe, rational consequences of a set of established and tested theories, constructs, and techniques. Rather, we are the inheritors of abstractions and concepts—a professional language comprised of value-laden metaphors and idioms. It is a language that has far more to do with philosophic assumptions about the human state, ideologies of professionalism, and not the least, politics of practice than they do with some kind of objective rationality. In general, the rhetoric expressed by the two perspectives inevitably takes the form of prescriptions for action. That is, they dictate (at least in broad terms) the professional's role vis-a-vis that of the client's. In so doing, unavoidable ethical questions come forward relative to the allocation of power and authority (and the matter of self-determination) in the helping experience. As in the case of a medico-scientific approach to practice, should the weight of influence be balanced by the human relations expert? Or, as in the case of the humanistic, strength-oriented approach, should the issues of power and authority be seen as conditions of the helping process that, as much as possible, can be shared by client and worker?

With these questions in mind, the balance of this paper will attempt to cast some light on the premises sketched thus far. First, I will develop the proposition that neither the concept of pathology nor that of strength are objective facts, but are instead social constructions that reflect public and professional attitudes and beliefs. Second, I will consider how well each of these models and their constructions serve us in our work with people; that is, the extent to which they approximate the types of human circumstances we encounter in practice. As a consequence of this analysis, consideration will be given to the influence of these models on the ethical and political climate of the social worker–client relationship.

Before proceeding with this analysis, it is important to point out a qualification of the discussion of how these models might affect practice (taking account of the practitioner's role, status, and actions). First, the comparison of the two models will be framed in rather polar terms to elucidate their essential contrasts. Second, they will be considered in prototypical terms so as to show what each form of practice would look like if the practitioner adhered to its contours and rules. It is doubtful that these conditions would actually reflect any one practice event. It is evident that a considerable gap exists between workers' expressed commitment to a particular theory and the way the theory is implemented.

STRENGTH AND PATHOLOGY
AS SOCIAL CONSTRUCTIONS

As defined by Gergen (Gergen, 1985) social constructionist inquiry attempts to understand the processes by which people explain and define themselves and their world. Dismissing the notion that there is a firm and objective basis for conventional knowledge and language, social constructionism argues that the terms in which the world is understood are social artifacts, the products of cultural, symbolic, and historical interchanges among people. Such artifacts have currency only as long as there is consensus about their value: Quite simply, we continue to depend on the conventional knowledge and language as long as they serve our varied social, adaptive, and professional purposes.

Let us consider the language of the two models as social constructions to see what they imply about the human condition. *Strength* and *pathology* denote antithetical states of being. According to Webster's Third Dictionary, the former refers to moral courage, fortitude, physical force, and vigor. Pathology, in contrast, covers abnormality, disorder, and disease.

These contrasts become even more striking in terms of their current usage when we examine the root derivations of these terms. *Strength* is a word that derives from the Anglo-Saxon, an earthy and unadorned language that depicts the natural world of living. Etymologically, it is a relative of other terms that express normalcy, assertiveness, proactiveness, and integrity.

Pathology, in contrast, derives from the early Greek, which tends to be more elite, scholarly, and abstract and in some ways detached from worldly experience. Its root is *pathos,* which connotes suffering, endurance, and sorrow.

Since the social constructions we inherit are rarely subject to inquiry, it is also important to ask how the biomedical term *pathology* came to be applied to something as ambiguous as human mental states. Although the term has a long history in general medicine, it was not used by medical psychiatry until the mid-nineteenth century. At that point, its adoption as a medical classification and its consequences were far more political than medical. Essentially, it had the effect of abolishing the perspectives of strength and normalcy that characterized the way psychiatry was practiced up to that time.

Until the mid-nineteenth century, psychiatry was somewhat philosophical and romantic. In ways that we might now see as quaint and arcane, various forms of prescientific psychiatry anticipated modern humanistic and cognitive psychology. Some of its practitioners used forms of what is now called psychodrama for purposes of what they termed "reeducation of perceptions." Others saw health as being consonant with freedom and perfectibility; thus, mental illness was considered a result of the loss of freedom and self-control. Still others considered morality as a condition directly linked with one's mental state. Although psychiatry was certainly idiosyncratic during this era, the various practitioners did share a common conviction that mind and body constituted an inseparable whole, a system; that psychiatric classifications should not be trusted; and that each individual deserved to be understood in his or her own right (Ellenberger, 1970, pp. 212–214).

By mid-century, however, the work of these pioneers fell into disrepute or oblivion as the study of brain anatomy took over and the positivistic sciences came into ascendance. Within this scientific revolution, medicine became institutionalized and standardized. Swept along with this change was the formal medicalization of mental disorders (Ellenberger, 1970, pp. 226–228).

On tracing the ascendance of medical psychiatry and its annexation of mental malfunctioning as a medical prerogative, Ernest Becker observes the following:

> Nineteenth-century diagnosticians redoubled efforts to keep man under medical wraps and dress his behavior disorder in Greco-Latin cant. Thus the science that knew least about total symbolic man and most about the animal body fully established its sacrosanct domain. We are coming to know that it had no business there. . . . The result of this lopsided jurisdictional development was that human malfunction has continued to be treated largely in nineteenth century disease categories up to the present day (1964, pp. 9–10).

In contrast, strength as a social construction did not have to be invented, and therefore offers less historical or political interest. Yet, this unpretentious term, tied as it is to judgments of virtue, willpower, integrity, and fortitude, has long been the metaphor used by individuals, groups, and cultures to define character and worth. Inevitably, if we are at all introspective, it is the term we use, often in private moments, to rate and evaluate our ability to cope with and survive the travails of living. It is a universal term, an unsophisticated term that requires little interpretation. And, as an estimate of personal worth and ability, it is powerful. We are, for example, more cautious about telling a troubled friend that he perhaps lacks the strength to cope than in suggesting that he may be suffering from depression, anxiety, or some other psychological disorder.

In this regard, the two metaphors clearly stand for much more than their semantic and rhetorical differences. More than just speculative theoretical abstractions about the human state, they have a functional purpose insofar as they are intended as guides for how practitioners ought to think about and therefore deal with the circumstances they encounter.

For example, the medico-diagnostic labels that are appended to designated mental states or behaviors purport to be purely descriptive and, therefore, meaningless and value-free. In other words, the diagnosis of schizophrenia or behavior disorder ought to have the same order of scientific objectivity as a diagnosis of arthritis or anemia. We know this is not the case. As Susan Sontag observes (1978), even physical illnesses such as cancer and tuberculosis have long been used metaphorically for all sorts of social and political purposes. This possibility is fostered by the reductionist quality of the diagnostic process, whereby utterly complex human conditions are narrowly enveloped by a specific category.

Labeling theory tells us that people bearing particular psychiatric diagnoses are likely to be subjected to judgments and attitudes that further embellish the caste in which the patient has already been installed. Such attributions may be outwardly benign, as when we see the individual as a patient, a victim, or in need of care; or they might be alienating, as when the patient is seen as deviant, dangerous, or just plain crazy. In short, medico-scientific classifications are readily transformed into other powerful social constructions. They not only define a person's station, but can also serve as a justification for the control and the determination of how a person ought to be regarded and treated.

On the other hand, the metaphor "strength" frankly is a value-laden, subjective term, since it is a judgment made in accord with certain personal or social norms or standards. At the same time, it is an expansive rather than a reductionist concept. When we attempt to gauge another person's attributes in a fair and caring fashion, we are bound to take account of a number of mitigating human and social factors. Some examples: *context,* the peculiar circumstances surrounding the person; *history,* awareness of how the person has coped with dilemmas in the past; *potential,* indices of untapped capabilities; *expectations,* what the person hopes for and wants; *meaning,* personal interpretations of the person's state; *relationship,* how we perceive and value one another; and, over all, *introspection,* our personal, humble reflections about the extent to which we can really comprehend another's life.

It follows that since our language of perception and understanding determines how we act, the worker's active role in the helping process will be influenced by her choice of model and metaphor. Out of this choice will emerge a peculiar social arrangement (more commonly called a therapy, counseling, or treatment relationship) that begins to inform and influence the client in ways that are not immediately apparent.

For example, if I as the worker focus more on your problems and disabilities than your strengths, my perceptions will narrow as I search for clues and causes to figure out what you and I will need to do to resolve or cure your malaise. However, if I am persuaded by your strengths and fortitude, then my scope will broaden as I attempt to learn from you how you have survived thus far and where you believe we ought to be heading in our work together. Although I am not disinterested in your distress, my inquiry would include, but also reach beyond, the central problem to understand what keeps you going. If how we understand determines how we act, how we act influences the response of the other in the human relationship that begins to take shape.

In the first instance, the focus on problems and inadequacies creates an analog of distance and control. The posture of detached objectivity required to construct a "case history" and diagnose another person's condition poses the risk of creating an aura of separateness. Such an approach becomes even more elitist should I intimate that I have the special knowledge of the professional, which grants me the authority to define your problems and, out of this definition, determine the plan that should produce the desired results. A moral and ethical distance might also result from such an outlook, particularly when questions of personal responsibility become diffused by my clinical lens.

Conversely, a more egalitarian relationship becomes possible when I am intrigued by the remnants of hope and vision that you still harbor as faint shadows of your strength. Your story interests me, not as a set of facts to be ordered into a rational explanation of your problem, but as a personal narrative that expresses the meaning of your existence. Thus, I invite you to regard me as a comrade more than as an expert as we both learn how to set the ethical, moral, and value terms of our relationship.

Thus far, I have tried to show that within the culture that we call social work, the ritual terms that shape theory and practice are not concise concepts purified by the scientific method, but rather socially constructed abstractions. These constructions have something to say about the allocation of power, authority, personal rights, and obligations, and about self-determination. As well-meaning as a preoccupation with problems and deficits may be, this focus can lead to an uneven distribution of control. In its most elemental form, a relationship that focuses on one member's failings or pathology must, in some way, elevate the others' power and status. Conversely, a strength-oriented relationship by its nature and intent presses for equality and sharing. I observe that the helping relationship, typically thought of as benign and altruistic, can also embrace the political attributes of authority and control.

PATHOLOGY OR STRENGTH AS A MODEL OF PRACTICE?

The argument takes a different turn, however, when we ask which model most accurately corresponds with the structure and processes of the change experience itself. This question leads to an even more elemental question that, as yet, has not been conclusively answered: What is the nature of the change experience and how does it unfold?

Over the past decades, the evolvement of systems of change has shown a greater resemblance to the fashion industry than to progress in science. Rather than progressing in an incremental manner built on research and scholarship, there has been a series of alternating shifts in prevailing paradigms—or more accurately, ideologies, styles, and fads.

Allen Buss, in his book *A Dialectical Psychology* (1979, p. 5), explains the complexities of these swings by observing that they involve radical shifts between two prototypical statements: (1) person constructs reality and (2) reality constructs person. To illustrate this argument he shows that in psychology, early structuralism was replaced by Watsonian behaviorism which was succeeded by cognitive psychology—shifts from person creates reality to reality creates person and back again. At the same time, humanistic or third force psychology (person constructs reality) was a reaction both to psychoanalysis and behaviorism each in their respective ways expressing the statement that reality constructs the person. Each of these shifts represented something less than an improvement in theory or research: They posed contrasting ideological or philosophical positions about questions of brain versus mind, biology versus culture, determinism versus free will, cause versus function, and reality as fact versus reality as a construction.

This dualistic, either/or debate has proved to be futile since it is apparent that person and reality have a dialectical rather than a linear relationship. Our best understanding of how people live and change (in and out of the helping relationship) comes from our appreciation of the process that is created when person and environment converge.

One reason the either/or debate has persisted is that the dynamics of this convergence are easier to label than they are to define and comprehend. To be sure, we have a number of handy terms, such as *interface, dialectic, person-in-situation,* and *transaction.* But they are about as informing for our social work purposes as terms such as *big bang, quarks,* and *black holes* are for our personal understanding of the universe. In both instances, using these terms shows more sophistication than substance.

The dilemma, it seems to me, has to do with the tacit problems of language, concepts, and the assumptions that have been willed to us. First of all, although any one human experience is a unitary, holistic event, the language we use to report it is linear: The description follows a sequential line as if thoughts, feelings, and actions unrolled like a carpet. Not by coincidence, our horizons of understanding are also cramped by the nature of the concepts that we have inherited, which are also linear in nature. If life is defined as a chain of events, then this chain is forged by the idea that every effect must have its cause. In other words, if someone behaves, thinks, or feels in a peculiar way, then we all too naturally assume there must be some predisposing conditions and that this cause—whether it is called repression, trauma, conditioning, or deprivation—must be identified if we are to determine how we might bring about change. To be sure, we have had a romance with a social systems or ecological model that intends to capture the interplay of forces within the human field. Informative as these models are, they offer no prescriptions for what to do, and all too often, the practitioner falls back on traditional methods to get something done.

Second, standard theories support the myth that the human state is relatively uniform, consistent, and as we find in the more empirical approaches to research and practice, predictable. These assumptions are evident in concepts of personality, traits, syndromes, measurement variables and scales, and obviously, in the very notion of diagnostic categories.

Consistent with the first two assumptions about cause–effect and uniformity is the third assumption that the ideal for whatever we call well-being—adaptation, adjustment, freedom from stress, absence of symptoms, or working through—is commensurate with doctrines of balance, equilibrium, or even homeostasis. In other words, the ideal state of being is the absence of stress and the presence of rest, stability, and symmetry.

Are these assumptions valid? Do they explain in useful ways human and social experiences? Common sense, just some reflections on how we get through an ordinary day, tell us that our lives are not linear sequences of events, each episode a precondition of the next. Surely our minds can and do invent scenarios in which we conveniently order reality in a way that makes it look like one happenstance seemed to predict another. This is the mind's way of simulating order, a process that can be revised any time we decide to think about our circumstances in another way.

Next, we are acutely aware that our patterns of living are neither uniform nor consistent. Despite the habit patterns that very roughly characterize the way we go about the ordinary tasks of living, the next novel situation we encounter is likely to evoke responses that surprise even ourselves. And to most of us, predictability as it pertains to ourselves is an abhorrent idea since it suggests possible control and power on the part of the one who predicts. Thus, we would prefer to be seen as more enigmatic and opaque rather than transparent.

And finally, given the contingencies, quirks, and sometime risks of daily life, it is safe to say that mind and body are altogether restless, in motion, at least slightly out of balance, and watchful to monitor and cope with whatever may come along next. Interestingly, while the human sciences pursue the myth of linear cause–effect relations, notions of lawful uniformity, predictability, and stability, the physical sciences—particularly quantum and mathematical physics—provide us with a new and radical picture of what the universe and its material, organic, and human elements are really like. The newest of these sciences, aptly called *chaos*, marks the end of the compartmentalization and reductionism of science (Gleick, 1987). It suspends the illusion that science will provide us with universal laws to help reinforce our need to believe that the universe is ultimately comprehensible and manageable. In fact, the systems around us (ecological, physiological, and economic, for example) are lacking the order, regularity, and pre-dictability that has long characterized the Newtonian version of the real world. If we are to find comfort in this chaotic version of reality, then we must settle for a revision that allows us to search for the variable and unpredictable patterns in the human state. In so doing, we would give up the illusion of regularity and dependable predictability in how we work with other human beings and their predicaments.

Returning to the questions about the nature of the change process, the preceding discussion offers yet another perspective on the attributes of the psychopathological and the strength approaches as they bear on practice. The former can be seen as a relic of an earlier scientific era that practiced positivistic reductionism and the compartmentaliza-tion of phenomena. Essentially, the complexities of the personal, cultural, physiologi-cal, and environmental conglomeration that marks the human state tend to be reduced to narrow compartments of a diagnostic scheme, and are treated accordingly.

By contrast, a health or strength perspective, although rooted in the philosophy of humanism, is also sympathetic to the knowledge of the new science. Coincidentally or otherwise, it is less concerned with control, classification, and precision. With its em-phasis on capability and potential, it discards notions of causality that may define the client as a hapless victim of conditions beyond his control in favor of an approach that centers on the client's values, hopes, and desired goals.

The idea that living is a chaotic and unpredictable venture means that the strength of the individual or collective is not tied to the wistful hope for a static state of tranquil-lity; rather, it is found in the vitality of the search of at least some periodic states of security and structure within the turbulence that is living.

In these terms, one's strengths cannot be cataloged, compared, or measured in line with one scale or another. In response to the same dire circumstances, strength for one person may be merely an active hope for survival; for another, it may be the willingness to risk untried solutions. Accordingly, a strengths approach to practice does not impose plans and programs; rather, it encourages clients to discover their own abilities to ex-plore every possibility, to discover the richness of choice and the cornucopia of oppor-tunity. Just as important, such an approach also frees workers to be at ease with their own humanness. They are then able to share their understanding of the challenge of finding meaning in a baffling world in a liberated and creative fashion.

When we peel back the layers of theory, technique, style, and other characteristics that give the change experience its own visibility and movement, we find two or more human beings, in many ways alike, who are basically engaged in conversation. This is the core aspect of the experience. No doubt, this is how it is perceived or sensed by the client: having no explanatory theoretical framework, he or she would see the occasion in a natural and unsophisticated way.

If all goes well, something called a relationship will grow out of this conversation. And, as is true of all important human relationships, it is (or should be) governed not by professional methods or protocols alone but by certain ethics. In this instance, they are the personal norms and ideals that have to do with obligation and responsibility and that guide how we treat others and how we expect to be treated. Perhaps more so than in other professions where the required skills, the concreteness of services sought, and the outcomes are more conspicuous, these ethical and moral standards have a par-ticularly critical role in the social work relationship. The naive client who enters the social work setting has little more to rely on than a one-sided and enigmatic relationship that appears to have no other purpose or activity than conversation. Lopsided as this partnership is, the risk is ever present that subtle political forces of power and authority will intrude.

In these instances, the worker must be certain that her ethics stand in tension with the politics of helping: the political dimension embodies the constant risk of encroachment of unwarranted influence and control that is a consequence of the unbalanced relationship; the ethical dimension serves as the conscience of the experience that jogs awareness of the need for prudence and care as to how the politics of helping are played out.

Margaret Rhodes, in her fine book *Ethical Dilemmas in Social Work Practice* (1986), not only covers much the same ground but also inspires many of the ideas of this essay. As she sums up:

> . . . the ideal of value-free counseling is impossible and dangerous. The non-political stand is misleadingly political, and the detached worker conveys values despite her detachment. If we do not recognize these assumptions, we (and our clients) cannot fully examine or challenge them (p. 87).

This brief foray into the political-ethical domain of practice is not a side-trip from or an add-on to the preceding arguments of this essay. Rather, these assumptions that touch on the risks of power and the centrality of ethical awareness in themselves call for a strength-oriented approach to our work with people. I argue that social work is, fundamentally, an ethical and moral enterprise that is all too often obscured by all sorts of technical, faddish, or theoretical embroidery. All this jargon and pseudo-technology becomes irrelevant, however, once we are willing and able to enter the client's metaphoric and moral world.

For it is not symptoms or defects that are expressed by these metaphors; rather they often symbolize a struggle with moral anguish, value conflicts, or the conditions of living that impede growth and achievement. As a colleague and perhaps as a mentor, the social worker appreciates that, in most instances, it is not a disorder of the psyche or mind that is at the root of suffering or a personal sense of failure. Instead, it is the discord and strife that come into being when life seems too chaotic and out of control, when the integrity of self is at risk, and when former values and beliefs seem to be no longer reliable.

A PERSONAL FOOTNOTE

If we can put aside our cherished theories and other presumptive notions about the human state and listen carefully to how people frame and define their own lives, it is then that we might truly learn something about the meaning of strength, the limits of a medico-scientific framework. As well, we might understand the ethical and moral incentives that shape the quality of life. The most reliable text cannot be found in the universal and abstract features of the theory; rather, it is contained within the story our clients will tell us about their lives.

A study of lives in which I am now involved is most instructive in this regard. The lives in question are those of a number of older people who spent most of their childhood in an institution for dependent children that existed for many years prior to World War II. Although the early experiences of my respondents varied, on one point there is complete agreement: life in the institution was harsh and deprived. Physical punishment was not uncommon, parental care and professional services were lacking as were other conditions we believe are necessary for proper development.

Contradicting standard developmental theories is the remarkable evidence that, almost without exception, all who endured their years in this institution succeeded in building lives that were and are successful by most standards. Most lives were ordinary and uneventful. Some did well in business, others entered the professions, and a number became social workers. Their families appear to be close-knit and secure, and their own children are now achieving their own successes.

In my conversations with these folks, I ask why they think things turned out so well for them, asking my question after they have recounted their vivid recollections of pain and hardship in institutional life. Their responses are fascinating, revealing personal sketches of strength, mastery, and will fortified by commitment to certain values—some religious, others about caring for and obligation to others.

A few were puzzled by my question, since they had never considered there was any other alternative but to do well. Others gave the question some thought and observed, "It was hard, but it was also good since I learned that I had to depend on myself," or "I learned how important self-discipline is," or "Because religion was so heavily stressed, I did get some values that helped me when I became an adult," or "It helped me understand how people should be treated." Still others who vividly recalled how hurt and angry they were as children said things such as, "I had to do OK in spite of the way I was treated," or "I promised myself that I would do the best I could just to show them."

There was one exception to these fairly consistent stories which leaves me wondering whether the good fortune of these people resulted from the absence of mental health services. This one exception was a woman, now in her early sixties, whom I will call Betty. By all accounts, her life was fulfilling and secure. I could see that her home was lovely, that her husband adored her, and that both had great pride in their children's success. Betty was about ready to retire from her long and rewarding career as a teacher of handicapped children.

However, when she finally spoke about her childhood years in the home, she did so with unexpected bitterness and resentment, pouring forth a litany of hurts and rejections. Puzzled and surprised, I asked my question: Then how did things turn out as they did? How did she see the connection between a wretched past and the pride that she expressed about her life?

She started to respond and then paused—obviously reflecting on what she had just told me. A bit bewildered, she mentioned, almost out of context, that she had been seeing a therapist for a while. Her beloved father had died a few years before, and since that loss, which she felt so deeply, she had not been able to shake off some feelings of depression. Then she added, as a rather solemn response to my question: "You know, I had never given much thought to my childhood in the home until I went into therapy. It never seemed that important to me until my therapist asked me about my childhood. When I told her about the institution, my therapist got really upset and told me that I had the most pathological childhood she had ever heard!" She thought for a moment, and then wistfully asked of no one, "Was it?"

REFERENCES

Becker, A. (1964). *The revolution in psychiatry*. New York: Free Press.

Buss, A. R. (1979). *A dialectical psychology*. New York: Irvington Publishers.

Ellenberger, H. (1970). *The discovery of the unconscious*. New York: Basic Books.

Gazzaniga, M. S. (1988). *Mind matters*. Boston: Houghton Mifflin.

Gergen, K. J. (1985). The social constructionist movement in modern psychology. *American Psychologist, 40,* 266–275.

Gleick, J. (1987). *Chaos: Making a new science*. New York: Viking Press.

Heisenberg, W. (1958). *Physics and philosophy: The revolution in modern science*. New York: Harper & Brothers.

Rhodes, M. (1986). *Ethical dilemmas in social work practice*. Boston: Routledge and Kegan Paul.

Sontag, S. (1978). *Illness as metaphor*. New York: Farrar, Straus and Giroux.

PART II

Practice Ideology, Principles, and Methods in the Strengths Perspective

CHAPTER 4

Introduction:
Beginnings of a Strengths Approach to Practice

Dennis Saleebey

> *If we scrutinize a person selectively to discover his weaknesses, his faults, or the ways in which he is deficient, we can always find some, although certainly this may vary in some degree or obviousness. If, on the other hand, we look to the ways in which that same person is whole or healthy, we may also be able to discover many things. So it will appear that the point of reference will determine which of the characteristics we will find. "Seek and ye shall find."*
>
> *(Beisser, 1990, p. 181)*

Arnold Beisser, a practicing physician who has been quadriplegic for thirty years, wrote these words in his wonderful little book *Flying Without Wings*. This is a poignant declaration of the root appreciation of the strengths perspective: if you want to find strengths you have to assume they are there, and then you have to look for them. The scales may have to fall from your eyes, and you may have to suspend cognitive and professional judgments and assessments in order to find the capabilities within this individual, group, or family. As a practitioner, the pressure often is on you to make little more than a rigorous evaluation of the problems you confront. Once you have made a move in that direction, however, you have also moved away from discerning the strengths of the individual. Understanding the snares, barriers, and pitfalls that individuals face and/or create for themselves in everyday life may be important. However, the presumption that this is the most important information sends you down a path that veers dramatically away from the one indicated by a strengths appreciation.

You will see throughout this section a vital and unmistakable belief in the capabilities of individuals, groups, and families. It comes across in many different ways, but the following ideas are resoundingly clear:

Copyright © 1992 by Longman Publishing Group.

- People are often doing amazingly well, the best they can at the time, given the difficulties they face and the *known* resources available to them.
- People have survived to this point—certainly, not without pain—but with ideas, will, hopes, skills, and other people, all of which we need to understand and appreciate in order to help.
- Change can only happen when you collaborate with clients' aspirations, perceptions, and strengths and when you firmly believe in them.

To work within an empowering ideology requires us to identify (for ourselves, for others, and for the people with whom we work) the abilities they possess which may not be obvious, even to themselves. . . . It is always easier to see what is wrong, and what people lack. Empowering research [and practice] attempts to identify what is right with people, and what resources are already available, so as to encourage their use and expansion under the control of the people of concern (Rappaport, 1990, p. 12).

To find the strengths in people and their situation requires that we give credence to the way clients experience and construct social realities. We cannot impose from without our versions (or those of the agency or some larger social institution) of the world. This appreciation of context is an acknowledgment of the special and unique social circumstances of each client (Rose, 1990). That acknowledgment is essential to discovering the hopes and the possibilities of the individuals you seek to help. You will see in the chapters that follow that a high level of commitment and resolve is required to "get you into the client's world" authentically and respectfully.

Though I do not think that any of the authors of chapters 5–10 use the term, it seems apparent that their approach to helping consumers occurs through a kind of *dialogue;* a give-and-take that begins with the demystification of the professional as expert, an operating sense of humility on the part of the helper, the establishment of an egalitarian transaction, the desire to engage clients on their own terms, and a willingness to disclose and share (Freire, 1973; Rose, 1990).

. . . empowerment means a process of dialogue through which the client is continuously supported to produce the range of possibility that she/he sees appropriate to his/her needs; that the client is the center for all decisions that affect her/his life (Rose, 1990, p. 49).

Another theme that runs throughout these chapters, though not specifically identified as such, is consciousness raising. As a result of the strengths approach, consumers begin to develop a less contaminated and constricted view of their situation and identity, and they take on a firmer appreciation of how their lives have been shackled by institutions, agencies, and ideologies. In other words, consumers are assisted in coming to a more authentic sense of who they are, what they can do, and what they want to do.

There *is* strength in numbers. While Rappaport, Reischl, and Zimmerman's chapter is the clearest expression of this, those who have used the strengths perspective of case management report that conventional mental health services tend to isolate and alienate those who use them. Once a consumer is engaged in a strengths approach, a desire to "normalize" life often develops. That may mean learning from and being with others who have experienced the same kind of treatment (Rapp and Kisthardt, personal communication). These contacts also become an opportunity for further consciousness-raising and confidence building.

For the social worker, a strengths perspective inevitably leads one out into the world of the client and out from behind the desk. Not only is it important to understand clients' constructed worlds of experience, but it is important to identify and encourage naturally occurring resources in the clients' world. In all cases, the resources that are a part of the "natural" social community are to be sought before relying upon the more formal agency network of social services. Why? Because they are a part of the clients' everyday milieu, and will be there when the client needs them. Also, these resources typically do not foster detachment and separation from the community, nor do they usually stigmatize participants and consumers.

A final theme I would like the reader to be alert for is that the strengths perspective as these authors reveal and elaborate it *is good, basic social work practice.* There is nothing here that is not coincidental with the core of social work values that energizes the profession. All that we do within these pages is to try to give these principles more conceptual and practical invigoration.

The opening chapter, by Charles Rapp, sets the tone of our new commitment; in essence what Rapp is doing is laying down another, better paradigm (as opposed to the heavily medicalized current one) for practice in the mental health field. Walter Kisthardt, in his chapter, breathes life into the principles laid down by Rapp, lacing them with many instructive examples. Julian Rappaport, Thomas Reischl, and Marc Zimmerman lay out an array of principles that explain the success of GROW, and then illustrate those principles with vivid case examples. Eloise Rathbone-McCuan follows with a chapter that, among other things, demonstrates the real potency of a strengths approach. She describes its application with clients rarely considered in positive terms: elderly women who are thought to be neglectful of themselves. John Poertner and John Ronnau recount similar successes that have occurred with another population often evaluated in unremittingly negative terms: youth with emotional disabilities. Finally, Mary Bricker-Jenkins describes a program she is helping to develop for women on public welfare to help them move toward less dependence and greater self-esteem: a program based upon what she and her colleagues *have learned from the consumers.* And that is, again, of singular importance in this approach: we do not impose our system of understanding, evaluation, or intervention, however beguiling or popular, upon clients. Instead, we try to learn as much as we can about how they are managing and how they have done things right so that we can begin from that point and collaborate with them as they move in directions that they have identified.

As you read these chapters, remember that preliminary research conducted at the University of Kansas shows that the strengths model of case management for individuals with chronic mental illness is successful in that most consumers have moved toward independent living in the community and the "normalization" (using naturally occurring community resources) of life style.

REFERENCES

Beisser, A. (1990). *Flying without wings: Personal reflections on loss, disability, and healing.* New York: Bantam.

Freire, P. (1973). *Pedagogy of the oppressed.* New York: Seabury.

Rappaport, J. (1990). Research methods and the empowerment agenda. In P. Tolan, C. Keys, F. Chertak, and L. Jason, eds., *Researching community psychology.* Washington, DC: American Psychological Association.

Rose, S. M. (1990). Advocacy/empowerment: An approach to clinical practice for social work. *Journal of Sociology and Social Welfare, 17,* 41–52.

CHAPTER 5

The Strengths Perspective of Case Management with Persons Suffering from Severe Mental Illness

Charles A. Rapp

A research team from the University of Kansas School of Social Welfare has devoted much of the last eight years to developing, testing, and disseminating a strengths perspective of case management for people suffering with severe and persistent mental illness. This paper will describe the principles underlying the perspective and several consequences of its implementation.

BACKGROUND

The development and use of psychotropic medications in the 1950s allowed previously intractable symptoms to be reduced if not controlled. This contributed to the massive discharge of patients from psychiatric hospitals to community settings with the promise of a better quality of life. From 1955 to 1980 the population in state hospitals was reduced from 558,992 to 175,000 (Foley and Sharpstein, 1983). Unfortunately, the hope of deinstitutionalization was gradually replaced by despair as patients were discharged to urban ghettos without access to adequate housing and services, a large homeless population was created, a huge burden was placed on families who often did not have the personal or financial resources to cope with such demands, unemployment rates for these people exceeded 80 percent, and few were involved in any vocational training. For many, the quality of life was far worse than in the hospitals. One result of the situation was the creation of the "revolving door" where extended hospital stays of the past were replaced with more frequent but briefer hospitalizations. In fact, in recent years, hospital readmissions approximate 70 percent of all admissions (Goldman, Adams, and Taube, 1983).

Copyright © 1992 by Longman Publishing Group.

These scandalous conditions helped unmask the inadequacies of the community mental health "system." The central deficit was the ineffectiveness and irrelevance of traditional mental health services for this population. Psychotherapy practiced within the mental health center was adequate neither to address a disease with biosociological roots nor to ease the oppressive economic social conditions under which these people lived. Overlaid on this was the apathy of many professionals toward serving this population.

In 1978, the National Institute of Mental Health (NIMH) launched the Community Support Program (CSP) as an effort to remedy the situation. CSP was defined as "a network of caring and responsible people committed to assisting a vulnerable population to meet their needs and develop their potentials without being necessarily isolated or excluded from their community" (Turner and Shifren, 1979, p. 2). NIMH guidelines specified the CSP components as essential for work with persons suffering from severe mental illness including crisis stabilization, assistance with entitlements, psychosocial rehabilitation, housing and work opportunities, and support to caregivers. The centerpiece of these recommendations was the establishment of case management to guarantee each person the continuous availability of appropriate forms of assistance (Turner and Ten Hoor, 1978).

Despite the importance ascribed to case management and its popularity with state and local policymakers, the concept lacks clarity and definition. The most common description posits five functions: assessment, case planning, brokerage, advocacy, and monitoring and evaluation. There are, however, few well-specified models detailing the methodologies for each function. The result has been proliferation of services and practices now labeled case management but which vary from in-office counseling to crisis intervention to information and referral to assertive outreach. The research examining the efficacy of case management has produced generally positive results using rather primitive designs, questionable measures, and a prevalent failure to specify the independent variable. In addition, there have been studies that suggest case management is ineffective and perhaps toxic to clients (Fisher, Landis, and Clark, 1988; Franklin et al., 1987).

THE STRENGTHS PERSPECTIVE

The strengths perspective of case management is based on six principles and a set of procedures that operationalize the principles throughout the helping process (see Modrcin, Rapp, and Chamberlain, 1985). The six principles act as the driving force of the model:

1. The focus is on individual strengths rather than pathology.
2. The case manager–client relationship is primary and essential.
3. Interventions are based on client self-determination.
4. The community is viewed as an oasis of resources, not as an obstacle.
5. Aggressive outreach is the preferred mode of intervention.
6. People suffering from severe mental illness can continue to learn, grow, and change.

Principle 1: The Focus Is on Individual Strengths Rather Than Pathology

Underlying this principle is the assumption that people tend to develop and grow based on their individual interests, aspirations, and strengths. We tend to spend time doing things that we do well and that have meaning. We tend to avoid things we do poorly or that we think we will do poorly. At best, solving problems returns us to an equilibrium, but exploiting strengths and opportunities promotes growth.

Based on these assumptions, the work with clients should not be directed at their symptomatology, psychosis, or, for that matter, problems, weaknesses, and deficits. Rather, the work should focus on what the client has done, what resources have been or are currently available to the client, what the client knows, and what aspirations and dreams she may hold.

A focus on strengths should also enhance motivation. The typical assessment process, for example, subverts client motivation with its obsession with problems, weaknesses, and deficits; it is a process clients undergo every time they confront yet another mental health professional. If the client has not entered the encounter depressed, by the time she has completed the process, she is sure to be depressed and unmotivated. As Disraeli stated, "The greatest good you can do for another is not just to share your riches but to reveal to him his own."

Principle 2: The Case Manager–Client Relationship Is Primary and Essential

Most models of case management do not attend to the importance of the relationship or prohibit a relationship. The crisis model and the brokerage model of case management are built with an assumption that the work can be done without a close relationship. Nationally, case management caseloads often exceed 80 to 1 and have even reached 200 to 1. A close collaborative relationship cannot be established with 80 people. In contrast, Richard Lamb (1980) advocates a therapist-case manager model for the central reason that a therapist is the one professional with a relationship of sufficient intensity and intimacy necessary to carry out case management. Unfortunately, Lamb's position has been interpreted narrowly in terms of the model rather than the underlying assumption.

As Deitchman (1980) stated:

> Economic survival is not successfully dealt with by referral; neither is psychological survival. For the chronic client to survive psychologically, he needs someone he can have a relationship with, someone he can confide in, someone he can depend on. The chronic client in the community needs a traveling companion, not a travel agent. The travel agent's only function is to make the client's reservation. The client has to get ready, get to the airport, and traverse foreign terrain by himself. The traveling companion, on the other hand, celebrates the fact that his friend was able to get seats on the plane, talks about his fear of flying, and then goes on the trip with him, sharing the joys and sorrows that occur during the venture (p. 789).

It is the relationship that buffers the demands of the tough times, anxious times. It is the relationship that attenuates the stress, and prevents or mitigates the exacerbation of symptoms. It is the relationship that supports the client's confidence in tackling the multiple requirements of the environment and other people.

Principle 3: Interventions Are Based on Client Self-Determination

A cornerstone of the strengths perspective of case management is the belief that it is a client's right to determine the form, direction, and substance of the case management help she is to receive. People with major mental illness are capable of this determination, and adhering to this principle contributes to the effectiveness of case management. Case managers should do nothing without the client's approval, involving clients in decisions regarding every step of the process. Opportunities to move each client closer to being the director of the case management scenario should be found, created, and exploited. One benefit of this stance is that it protects case managers from asking too much of clients or from asking the client to do something that would be the "wrong" thing for the client; both of which can contribute to symptom exacerbation. It also foreshortens tension between clients and case managers.

People often ask, "What do persons with major mental illness need?" The answer is, "What such people need is what they want. What they want is what any of us want: a decent place to live and adequate income; friends and opportunities to recreate; an opportunity to contribute (work, family, helping others) and recognition for that contribution." A study by Ewalt and Honeyfield (1981) found that hospitalized psychotic patients viewed the following as their needs to "make it" in the community: (1) money, (2) availability of health care, (3) a decent place to live, (4) transportation, (5) opportunities for socialization, (6) availability of help if needed. Thirty-three percent of those interviewed (N = 253) also stated the importance of the need to "be of help to others." These findings parallel the recent findings of successful programs (Gowdy, Rapp, and Poertner, 1987). That is, the programs that have produced the best results are those that conscientiously address these areas of need. In contrast, "Efforts at deinstitutionalization that rely primarily on professional judgments, at least in the mental health field, have failed miserably, with an overwhelming proportion of discharged long-term residents unable to maintain ongoing community tenure" (Ewalt and Honeyfield, 1981, p. 223).

Contrast the language, if not the substance, of the above list reflecting client perceptions with the following list generated by researchers and professionals at the Research Meeting on Community Support and Rehabilitation Services (1988). Outcomes areas included (1) service integration, (2) access to mental health services, (3) service coordination, (4) brokerage, (5) service availability, (6) interagency cooperation, (7) systems level support, and (8) systems interface issues in relation to case management. Whether taken literally or metaphorically, selecting one language over another will inevitably lead down a very different path. The position here is that if client self-determination is to be taken seriously, the client's desires must be given absolute primacy.

Principle 4: The Community Is Viewed as a Resource and Not an Obstacle

Two assumptions underlie this principle. First, a person's behavior and well-being is in large part determined by the resources available and the expectations of others toward the person. Second, clients have a right to the societal resources they need (Davidson and Rapp, 1976; Rappaport, 1977). The case manager's task is to create community collaborators; to become a catalyst for others in the community who care. Juxtapose this position with the more common stance blaming the community for lack of employment, housing, and recreation opportunities. The community as scapegoat can be just as inimical to effective helping as blaming the clients. Both can lead to a sense of paralysis, frustration, and impotence.

The task of resource acquisition should emphasize normal or natural resources, not mental health services, because community integration can occur only apart from mental health and segregated services. The assumption which has been largely confirmed in our experience is that in any population there are a sufficient number of caring and potentially helpful people available to assist and support clients. The burden of proof on case managers should be that to use a mental health service, it must be first demonstrated that, natural helpers, community services (e.g., recreation department) and social services (in that order) cannot be organized on behalf of the client.

The essentiality of this principle has been underscored by one of the more rigorous studies of case management to date. Franklin et al. (1987) randomly divided 417 patients with major mental illness who were discharged from a psychiatric hospital at least twice and at least once within two years prior to the study into an experimental group who received case management and a control group who did not receive this service. Here are the results at the one year follow-up:

- CM clients received 71 percent (18,250) of all services (25,707) reported for both groups.
- Ninety-six percent (24,678) of all services were given by TCMHMR Services:
  Ninety-six percent (17,607) of all services received by CM clients
  Ninety-five percent (7,071) of all services received by control clients
- Twenty-nine percent (62) of the CM group and 19 percent (38) of the control group were hospitalized.
- Twice as many CM clients (20 versus 10) were admitted to state hospitals, and they stayed longer (average 118.5 versus 112.7 days).
- More CM clients (42 versus 28) were admitted to county hospitals, but they stayed 19.1 days as compared with 19.4 days for controls.
- Inpatient services cost $441,434 for the CM group (average $7,120) and $237,480 for the control group (average $6,249).
  State hospital costs per client @ $128.66 per day
  CM: *$15,246* (N = 20, 2, 370 bed days, $304,924 total)
  Controls: *$14,500* (N = 10, 1, 127 bed days, $145,000 total)

County hospital costs per client @ $170 per day
  CM: *$3,250* (N = 42, 803 bed days, $136,510 total)
  Controls: *$3,303* (N = 28, 544 bed days, $29,480 total)
No significant differences in quality of life between CM group and control
group at the beginning and at the end of study.

The irony of the study is that the case managers were incredibly successful by standard definitions of case management—linking clients to mental health services. Yet the success produced a consistent array of iatrogenic consequences for clients (e.g., increased hospitalization) at more cost, usually, to the community.

Principle 5: Aggressive Outreach Is the Preferred Mode of Intervention

Given the above principles of client self-determination and the priority of naturally occurring resources, it should be clear that office-based involvement and interventions are contraindicated. A case manager cannot sit in the office and locate, arrange, and support an employer with a job the client desires. The work must occur in apartments, restaurants, businesses, parks, and community agencies. Office contact with clients should be limited to the few cases when the client prefers it (usually for psychological safety), and this is rare.

An outreach mode offers rich opportunities for assessment and intervention. Office-bound assessment limits the sources of data to what the client says, the case manager's observations of the client, and the ten-inch stack of paper referred to as a case file. This is simply not enough for a variety of reasons.

First, a client's behavior in a mental health program is often different from her behavior in other settings. "Thorazine shuffle" disappears in many cases once the individual leaves the mental health center and work on developing strengths begins. The opposite is also true. Many clients can and do cook, clean, and socialize while in structured day treatment or partial hospitalization programs, but fail to do so in their own apartments and neighborhoods (Rapp and Wintersteen, 1986a). Skills learned inside agencies do not appear to easily generalize to more normalized settings (Gutride, Goldstein, and Hunter, 1973; Jaffe and Carlson, 1976; Liberman et al., 1985).

Second, the client's perception of resources available is just that, a perception. Most people are unaware of the potential resources available. There have been many examples of this in the eight years of our program. In one case, a client wanted to earn his GED certificate and attend classes to do so. The case manager helped the client arrange such classes only two blocks from the boardinghouse, but discovered that the client did not go to the first two sessions. The indication was that the client was scared. Because the case manager was doing the work in the community and more specifically in the boardinghouse, he came to know another resident (not suffering from mental illness) who was more than willing to walk the client to class. After three sessions, this was no longer needed and the client went on to earn his certificate. The point is that it was unlikely that successful resolution of this problem would have occurred if the work had been done in an office.

Finally, part of a case manager's job is to provide direction to clients, to model certain behaviors, and to teach others. Given the sometimes disorganized and jumbled cognitions of people suffering from major mental illness, each new encounter may produce new anxiety and an inability to use skills in their repertoire (Jaffe and Carlson, 1976; Liberman et al., 1985). As has been already suggested, teaching a client to cook spaghetti for twenty people in a day treatment program on a gas stove can be perceived as very different than cooking spaghetti for one on a hot plate. In vivo instruction removes many of the conditions that impede generalization.

Principle 6: People Suffering from Major Mental Illness Can Continue to Learn, Grow, and Change

This principle overlays the entire perspective. The central belief of our program is that these people are not schizophrenic or chronically mentally ill but that they are people with schizophrenia. It is only one part of their being. They, like us, have a history of pain as well as accomplishment, of talents and foibles, of dreams and aspirations. Interestingly, a recent study of effective programs in Kansas found that the most prevalent common denominator was the managerial and direct service staffs' holistic view of clients (Gowdy and Rapp, 1988).

In so many ways, the mental health system has institutionalized low expectations. In contrast, recent data from the twenty-year follow-up study in Vermont more than suggests that most people suffering from major mental illness can eventually merge into the fabric of a community having jobs, families, friends, and homes (Harding et al., 1987a, 1987b; Harding, Zubin, and Strauss, 1987). What has to be built into any strengths perspective of social work practice is an absolute belief in individuals' capacity to better their lives. With a little help, they will do so. The practice perspective must reek of "can do" in every stage of the helping process.

CONSEQUENCES

Eight years of work on the strengths perspective of case management has led to several insights on the perspective and the process of helping. These lessons are briefly described below.

Insight 1: The Strengths Perspective Enhances Individualization of Clients

The last six years have provided us with the opportunity to witness the professional practice of hundreds of mental health personnel in scores of agencies in over a dozen states. The development of case plans is central to virtually all efforts at helping and, despite great variations in formats, all case plans include as their centerpiece a delineation of goals. In the more typical program one might conclude that there are only two or three clients being served in all these venues because the case plans and goals vary little or are all the same; they are generic. Ninety percent of the goals are included in this listing of the typical case plan: (1) improve personal hygiene, (2) improve daily living skills, (3) improve socialization skills, (4) improve prevocational skills or work readiness, (5) take medication as prescribed, and (6) show up for appointments and follow through with treatment plan. While these case plans can often be criticized for lack of specificity and behavioral referents, inadequate specification of the actions to be taken to reach these goals, and the absence of time frames and client participation in their designation, the most abhorrent observation is that they reflect a form of practice which sees all clients as the same.

Our first reaction to the generality of case plans was that it reflected poor practice, poor supervision, and poor training. In other words, it was technical in nature. The prevalence of these plans, however, suggested that it may be less technical than conceptual. This explanation gained plausibility when we found that "generic brand" client case plans were found in some of the best agencies and written by otherwise exceptional professionals.

We therefore believe that the problem or pathology model of practice promotes the homogenization of clients and prohibits individualization. Consider the following two sets of questions which we use in training to make this point. Envision a group of one hundred people responding to these questions.

How many of you have arguments with your partner?

How many of you have arguments concerning money or finances?

How many of these arguments are based on one partner spending too much money on the wrong things?

How many of these arguments are based on spending too much money on clothing?

How many people like music?

How many people can play an instrument?

How many people can play a horn?

How many can play a saxophone?

There will be at least ten people who would still be included after the first four questions. After the second four, there will be one, two, or occasionally three.

The lesson seems to be that human problems are finite and shared by many of us, although how we experience these problems may be highly personal. On the other hand, our uniqueness as individuals seems to be more a function of strengths that are highly idiosyncratic; the configuration of these strengths in a given individual is even more so.

To enhance and expose the client as individual, then, assessment and case planning methods need to be based on an exploration of a person's strengths. To do otherwise is to direct our minds and our practice toward "standardized" human beings and thereby do injustice to the cardinal value of social work, which places the individual, in all of his or her elegance and uniqueness, at the center of our concerns, and ultimately to reduce the effectiveness of our efforts.

The dominance of the generic client idea can be experienced through talking with long-time clients. In the vocational domain, for example, women clients will often state their job interests as some form of domestic or secretary, despite one woman having a profound interest in art, another having a long-time gardening hobby, and still another being devoted to animals. But they have all been socialized to accept that the job for them is a maid at Holiday Inn, at minimum wage. The irony is that these women are not even interested in keeping their apartments or room in a group home orderly and clean. Then we wonder why our clients do not follow through on job opportunities or fail to keep jobs for more than the briefest times. They do not need more skill development or more medication to control their symptoms, but jobs that they are interested in if not passionate about. And this kind of job can only be arranged by being fully apprised of a client's unique strengths.

We, as professionals, can sometimes deceive ourselves by thinking that we are using a strengths assessment perspective when we actually are reframing problems positively and thereby operating from a problem (or deficit) assessment perspective. For example, a professional who has assessed a client as being overly dependent on her parents may discuss with the client her enormous capacity for caring about others as exemplified by her relationship with her parents. This would represent a positive reframing of a problem to make it more palatable for the client to hear and therefore grapple with the problem. It is a problem focus leading to a set of case plans aimed at the parent–child relationship. A strengths assessment would identify and develop strengths that may have little to do with parent–child relationships and issues. The case plans for strengths development lead in an entirely different direction, and a result of developing strengths is usually greater autonomy. The diminution of the identified problem—reframed or not—occurs spontaneously in the process of human growth. The initial focus of the professional's work, not a reframing of that focus, is the determinant of whether the strengths or problem orientation is being employed.

Insight 2: Strengths Facilitate Partners Not Adversaries

The tension between clients and workers is often obscured by the professional lexicon, including such phrases as "resistance to therapy" and "setting up the client to fail." The first phrase has the wonderful effect of camouflaging the conflict by explaining the behavior as a rather natural occurrence in the helping process and as a function of the client's personality. It is therefore neither upsetting nor remediable by the professional attempting to change the client's behavior.

The second phrase is heard when a client suggests a goal or aspiration that the professional views as unrealistic and thinks giving permission to pursue it could lead to pain, suffering, exacerbation of symptoms, and regression. Its effect is to deprive the person of one of the most precious elements of humanness—the need for a dream. It further suggests a parent–child relationship of unequal knowledge, power, and protection; guarantees not of a partnership but of an adversarial relationship.

Believing and adhering to a strict code of client self-determination and the skillfully assessing strengths seem to facilitate a partnership between client and worker. The professional works on behalf of the client, and the client's goals and aspirations become the centerpiece of the work. Why do clients not follow through on medication regimens? Why does a client refuse to take a bath? Why doesn't this person show up for her group session and when she does, why is she disruptive? Clients' lack of compliance and lack of progress seem as much a function of their hostility toward a system that is irrelevant to their needs and hopes as it is a function of their personalities and their disability. In fact, failing to follow alien prescriptive demands is often the only way we allow them to express their opinion and their sense of power.

A cooperative relationship often starts with playing basketball or doing the dishes or going shopping together as the client tests the worker's promises, interests, and sincerity. As confidence in the relationship replaces skepticism and the client becomes reaffirmed as a person with assets and valid aspirations, goals become more ambitious, communication more honest, and assistance more accessible.

Insight 3: Strengths Orientation Fosters Empowerment

Two of the most oppressed groups in mental health are clients and their case managers. While the oppression of clients has been well documented (Brandt, 1975; Szasz, 1970), that of case managers has not. Basically, they are the lowest paid, the lowest on the organizational hierarchy, and the least credentialed, yet have the most cases and the most ambitious goals set out for them. They also have to complete the most paperwork, go to the same meetings as others, and are the most supervised members of the organization. They have the least control over their jobs and have the least influence over organizational or client matters.

The strengths orientation cannot address this body of factors. In some small way, however, it may provide some enhanced sense of power for both clients and case managers by (1) replacing the mutual conflict with a partnership; (2) encouraging the vigilance needed to identify strengths, which forces the individual to look for the good rather than the bad and to enhance the positiveness of worker activities; (3) defining the community as oasis, allowing individuals to see possibilities where only limitations were seen before; (4) leading to improved client outcomes, so that both worker and client can see results and experience the satisfaction they can bring. In short, we have seen workers (and clients) with a new sense that they can make a difference.

One indicator of the perspective as an empowerer of clients is the consistent phenomenon of client achievements in areas not targeted or attended to by the case manager. Here is an example:

> John R. is a twenty-seven-year-old man who has a diagnosis of Schizophrenia, Paranoid Type. In the absence of a group home bed or transitional apartment in the community, John was discharged from a three-month admission to the state hospital to his parents' home. Upon intake, the following problems were recorded for attention by the treatment team at the Community Support Program where he was referred for aftercare: (1) lacks motivation to engage in social activities; (2) displays poor judgment regarding how he manages his money; (3) needs to improve communication skills with peers; (4) needs to become more compliant with medication regimen and reduce abusing alcohol; and (5) needs to effectively individuate from family of origin. The chart also noted that John enjoyed sports, was in good physical health, and was assertive with staff in expressing his wants and needs. In order to achieve these treatment goals, John was scheduled to attend the partial hospitalization program, attend a medication clinic, and work with a case manager.

During the subsequent weeks, John's behavior began to concern the staff. His parents were reporting that he was staying up very late watching TV, drinking despite their protests, and not attending the partial program on a regular basis. The case manager made a home visit, and reluctantly John agreed to come downstairs to talk with her. At this meeting the case manager conducted a strengths assessment with John and learned several things: he did not want to move into his own apartment at this time, and he did not want to go to the partial program and spend all day with "those crazy people." What he did want to do was to get his driver's license and save up enough money to buy a car. This information led to a discussion of cars, John showed the case manager the many model cars he had put together, and they talked of how much he enjoyed the auto mechanics class he had taken in high school. They agreed to meet the following week at a local gas station, where the case manager knew the manager. The manager agreed to allow John to volunteer for two hours each day, doing odd jobs and going to pick up needed parts at the nearby parts dealership. During the next few weeks, John began to take his medication more regularly, and his attendance and participation at the partial program showed marked improvement. His parents also reported that he was no longer staying up late watching TV and that he was not abusing alcohol at home. After three months of volunteering at the gas station, John began to talk of trying to move to his own apartment with a roommate, a mechanic he had met at the station. The owner of the station was also considering hiring John as a part-time paid employee.

The observed pattern over the last eight years of our program is so strong as to demand an explanation: Regular trips to the library lead to working on grooming; working on joining a bowling league leads to better maintenance of an apartment; participation in the local theater group leads to work on weight loss and nutrition; work on moving to an apartment leads to better medication compliance. These secondary achievements occur without explicit attention by the case manager. Rather than appealing to the notion of "spontaneous recovery," it may be that success in one area breeds efforts and success in others; that success empowers clients to try areas where they lacked the confidence or willingness to try before.

Insight 4: Blending Societal, Programmatic, and Client Goals

The helping relationship occurs in an arena of competing demands and agenda by multiple constituencies (Martin, 1980). As Taber (1987) has said, social work not only is a servant of the client but of a larger society which "foots the bill" to remediate some social problem. There is an emerging consensus that the core outcomes for case management are improving vocational and independent living status or functioning, increasing social supports, and securing community tenure. These outcomes speak directly to the interests of legislators, citizens, many professionals, and most clients. Program evaluation and management information systems are being designed to capture these dimensions as a way of measuring performance (Rapp et al., 1988).

Into this arena comes a case manager who has been taught about client self-determination and a client whose only goal is to learn how to play the guitar better. Success will not show up on any evaluation except perhaps a reference in the case file. All of a sudden, the client's goal is not consonant with those of other interested parties. It is credible but all too easy to see the problem as society or technically in terms of inadequate management information systems (MIS) or evaluation systems.

Rather, the problem is often that the case manager assumes a passive posture in the helping relationship by becoming a servant to the client: If the client wants a donut, I will run and get him a donut. This is no more a partnership than when the professional dictates to the client. In almost all cases, this perspective comes from a sincere acceptance of client self-determination. It also assumes the client knows all rather than the client knows best; two very different ideas.

An alternative perspective is for the case manager to help the client explore new vistas. Guitar lessons can turn into getting paid for working in a music store or giving lessons or performing; ideas that the client may never have considered or may have discarded years earlier. This is not talking a client into something, but creating new possibilities by blending different strengths. In some cases it may be nothing more than "planting seeds" that can be regularly watered. It may mean visiting a music store, talking to musicians, attending performances, or scanning classified ads for gigs. The client has the right to make the choices, but freedom may best be served by knowledge of the choices possible and the confidence that the person could successfully select from among these choices.

CONCLUSION

The strengths perspective of case management has been the subject of several research efforts (Rapp and Chamberlain, 1985; Rapp and Wintersteen, 1986b; Modrcin, Rapp, and Poertner, 1988). Consistently positive findings have been produced in reducing the incidence of hospitalization and the length of hospitalization, and in increasing individual case goal attainment, client satisfaction, and quality of clients' lives. Additional research is continuing with a particular focus on assessing the contribution various elements make to the positive results.

I think it is fair to say that we underestimated the differences between working from a strengths perspective and from a problem or pathological perspective. This naiveté most clearly manifests itself in two ways. First, despite our rhetoric, admonitions, training, and passion, trainees have had trouble translating client strengths into case plans or working agreements between the client and worker. Thus, the woman who says she wants a housekeeping job will be helped to find a housekeeping job, and the fact that this woman is driven by a passion for art is not usually a part of such discussions. This is probably a function of our tendency to compartmentalize clients' lives rather than looking at them holistically. It is an outgrowth of the problem orientation where the problem (e.g., inadequate social skills) leads to a rather automatic and particular solution (e.g., teach social skills). Helping trainees consider strengths in one part of a person's life when attending to issues and possibilities in another domain is difficult. A second manifestation of naiveté is to view a strengths approach as positively reframing deficits, excesses, and problems. A person's seeming obsession with illness and psychosomatic sickness is now viewed as a strong and measurable concern with her health. A person who does not attend scheduled group or therapy sessions is now asserting independence. Lack of interest in friends or group activities is now an indicator of self-reliance. Part of a strengths perspective is reframing; but here it is reframing the professional's understanding of behavior from the client's perspective as serving a useful purpose and reflecting a possible strength. And a strengths perspective is much more than reframing problems and deficits; a strengths perspective identifies the real talents, histories, and aspirations unique to each individual, and often unrecognized and unappreciated by them.

We frequently confront resistance and downright hostility when presenting these ideas to groups of veteran mental health professionals. Although it plays itself out in a myriad of ways, it seems at its root to reflect a fear of loss of status (the all-knowing professional) and the comfort received from perceiving clients as inferior, lacking, and/or ignorant. The pain mental health professionals feel because of their ineffectiveness can be assuaged by ascribing the responsibility for it to the schizophrenic client or to the hostile environment. But resistance to the idea of building on the potential of clients and communities may be based on the recognition that it would require a form of practice that is not as safe as fifty-minute hours in a comfortable office, but is a mode of helping that delivers in the community, often during nontraditional hours, and frequently with many unknowns.

The nascent formulation of a strengths perspective for case management services to persons with long-term mental illness offers a means by which mental health practice can become more congruent with the core values of social work and thereby better delineate the unique role of the profession in mental health. Our early research evidence also indicates that client outcomes and service effectiveness can be enhanced by the adoption of such a practice perspective. It is hoped that the ideas presented herein can contribute to the further development and refinement of a perspective of social work practice that can be applied to other populations and stand as a viable alternative to pathology-based practice.

REFERENCES

Brandt, A. (1975). *Reality police: The experience of insanity in America.* New York: William Morrow.

Davidson, W. and Rapp, C. (1976). Child advocacy in the justice system. *Social Work, 21*(3), 225–232.

Deitchman, W. S. (1980). How many case managers does it take to screw in a light bulb? *Hospital and Community Psychiatry, 31*(11), 788–789.

Ewalt, P. L. and Honeyfield, R. M. (1981). Needs of persons in long term care. *Social Work, 26*(3), 223–231.

Fisher, G., Landis, D., and Clark, K. (1988). Case management service provision and client change. *Community Mental Health Journal, 24*(2), 134–142.

Franklin, J., Solovitz, B., Mason, M., Clemmons, J., and Mitler, D. (1987). An evaluation of case management. *American Journal of Public Health, 77*(6), 674–678.

Foley, H. and Sharpstein, S. (1983). *Madness and government.* Washington, DC: American Psychiatric Press.

Goldman, H. H., Adams, N. H., and Taube, C. A. (1983). Deinstitutionalization: The data demythologized. *Hospital and Community Psychiatry, 34*(2), 129–134.

Gowdy, E., and Rapp, C. A. (1988). *Managerial behavior: The common denominators of successful community based programs.* Unpublished manuscript. Lawrence: University of Kansas, School of Social Welfare.

Gowdy, E., Rapp, C. A., and Poertner, J. (1987). *Managing for performance: Using information to enhance community integration of the chronically mentally ill.* Unpublished manuscript. Lawrence: University of Kansas, School of Social Welfare.

Gutride, M. E., Goldstein, G. P., and Hunter, G. F. (1973). The use of modeling and role playing to increase social interaction among social psychiatric patients. *Journal of Consulting and Clinical Psychology, 40,* 408–415.

Harding, C. M., Brooks, G. W., Takamaru, A., Strauss, J. S., and Breier, A. (June, 1987a). The Vermont longitudinal study of persons with severe mental illness I: Methodology, study sample, and overall status 32 years later. *American Journal of Psychiatry, 144*(6), 718–726.

Harding, C. M., Brooks, G. W., Takamaru, A., Strauss, J. S., and Breier, A. (June, 1987b). The Vermont longitudinal study of persons with severe mental illness II: Long-term outcome of subjects who retrospectively met DSM-III criteria for schizophrenia. *American Journal of Psychiatry, 144*(6), 727–735.

Harding, C. M., Zubin, J., and Strauss, J. S. (May, 1987). Chronicity in schizophrenia: Fact, partial fact or artifact? *Hospital and Community Psychiatry, 38*(5), 477–486.

Jaffe, P. G. and Carlson, P. M. (1976). Relative efficacy of modeling and instructions in eliciting social behavior from chronic psychiatric patients. *Journal of Consulting and Clinical Psychology, 44,* 200–207.

Lamb, R. H. (1980). Therapist-case managers: More than brokers of service. *Hospital and Community Psychiatry, 31*(11), 762–764.

Liberman, R. P., Massel, H. K., Mosk, M. D., and Wong, S. E. (1985). Social skills training for chronic mental patients. *Hospital and Community Psychiatry, 36*(4), 396–403.

Martin, P. Y. (1980). Multiple constituencies, dominant societal values, and human service administrators. *Administration in Social Work, 4,* 15–27.

Modrcin, M., Rapp, C. A., and Chamberlain, R. (1985). *Case management with psychiatrically disabled individuals: Curriculum and training program.* Unpublished manuscript. Lawrence: University of Kansas, School of Social Welfare.

Modrcin, M., Rapp, C. A., and Poertner, J. (1988). The evaluation of case management services with the chronically mentally ill. *Evaluation and Program Planning, 11*(4).

Rapp, C. A. and Chamberlain, R. (1985). Case management services to the chronically mentally ill. *Social Work, 30*(5), 417–422.

Rapp, C. A., Gowdy, E., Sullivan, W. P., and Wintersteen, R. (1988). Client outcome reporting: The status method. *Community Mental Health Journal, 24*(2), 118–133.

Rapp, C. A. and Wintersteen, R. (1986a). *Client outcome monitoring and evaluation systems.* Unpublished manuscript. Lawrence: University of Kansas, School of Social Welfare.

Rapp, C. A. and Wintersteen, R. (1986b). *Case management with the chronically mentally ill: The results of seven replications.* Unpublished manuscript. Lawrence: University of Kansas, School of Social Welfare.

Rappaport, J. (1977). *Community psychology: Values, research, and action.* New York: Holt, Rinehart and Winston.

Report of the research meeting on community support and rehabilitation service. (May 3–5, 1988). Bethesda, MD: National Institute of Mental Health Community Support Program and National Institute on Disability and Rehabilitation Research.

Szasz, T. B. (1970). *The manufacture of madness.* New York: Harper & Row.

Taber, M. (1987). A theory of accountability for human service and the implications for program design. *Administration in Social Work, 11*(3/4), 115–126.

Turner, J. E. and Shifren, I. (1979). Community support system: How comprehensive? *New Directions for Mental Health Services, 2,* 1–13.

Turner, J. E. and Ten Hoor, W. J. (1978). The NIMH community support program: Pilot approach to a needed social reform. *Schizophrenia Bulletin, 4*(3), 319–348.

CHAPTER 6

A Strengths Model of Case Management:

The Principles and Functions of a Helping Partnership with Persons with Persistent Mental Illness

Walter E. Kisthardt

Thus far in this text the reader has been exposed to the philosophical foundations and some applications of a strengths perspective. Both suggest a fundamental change in the way we view, evaluate, and treat individuals, families, and environments. The shifts in professional values inherent in this perspective inevitably must bring changes in the way we provide helping services. Evidence of service delivery based upon consumer empowerment and personal strengths may be seen in the growing sanction for, and employment of, case management with persons who experience persistent mental illness.

States around the country are currently developing plans to provide individualized case management for this population as a consequence of the passage of Public Law 99-660 in 1986. The "strengths model" of case management, developed out of continuing research at the University of Kansas School of Social Welfare, has been disseminated, through training and ongoing technical assistance, in sixteen states during the past five years. Hundreds of case managers and supervisors are attempting to incorporate this model in their work (Rapp and Chamberlain, 1985; Rapp and Wintersteen, 1989; Kisthardt and Rapp, 1989).

This chapter describes specifically how a strengths model of case management is implemented with individuals suffering from persistent mental illness. The data that support the positions taken in this chapter have been gathered from two converging perspectives. First, the author's own experience in providing case management training and technical assistance has yielded input from case managers and supervisors working in many different states and organizational arrangements. The common struggles in attempting to provide assistance based upon the unique capacities and desires of individuals within a system requiring attention to illness and coping deficits are obvious.

Copyright © 1992 by Longman Publishing Group.

The second perspective is provided by the consumers themselves. Extensive loosely structured individual interviews with consumers who received the strengths model of case management at four different agencies provide insights that may help professionals develop the principles and practices needed to design and deliver effective case management services.

The first section of this chapter focuses upon six principles that guide and direct the helping efforts. The second section demonstrates how these principles come to life during the helping process. Actual case examples and illustrations of practice strategies will be employed to provide sharper focus relative to strengths-oriented practice. It is suggested that the primacy of consumers' strengths and desire to determine the course of their own lives has fostered a broader and more complex helping role. Consequently, the implementation of this role must integrate mental health, social welfare, and social action strategies. The core functions of the strengths model of case management are discussed following the presentation of the guiding principles.

PRINCIPLES OF THE STRENGTHS MODEL: REDISCOVERING THE CAPACITIES OF PEOPLE AND COMMUNITIES

The strengths model rests upon six principles which have been espoused by theoreticians in social work, psychology, biology, and other disciplines for many years. Writers such as Mary Richmond (1922), Bertha Reynolds (1964), Gordon Allport (1955), and Rene Dubos (1965), have had a profound influence upon the view that human beings possess the inherent capacity to adapt, learn, grow, change, and use their internal resources to confront and respond to daily challenges in their lives. Terms such as *motivation,* (White, 1963), *competence,* (Maluccio, 1981), *health,* (Weick, 1986), and *strengths,* (Weick et al., 1989), have increasingly been employed to promote a form of practice which strives to enhance self-efficacy (Bandura, 1977).

Attempting to incorporate this strengths philosophy in practice with a group of consumers who are frequently described as possessing precious few strengths as a consequence of their illness begins with a discussion of six principles of practice.

The Helping Effort Focuses on the Strengths, Interests, and Aspirations of the Consumer

Anyone who has worked with people with persistent mental illness knows that this condition may lead to difficulties in thinking, feeling, and behaving. The consequences for these people often take the form of difficulty in finding and maintaining gainful employment. This in turn creates dependence on the public welfare system to obtain the necessities of life. Some have argued that "the chronically mentally ill don't need case management because they are schizophrenic, they need it because they are poor." (Deitchman, 1980, p. 788).

Despite the presence of multiple problems experienced by those with persistent mental illness, both personally and in the sociocultural environment, the task remains for practitioners to develop and provide an individualized plan of care. An orientation to, and appreciation of, the uniqueness, skills, interests, hopes, and desires of each consumer, rather than a categorical litany of deficits (such as "lack of social skills," "resistance to treatment," and "noncompliance with medication regimen"), will best accomplish this task.

Practitioners who value this principle understand the nature of mental illness generally. But more than this, they recognize the uniqueness of each consumer; a difference that sets each consumer apart from every other person who happens to share a similar diagnosis. They do not attempt to explain and understand people in terms of illness. They know that the expression of the illness is an outgrowth of the complex interplay of a multitude of factors that relate to both individual and social pressures. Likewise, they understand that the strengths of people also evolve from the interplay of many factors, including individual talents, desires, and hopes, and the availability of environmental resources.

The degree to which practitioners believe in and attempt to harness and recognize individual strengths and competencies may be evidenced in subtle yet powerful ways. Consider the following illustration, which captures both a strengths perspective and an illness perspective within the same consumer situation:

A case manager was working with a twenty-seven-year-old woman who was diagnosed as having bipolar disorder. The consumer had been showing little signs of improvement in her involvement with the partial hospital program and regular meetings with a therapist for outpatient work. She was described as being "lethargic, unmotivated, difficult to engage as a function of lability and frequent shifts in mood." She was then assigned to work with a case manager who was trained in the strengths model. The initial meetings between the consumer and the case manager took place at the local pizza restaurant, where they spent time smoking, drinking soda, and getting to know each other. The case manager explained the strengths assessment, and told the consumer that she wanted to do everything she could to help her achieve the things she wanted. She learned that the consumer had done very well in high school, and that she always wanted to be a licensed practical nurse. They agreed to work on this goal together. Despite concerns expressed by the staff at the partial program and by the therapist that this goal was "unrealistic" and was a function of the consumer's desire to "manipulate," the case manager persisted. The staff agreed to cooperate by modifying the requirement that the consumer attend partial as long as she continued in outpatient therapy. Over the course of the next few months the consumer set goals to become enrolled in LPN classes, and she was able to complete four out of five modules in the course. When the case manager shared these gains with the therapist, her response was, "Well, that's just a function of her manic phase." The consumer continued to work on her goal with the case manager, and she even obtained part-time work in a doctor's office to become more familiar with the routine of providing health care.

The implicit meaning of this therapist's comment demonstrates the differences in perceiving consumer behavior in terms of personal strengths versus illness. The therapist did not credit this woman with obvious goal-directed and purposive behavior. Rather, her accomplishments were viewed as a consequence of her illness, over which the consumer was thought to have little control. The gains made by this consumer resulted from the affirmation and support of a professional who was willing to place the woman's desires at the forefront of the work they did together. The energy that fueled the process was generated from a focus upon the uniqueness, interests, and capabilities of the consumer, not upon what the partial staff and therapist perceived as weaknesses and pathology.

People Possess the Inherent Capacity to Learn, Grow, and Change

This principle expresses the belief that persons with persistent mental illness do not lose their hopes and dreams as a consequence of their diagnoses. It reflects the promotion of the possible, and conveys positive expectations of reaching goals seen by consumers of case management services as desirable. The impact of a helping perspective that sets predetermined limits upon consumer functioning was alluded to by a consumer with whom I spoke:

> The nurse at the hospital (psychiatric) was telling people that they would always be in and out of the hospital for the rest of their lives, which is not good to tell somebody who is trying to get well. When you hear that you'll always be like this it makes you feel sick instead of feeling well. My case manager helped me to feel good about myself again, not by telling me I didn't have a mental illness . . . I know that . . . but by telling me I was a talented person and she could help me get the things I wanted in life.

Belief in this principle leads practitioners of strengths-oriented helping to set positive expectations about clients' futures. Comments from a number of consumers interviewed suggest the importance of their perception that case managers "believed" in them. One consumer stated that his case manager "gave me the confidence to try new things and get what I wanted. I would probably have gotten them anyway, but he (the case manager) was the easiest route."

The belief in change as a consequence of normative human development may serve to remove obstacles to working with consumers in taking gradual, supported risks. The following example illustrates what can happen when professionals are willing to go with the directional change experienced by consumers rather than going against them:

> Mary, a thirty-two-year-old woman, had been diagnosed as schizophrenic, paranoid type. She had a long history of state hospital admissions, and her general prognosis was thought to be very poor. One day at the partial program Mary announced that she and a male member of the psychosocial club were engaged and going to be married. This news concerned the staff, as they felt that neither of these clients could take care of themselves, let alone each other. Mary wanted to get married "as soon as possible," but the staff attempted to persuade her and her partner to make this a long-term goal, so that they could learn more about what married life was like.
>
> During the next few weeks Mary and her partner did not come in to the partial program. A case manager was sent to do a home visit at Mary's apartment to find out how she was doing. When she arrived she found that Mary and her partner had decided to move in together, to "help us get ready for the wedding"; the plans for which they had already set in motion. The case manager was assigned to work with both of them, and during the next few

months many treatment plan goals were set and achieved as they prepared for the big event. The staff at the center changed their approach to more fully be with the couple "where they were"; the wedding was held at the program, and the staff and many consumers held a reception at the center.

People with persistent mental illness make decisions every day. To be sure, at times these decisions are influenced by the presence of symptoms related to major mental illness. Moreover, decisions consumers make, such as not taking prescribed medications, or using alcohol or drugs, may precipitate a recurrence of the positive symptoms of their illness. The task remains for mental health professionals to assist consumers in becoming aware of the power they possess to make decisions that will promote greater health and personal satsfaction. In our experience, this is rarely accomplished when the attempt is made, either implicitly or explicitly, to assume responsibility for directing the course of consumers' lives.

The Consumer Is the Director of the Helping Encounter

This principle breathes life into the time-honored maxim of self-determination in social work. There may be no other adult client population where the expression of this principle in practice has been so troublesome. One hundred and fifty years of social policies and medical practices that sequestered the mentally ill in asylums and state hospitals, or exiled them to partial hospital programming in community mental health centers, demonstrates that the belief that persons with a mental illness should direct their treatment planning is regarded as unwise and even unethical.

The idea of consumer-as-director is attracting increasing attention as a consequence of the consumerism movement, innovative community support programming, and the growing attention to helping strategies oriented to the strengths of people. To push this notion a bit further, consider that every director usually has the assistance of one or more advisers or consultants whose judgments are valued, and who ultimately influence decision-making. Case managers using the strengths perspective readily assume these important roles: adviser, consultant, educator, and even friend. Directions deemed desirable by consumers are openly discussed, not judged. Alternatives are generated, and potential consequences of each alternative explored. These collaborative activities more fully inform consumer choice and goal-directed activity. For, in the final analysis, consumers will make choices, even if this means not choosing a course of action, which may have a profound effect upon their health and well-being. We cannot make these decisions for them (even for those who are mandated to outpatient legal commitment; these individuals still must choose between being compliant with the outpatient order or returning to the hospital). Therefore, case managers must strive to provide the conditions, knowledge, and linkages with other resources, and must make conscious use of the collaborative strength of their relationship with consumers to assist them in charting and navigating their own course toward maximum health and well-being in the community. A key to unlocking the collaborative power of the helping relationship may be found in the level of trust case managers are able to earn through their efforts.

The Consumer/Case Manager Relationship
Becomes an Essential Factor in the Helping Process

Few would argue with the belief that the nature and quality of the helping relationship exerts considerable influence on the essence of outcomes experienced by consumers. Moreover, it is evident that the process of relationship building with any client group occurs gradually and is often characterized by initial feelings of uncertainty, doubt, and even suspicion. Case managers who understand the importance of relationship, and understand that for some consumers they must demonstrate their caring and reliability, know that to expect immediate compliance and cooperation from consumers may often lead to frustration. One consumer summed up her perceptions this way:

> When they told me I would be working with a case manager I didn't know what to expect. I felt like they (the program) were forcing her on me, and I didn't like it. I gave her [the CM] a hard time in the beginning, I guess I was testing her to see if she would do all of the things she said she would. She stayed with me even when I was not very nice to her, and now I'm glad I did. She has helped me to feel more comfortable going places in town, and when I said I didn't feel like doing anything she did not push me. I'm glad now that I had her to help me.

Research into the factors inherent in the helping relationship suggests several specific critical elements. Mutual trust, openness, clarity in terms of mutual expectations, caring, honesty, supportiveness, and genuineness are among the most frequently discussed. In fact, the perceived presence of these elements of the helping relationship are most frequently cited by clients as the most important factors in positive outcomes. As Maluccio (1981) found:

> In studies of client perception of treatment, the worker's human qualities seemed to be valued by clients more than technical skills . . . from the perspective of clients, the composite picture of the good or ideal worker is that of someone who is warm, accepting, understanding, involved, natural, genuine, competent, objective, and able to share him or herself with the client (p. 16).

In the strengths model of case management the idea of the case manager "sharing" with the consumer has proved to be both liberating and vexing. A professional helping relationship is largely forged of a mutual understanding of acceptable and unacceptable behavior in reciprocal roles. For example, the therapist typically does not help a client move furniture, and the psychiatrist does not go bowling with a patient. Frequently, these restrictions on "role appropriate" behaviors are discussed as professional boundaries.

Case managers, however, have discovered that assisting consumers in their daily lives, however valuable and genuine, has led to some conflict in terms of being perceived as a friend as opposed to being seen as a professional. In implementing a strengths perspective in case management practice, the traditional boundaries of mental health treatment are being reshaped and redefined. In this process some uncertainties are inevitable. One case manager expressed this ambiguity, while also alluding to the potential for real gains for her consumers:

I have seen how important it is for me to be a part of the clients' lives. We do things together like go for walks and play chess . . . we've even gone to the shopping mall together. These were things she wanted to do. When I first started working with Jane she wouldn't even let me in the house. Now she calls me to make sure I don't forget our appointment! It's gotten to the point where she calls me whenever she is having difficulties. She used to call her doctor, and invariably she would be admitted to the hospital. She now has been out for over a year, which is the longest time she has been able to stay well. I worry sometimes that she is too dependent on me, but I guess I'm kind of dependent on her too.

The dilemma illustrated in the words of this case manager leads to the following question: How do I keep from making consumers overly dependent upon me for support and assistance, especially when chances are I may be taking a new job or eventually needing to close her case? This question will be more fully addressed in the discussion of the advocacy and graduated disengagement functions later in the chapter. In any case, the nature of the case manager–consumer relationship must be recast, broadened, and in some ways, made more ordinary if we are to help the people we work with discover and use their strengths, pursue their own desires, and meet their needs.

It is obvious that this expanded helping relationship demands that case managers also expand the contexts in which they provide assistance. Evidence of the shift from office-based brokerage to in vivo engagement of consumers and community collaborators may be seen in case management systems throughout the nation.

Assertive Outreach Is the Preferred Mode of Case Management Helping

In the strengths model of case management, as well as in other models such as the Program for Assertive Community Training (Stein and Test, 1980; Bond et al., 1988) and the Psychiatric Rehabilitation Model (Goering et al., 1988), case managers are instructed to join with consumers in naturally occurring community contexts. This principle reflects the growing belief that significant numbers of people with persistent mental illness are voting with their feet—in effect denouncing structured aftercare programming for services more tailored to their unique goals and desires. Consequently, a shift is occurring that reflects the need to provide client-centered service programs rather than service-centered client programs (Rose, 1985).

In the delivery of the strengths model, we have found that the implementation of this principle needs to be flexible. For example, some consumers prefer to begin the helping process by meeting at the community support program. This desire is honored, but case managers continuously look for opportunities to spend time with consumers in the community as the relationship progresses. These efforts are typically tied to concrete wants and needs expressed by consumers, such as applying for Section Eight housing or getting more furniture and supplies for their apartment.

We have observed two positive outcomes which accrue from implementing this principle of assertive outreach. First, case managers tend to become more knowledgeable of the formally organized resources, as well as the naturally occurring helpers in their communities (for example, church groups and business organizations). Second, case managers report finding out important information about consumers' lives and living circumstances which they could not have learned by meeting with them only at the office. To be successful as a negotiator of resource systems, a different view of communities may be required.

The Community Is an Oasis of Potential Collaborators in the Helping Process

One of the most common concerns expressed by case managers is the perceived dearth of resources available in their communities to assist consumers. This principle of the strengths model invites case managers to challenge this assumption. It suggests that if one expects to see a desert, one will probably see sand and feel aridity. A strengths perspective, however, leads one to view the community in its broadest sense as a reservoir of untapped potentials and possibilities. For if the individual's relevant and immediate environment, which often includes family, is viewed as pathological, hostile, and even toxic, efforts to intervene in these contexts will likely be avoided.

In our observations of and discussions with case managers, two factors seem to influence a reluctance to integrate a strengths-oriented view of communities. The first is that case managers report a sense of inadequacy in terms of the training and skills needed to influence key resource people, such as landlords and potential employers. The second factor relates to a sense of anger and frustration around the generalized presence of the stigma associated with mental illness. Both concerns are valid, and if left unaltered will tend to minimize the extent of linkages that are attempted with, for, and on behalf of consumers.

Sometimes, activities need to change before perceptions are altered. Successful ventures as community advocate for consumers will tend to solidify the view that there are people "out there" who are willing to help and may benefit themselves for giving consumers a chance. The following excerpt from a case management training session conducted in Toledo, Ohio, typifies what can happen when potential resources are approached in a positive fashion:

> As an exercise in the resource acquisition module of the training, case managers were requested to go out into the city and talk with one person who represented an agency service that might help with a specific goal which had been developed during case manager–consumer roleplay exercises that morning. At first, there was some reluctance on the part of the case managers. They expressed various reasons why the exercise "would not work," such as "no one is ever around on a Friday afternoon," and "we don't have enough time to get this done." An hour later the group reconvened to report on the outcome of the experience. The enthusiasm and energy that was now evident stood in sharp contrast to the skepticism and reluctance displayed earlier. One after another, case managers eagerly shared stories of their successful efforts. From one, the agreement of a local health club to provide reduced rates for her consumer to work out, and even lower rates if she could get a group of three clients to join. Another shared the willingness of the owner of riding stables to exchange riding lessons for a client who would help groom the horses. Another case manager phoned a friend, who was a retired nun, who agreed to work with a client to help him learn to read. The excitement was electric, as case managers furiously struggled to get the names and phone numbers of these community resource people.

Collectively, these six principles of strengths-oriented case management converge within a practice framework that supports and directs each function of the helping process. They are interdependent and mutually reinforcing. The failure to integrate just one principle may serve to undermine the whole essence of the strengths approach. For example, viewing the consumer as the director of the helping effort may be compromised if the stated goal is to get a job and case managers restrict their work to prevocational group work within the confines of the mental health center.

In implementing these principles in strengths-oriented practice, skills in relationship-building, mutual negotiation, community collaboration, and interdisciplinary consultation become essential. We now turn to an examination of how these skills are expressed in the case management process. This is done by describing the mutual activities inherent in each of the six functions of the strengths model; engagement, strengths assessment, personal goal planning, implementation through advocacy and linkage, monitoring, and graduated disengagement.

FUNCTIONS OF THE STRENGTHS MODEL

Engagement: Establishing the Helping Partnership

Engagement is viewed in the strengths model as a series of unstructured, informal, conversational encounters that take place in the beginning of the helping process. For the most part, consumers who are known to the Community Support Program (CSP) based on their history of psychiatric hospitalization are identified as being appropriate for case management services. This does not automatically mean, however, that the potential consumer will recognize and accept this need as it has been perceived by someone else. Furthermore, consumers may not even want to have a case manager. Case managers should approach these initial meetings with these possibilities in mind, knowing that they cannot assume that consumers will readily engage with them. A strengths perspective suggests that initial reluctance on the part of consumers may be a normative response to a strange and uncertain social encounter. Typically, a less-than-enthusiastic response on the consumer's part might be viewed as "guarded," "suspicious," "resistive to treatment," or even diagnosed as "paranoia."

Interviews with consumers have tended to support specific helping strategies which may serve to increase the desire to engage in the case management process. When asked about the first meeting with case managers, consumers stated such things as "being easygoing and laid-back," "having a good sense of humor," "asking me about the things I wanted to do," "not asking me a lot of personal questions" (one consumer said that the case manager did not impress him as a snoopervisor), and "sharing things about themselves," as being important to them. The following approaches have yielded a fair amount of success in promoting the engagement function.

Attempt to contact consumers you will be working with prior to the first face-to-face meeting. This strategy appears to serve three purposes. First, it represents a nonthreatening way to introduce yourself and the case management process to potential consumers. Also, it demonstrates a respect for the individual's right to privacy, as well as the right to be informed regarding decisions made by the treatment team. Usually, case managers attempt to reach consumers by phone if this is possible. They have also used correspondence, and report that this seems to be valued by consumers. The following example of such contact attempts to incorporate the philosophy of a strengths approach:

> Dear Mr. (Ms.)_____
> My name is _____, and I am a case manager at (program's name). I wanted you to know that I have been assigned to contact you, to see if you would be interested in working with me. As a case manager, I might be able to help you with the things that you think are important for you in your life. I would like to meet you so that we can get to know each other, and answer any questions you might have. I can meet with you whenever, and wherever you like. If you want to call me to talk further about case management my number is _____. If I am not here please leave a message and I will call back. If I do not hear from you may I drop by your place on (day, date, and time)? I hope you'll consider working with me. I look forward to meeting you soon.
> Sincerely,
> (Case Manager's Name)

During the initial meetings, case managers attempt to model the belief in mutuality and a helping partnership by engaging in a normative social dialogue rather than a more formal question and answer interview. These meetings involve a bilateral information exchange. In contrast to the traditional mental health intake interview, where the clinician typically asks most of the questions from which the diagnosis or psychosocial assessment will be generated, the engagement process encourages mutual sharing and self-disclosure on the part of the case manager. These relate to efforts to establish areas of common interest, such as music, sports, television, or other interpersonal common denominators, which serve to establish an emerging helping relationship.

The engagement function is guided by the unique abilities, level of tolerance, and interest of each consumer. Consequently, there has been much variance in the nature of these first meetings. For example, some consumers who have been involved in the process before have little difficulty understanding and cooperating in beginning to develop the strengths assessment tool and even engage in setting some initial personal goals on the personal planning tool. Others want nothing to do with "more paperwork" and do not want to review these helping tools with the case manager. Since the explicit objective of these initial meetings is to get to know each other, and to be clear regarding the mutual expectations of the process, case managers must use their own knowledge, experience, and judgment in deciding how far to proceed.

Ideally, during engagement consumers are receptive and data is provided that will be recorded on the strengths assessment tool. Even when consumers are not overly receptive, case managers look for opportunities through observation and statements that are made which give some clues as to the consumer's uniqueness and interests. For example, in a first meeting with a consumer who was relatively nonverbal, one case manager noted that he had a car, listened to classical music, dressed sharply, seemed to be in good physical health, lived in his own apartment with a roommate, and asked well-informed questions.

Consumers with whom I spoke consistently expressed the perception that their case manager was "a real person." When asked to talk more about what this meant, many said such things as "they were right there with me, it wasn't a power thing, they were human, and I felt like I was on the same level with them." Case managers who are aware that consumers are doing their own assessment during these initial meetings may be more sanguine about sharing aspects of themselves during these interactions. The value of this approach was suggested by two consumer informants:

> Our relationship is real good, knowing that we could talk and share things. It took a while for me to gain trust, it's not just automatic. A lot of it is Fran's (CM) sense of humor, and she listens to me, and she shares a little about herself. It's not just all me, it's her too.

From another consumer:

> It really helped me to connect with her (CM) when she shared things that happened in her life. Our mothers have things in common, like pouring cold water on things that you want to do. I often feel isolated that something has never happened to anyone else but me. Knowing she had the same experience helped.

As consumers and case managers are getting to know each other, case managers are simultaneously beginning to develop the strengths assessment. This tool is used explicitly in the helping process to guide and inform the particular avenues the two will take together in the helping journey.

The Strengths Assessment: A Whole Personal Inventory

The strengths assessment is the tool designed to assist the case manager in developing an individualized helping plan for each consumer. The strengths assessment has been specifically tailored for the case management process, and is intended to supplement rather than to supplant existing assessments, such as diagnostic and psychotherapeutic assessments which may also be present in an interdisciplinary program approach. Figure 6.1 illustrates a strengths assessment which was developed by a case manager and consumer.

The strengths assessment documents information about consumers' lives in six interrelated and interdependent life domains. These are (1) daily living situation, (2) vocational/educational, (3) financial/insurance, (4) health, (5) social supports, and (6) leisure time. In each life domain, the case manager attempts to gather information regarding (1) what the consumer's present situation is in this area; (2) what, if anything, the consumer wants to change, achieve, or maintain; and (3) what the consumer has realized in these areas in the past.

This format takes into account the belief that human goal-directed behavior is related to current levels of social functioning and resources that are being used, personal aspirations for the way one would like things to be, and a sense of mastery that has been gained from efforts, both successful and unsuccessful, attempted in the past. Case managers have reported that this format works well, especially in helping them to organize the complex areas which interact to create difficulty for consumers.

Case Manager's Name _____ Barb R. _____ Consumer's Name _____ Ann P. _____

Date _____

CONSUMER STRENGTHS ASSESSMENT

CURRENT STATUS: What's going on today? What's available now?	INDIVIDUAL'S DESIRES ASPIRATIONS: What do I want?	RESOURCES, PERSONAL SOCIAL: What have I used in the past?
27-year-old white female lives in 2-bedroom apartment with 2-year-old son. Nicely decorated with paintings (landscapes) she did. Ann does not drive, uses public transportation—likes to cook, maintains apartment well. SRS involved re welfare of son.	*LIFE DOMAIN* *DAILY LIVING SITUATION* • Wants to stay out of the state hospital. • Wants to keep her son. • Wants to have "some time to myself" away from child care duties.	• Has been hospitalized 2 times in past. Longest admission 6 months. • Has lived in current apartment for 5 months. • Previously lived with family. • Lived with father of child for 2 years in San Francisco.
• Has ADC—Food Stamps. • SSI ($202.00 per month). • Section 8 apartment. • Medical card. • Family helps out occasionally. • No child support.	*FINANCIAL/INSURANCE* • Wants to increase monthly income. • Will consider applying for SSDI.	• Used to earn "good money" as a waitress (see vocational).
• Not employed presently. • Days are devoted to child care. This is her primary role now and Ann states that "sometimes I don't know how to handle him." • Has GED.	*VOCATIONAL/EDUCATION* • Would like to attend art classes. • Wants to be a "better parent."	• Worked as a waitress for "a couple of years" before onset of illness. Did not like "having to put up with customers' complaints."
• Son is very important to her. • Family (parents, 2 older sisters) live nearby—some support but "they want to take my son" and "they don't believe me when I tell them things."	*SOCIAL SUPPORTS* • Wants to keep son with her. • Wants to make more friends. • Wants family to "understand" her and "believe" her.	• Used to "have a lot" of friends. • Used to enjoy dancing, and painting was a source of support. • Her last case manager "really helped" and was very supportive. • Used to go to church.

Figure 6.1 Case Management

Figure 6.1 *(continued)*

Ann is in good heath—her DX is Bi-Polar, currently taking Lithium. She smokes cigarettes, says she has a beer "now and then." Some days feels "very anxious." No major medical concerns.	*HEALTH* • Wants to cut down on her smoking. • Wants to exercise more. • Wants to stay well and out of the hospital.	• Used to love to ride bikes. • Used to play on girls' softball team. • Used to meditate. • Used to be a vegetarian.
• Ann has little time to do "the things I like to." • She has painting supplies but lately has not been motivated and her time is taken taking care of her 2 year old. • Reads romance novels.	*LEISURE/RECREATIONAL SUPPORTS* • Wants to have a few hours during the week when she can do the things she wants to do.	• See (health).

WHAT ARE MY PRIORITIES?

1. "To keep my son."

2. "To stay out of the hospital." (psychiatric)

3. "To have some fun."

4. "To get back into my painting."

CASE MANAGER'S COMMENTS: Ann is a neat person; good sense of humor—devoted mother.	CONSUMER'S COMMENTS: "I'm glad I have a new C.M. who cares about me."
CASE MANAGER'S SIGNATURE DATE Barb R.	CONSUMER'S SIGNATURE DATE Ann P. 10/15/89

In reviewing the strengths assessment illustrated in Figure 6.1, the following points should be highlighted:

Information Is as Detailed as Possible.   Specificity promotes individuality. This detail is noted particularly in the information relative to current and previous circumstances. For example, we learn that this particular consumer relishes her role as a mother, yet has had some difficulty in caring for her two-year-old son. She is aware of the frustrations this role brings for her, and is currently working with a protective service worker to improve in this area. Certain primary areas of interest to the consumer are noted, which include maintaining her present apartment and being able to have some time to herself. The details provided in each of the six life domains, in this case, pointed out potential directions the consumer and case manager agreed to follow in the personal plan.

Wants and Desires Are Established and Discussed Prior to a Collective Determination of What the Consumer Needs to Do.   The strengths assessment, therefore, is not viewed as a "strengths/needs" assessment. The intent of the strengths assessment is to avoid imposing a professionally predetermined set of activities such as learning to manage money or becoming compliant with medication before establishing in the consumer's mind how decisions to attend to these areas relate directly to her own unique wants and desires. In the situation noted above, the consumer stated that she wanted to maintain her apartment and stay out of the psychiatric hospital. These personal motivations led her to a decision to attend medication clinic with the case manager and to become more consistent in taking her prescribed medication because she realized that this was an important factor in her ability to get what she wanted.

Problems in Consumers' Lives Are Reframed in Terms of What They Would Like to Happen. This strategy accomplishes three primary objectives: (1) it helps to generate a treatment goal founded upon the consumer's own perception of the areas of his life he feels motivated to work on, (2) it provides a standard by which short-term goals may be suggested by the case manager, and (3) it provides a benchmark from which inconsistencies in consumer behavior may be gently pointed out by the case manager.

In the example above, the consumer generated several tasks based on the case manager's suggestions regarding what she needed to do to stay out of the hospital and maintain custody of her son. These tasks included going to the mental health center for medication clinic (which she had not been doing prior to her last hospitalization) and attending parent education classes at the YWCA. Over time the consumer became more aware of how these activities were important to her desire to achieve her own goals.

Developing the Strengths Assessment May Suggest Immediate Planning and Implementation Helping Tasks. Typically in mental health practice the axiom of "never intervene prematurely" has dictated that a comprehensive psychosocial assessment and diagnosis be generated prior to the delivery of a particular treatment approach. Case managers, however, frequently find that there are basic human needs such as financial entitlements and instability in housing demanding immediate attention. Helping consumers meet these concrete needs early in the relationship tends to promote a sense of hopefulness, confidence, and trust in this goal-directed partnership.

The strengths assessment dialogue concludes with the setting of mutual priorities regarding specific "want" areas that have been expressed by the consumer. Case managers are active partners in this process, and use their own knowledge and experience in an effort to develop through negotiation the initial tasks of helping. For example, the client discussed above felt that taking steps to make more friends was her immediate desire. The case manager acknowledged this, agreed to work with her in this area, and also suggested that they make going in for a medication review one of their priorities, as this would be an important step in staying well. The consumer agreed, and they developed initial personal plans that would address both areas.

Personal Planning: Blending Needs with Consumer Aspirations

The personal planning tool (see Figure 6.2) is analogous to the case management treatment plan. In this stage of the helping partnership, the specific short-term activities that must be undertaken toward the realization of a consumer goal are recorded and continuously reviewed, modified, and expanded.

For: _____Ann P._____ Case Manager: _____Barb R._____ Date: _____

Planned Frequency of Contact _____1 x week_____

LIFE DOMAIN
FOCUSED UPON   ____ Daily Living Situations   ____ Vocational/Educational
                _X_ Social Supports   ____ Leisure/Recreational Supports
                ____ Financial/Insurance   ____ Health

CONSUMER'S LONG-TERM GOAL: "I want to keep my son."

MEASURABLE SHORT-TERM GOALS TOWARD ACHIEVEMENT	RESPONSIBILITY	DATE TO BE ACCOMPLISHED	DATE ACCOMPLISHED	COMMENTS:
1. Ann will attend med clinic next week with Barb.	Ann & Barb	10/20/89	10/20/89	Talked to Dr. Ordered blood level. Ann did great!
2. Ann and Barb will meet with SRS worker to review plan for maintaining custody. (Ann will call to make appointment.)	Ann & Barb	10/26/89	10/26/89	Good meeting. Ann in good spirits.
3. Ann will attend meeting for parent training skills at YMCA.	Ann	11/12/89	11/12/89	Ann attended. Knew one other person, said she learned a lot.
4. Ann will take one afternoon next week and work on her drawings (mother will watch baby).	Ann & Mom	11/19/89	11/18/89	Ann drew three pictures, feels great and enjoyed time to herself.

Ann P.		Barb R.	
CONSUMER SIGNATURE	DATE	CASE MANAGER SIGNATURE	DATE
		Mrs. P.	11/12/89
PSYCHIATRIST SIGNATURE	DATE	COLLATERAL SIGNATURE	DATE

Figure 6.2   University of Kansas School of Social Welfare Case Management Personal Plan

The essential task here is to assist consumers in recognizing that certain areas of their functioning, such as being compliant with prescribed medications and attending to personal hygiene, represent the means toward some desired end. Consumers should not be expected to comply with plans merely because someone else thinks that they should. Plans that are developed with minimal attention to the agenda of consumers are likely to fail. To illustrate, a case manager in one CSP told of a consumer who was informed by staff to improve his personal hygiene or he would not be allowed into the partial hospital program. Consequently, the staff did not see him for a number of weeks. When the case manager visited him in his apartment, he learned that the consumer did not want to attend the program anyway, because he did not want to be around "all those crazy people." The consumer did, however, want to keep working with the case manager regarding his own desire to "be more normal." They agreed that he would shower at least twice a week, as this is an activity most "normal" people do. As a result, the consumer's motivation to attend to personal hygiene improved.

The personal planning process is developed out of the work of Houts and Scott (1975). The objective in this collaborative planning effort is to break down a stated consumer want (long-term goal) into short-term tasks (Epstein, 1980). These tasks may be accomplished by the consumer alone, with the case manager, or with someone else, family, com-peer friend, or other consumer. The collective review of the short-term goals from week to week becomes the purposive focus of each helping visit.

Review of case management documentation suggests that writing short-term goals requires skills in which many case managers have not been trained. Four standards may be used to critique goal-setting:

Goals Should Be Measurable and Observable.   In writing such goals, we have found that three desirable outcomes may be realized. First, consumers begin to experience a sense of accomplishment, confidence, and motivation, and they begin to believe that working with a case manager may be to their benefit. Second, case managers report feeling a sense of accomplishment and personal/professional satisfaction. Third, this standard challenges case managers to bring the abstract to the concrete, the general to the specific in a manner reflecting the uniqueness and individuality of each consumer. Therefore, the goal of increasing self-esteem becomes walking one mile three times a week for one consumer, and reading one book a month for another.

Goals Are Stated in Positive Terms.   This standard requires skills in resetting problems and perceived deficits into individual wants. In keeping with a strengths philosophy, the atmosphere of positive expectations is promoted by focusing upon the beneficial outcomes desired instead of the negative factors one wishes to eliminate. For instance, the goal "decrease dependence on parents" would not meet this standard. It focuses on the negative. One way to restate this goal is to include a specific behavior that indicates greater independence. For example, "increase independence by contributing fifty dollars per month to the family."

Each Goal Contains Just One Evaluative Standard.   Compliance with this standard simplifies evaluation of goal attainment and acknowledges and fortifies successes, especially small and incremental ones. Too often goals incorporate several desired outcomes; for example; "Mary will attend the community meeting, participate in the discussion, and remain the entire time." As stated, if Mary attends the meeting (which may itself reflect considerable achievement), makes comments during the meeting, but leaves the meeting early, she will not have achieved all of the elements of the goal as written. This series of behaviors could be broken down into three separate goal statements. In so doing, Mary would receive positive affirmation for achieving two out of three of her goals; a very respectable .667 batting average!

The Short-Term Goal Should Have a High Probability of Success.   Knowledge of each consumer, including their skills and available resources and supports, is an essential component of goal setting. Armed with this knowledge, case managers attempt to generate goals with consumers consistent with their desires, abilities, and environmental accommodations. A consumer stated to a case manager that he wanted to buy a four-bedroom house in one of the more fashionable suburbs outside of the city. One cannot be certain that this consumer will ever realize this goal (just as one cannot be certain that he will not). If the consumer is motivated by this goal, however, a short-term goal such as "will develop budget with case manager to ensure apartment utilities are paid on time" is realistic and may be achieved in a relatively short time. If the consumer is motivated by such an aspiration, he may be more motivated to engage in activities that bring him closer to making his dream a reality.

The personal planning tool (Figure 6.2) operationalizes several of the principles of the strengths perspective. The expectation that people can learn, grow, and change is conveyed through the incremental steps delineated in the short-term goals and the inclusion of a target date (positive expectations). By naming the other collaborators in the plan, such as family members, friends, or other helping professionals, the notion of a caring collective of resources in the community is expressed. Finally, the fact that the short-term goals relate directly to a stated desire, couched in the consumers' own words, breathes life into the principle that consumers should play an active role in directing the course of the helping process. In a recent study of the impact of the strengths model, sixty-six consumers achieved an 83 percent achievement rate in goal planning activities in four separate mental health centers (Kisthardt, 1990). This may be due in part to consumers' perception that they experienced some degree of control and influence in their treatment plans.

This study also suggests that consumers ascribe value and meaning to the goal planning process. For example, 60.7 percent of the study sample stated that case management was "extremely helpful" in their goal of "keeping it together and staying out of the psychiatric hospital." The following statements reflect consumers' assessment of the utility of the goal planning process:

> Normally I wouldn't have liked the goal sheets. I was afraid to have goals, but there was a sense of accomplishment. Just reminding me that there were different areas of my life. Maybe I didn't want to be that positive, maybe that day I didn't feel like I had any strengths, but I do now.

Another consumer expressed this view:

> When I first met David (CM) all my goals were up here (points to his head). Now, when I see them on paper I can connect with them. I see I can do it, and I want to do more.

Finally, another consumer stated this:

> Goal planning is a process anybody can benefit from. Sometimes your life is like a rerun, it keeps going over and over, it just gets to be a constant pattern, and every now and then you got to change the channel. Don't let the future be twenty years down the road, you want

something a little bit sooner. Writing it (the goal) down where you don't just talk about it, but visually see it there in visual contact, my appointments or other things I got to do, anything that helps your mind stay improved, I'm all for it.

We have found that there is one important caveat to bear in mind during the goal planning process. Do not attempt to generate a comprehensive plan that includes a wide range of goals during the first planning meetings. Sometimes, in their enthusiasm to implement the goal planning function, case managers generate a lengthy list of goals, but soon discover that they have proceeded too quickly. Consumers may become overwhelmed if they feel that they have agreed to a plan where they are over-extended. The following example illustrates this point:

During a goal planning meeting a case manager recorded thirteen short-term goals with a consumer after having been working with her for only three weeks. (This session was videotaped for evaluation purposes.) During the meeting it was evident that the case manager was strongly directing the development of the plans by making suggestions regarding what the consumer could do. The consumer was agreeing, but her facial expression and body language indicated that she was becoming increasingly anxious as the case manager recorded each goal. The case manager, enthusiastically writing the goals on the form, missed these very important cues. That evening the consumer, feeling overwhelmed and fearful that she would "let the case manager down," called the crisis line. She received the reassurance she needed, and the plans were scaled down at the next meeting with the case manager.

In many instances, the planning and implementation function involves including other potential helpers in the completion of a desired goal. This function of case management has been generally defined as linkage. In actual practice, case managers have discovered that linkage constitutes far more than a referral. The knowledge and skills involved in influencing resource persons on behalf of consumers become essential elements of strengths-oriented practice around linkage.

Advocating for Community Connections: Expanding Resource Networks Through Influencing Systems

Case management has been described as a method of helping incorporate the dual focus on person and environment (Rapp and Chamberlain, 1985). Such a focus long has been a hallmark of social work (Gordon, 1969). Attempting to establish linkages on behalf of consumers necessitates the application of skills in community organization (Roberts-DeGennaro, 1987) as well as strategies to influence key actors in the community who control access to resources; for example, landlords, potential employers or volunteer coordinators, social welfare workers, and directors of community services such as the YM/YWCA. For case managers to become more effective in influencing these systems, they must continue to expand their understanding of, and receive agency sanction for, exercising power (Schwartz et al., 1982; Alinsky, 1972).

In operationalizing the advocacy function, case managers may benefit from a conceptual framework that guides their efforts in effecting resource acquisition for consumers. Power, within this framework, is defined as "the ability and willingness to affect the behavior, thoughts, physical well-being, and/or feelings of another (Claus and

Bailey, 1977, p. 17). In order to gain a deeper understanding of how power may be exercised in the advocacy role, the conceptualization proposed by French and Raven (1960) is useful. In this framework, the expression of power/influence is understood as taking five forms: (1) referent, (2) reward, (3) expert, (4) legitimate, and (5) coercive. The strategy involved in the process of advocacy suggests that case managers attempt to exercise these forms of power sequentially, beginning with the cooperative and collaborative and moving to the more confrontive only when the former have been ineffective.

Referent power refers to the ability to influence another as a function of the relationship which has been forged with potential resource providers. Case managers attempt to nurture and develop mutually satisfying relationships with community collaborators, and believe that the investment of time and energy in fostering these relationships is an important aspect of their overall role. Frequently, potential resources are not approached until there is an immediate crisis in consumers' lives. A more proactive posture suggests that getting to know local law enforcement, clergy, housing authorities and landlords, as well as vocational and volunteer representatives should be undertaken before crisis situations emerge. Case managers, especially those in rural areas, who maintain a professional, and on many occasions, social acquaintance with community collaborators, frequently report successful efforts in establishing needed and desired linkages for consumers.

Reward power is based on the idea of the exercise of power/influence as relational (Etzioni, 1970, p. 18). Thus, case managers, focusing upon consumers' strengths and abilities, attempt to demonstrate to potential providers that making the resource available to consumers may benefit them as well. One case manager shared the following illustration of this strategy:

> When I first approached the landlord and informed him of my role and the consumer's situation and involvement with the mental health center I could see him becoming reluctant and somewhat fearful about renting to him. I tried to affirm and tune in to these fears, and told him of the successes the consumer had in the past in taking care of his apartments. I reassured him that I would be working with the consumer on a regular basis to help with any difficulties he might experience. He seemed to become more receptive, but it was clear he was not sold. I then told him that he would never have to worry about rent being paid on time; that the consumer received guaranteed checks each month from the government, and a direct deposit could be arranged to the landlord's account. This did the trick! Now the landlord calls me periodically to see if I have any other clients who need an apartment.

Expert, or epistemic, power refers to the ability to influence a potential provider with the presentation of specialized knowledge that is viewed as meaningful by the target of the advocacy effort. Case managers who are knowledgeable about the strengths and capacities of consumers, the availability of formal and informal helping resources in their communities, entitlement regulations, and legislative initiatives designed to reduce discrimination and promote least restrictive alternatives, may use such information in their advocacy efforts.

Legitimate power also serves to promote successful linkage efforts. It is the capacity to exert influence based on the perception of a designated authority inherent in the professional role. Although this particular form of power has been troubling for case managers, who frequently report intimations of low status within the mental health hierarchy, the receptiveness of community providers in other systems may reflect a more positive view. Consider the following example, which illustrates the impact realized by a case manager who believed that she occupied a very important role in her community.

> A case manager, who was also the director of the community support program (which consisted of herself and one other half-time worker), was finding that apartments were relatively available to consumers in this rural community. Most were unfurnished, however, and she was having difficulty obtaining appliances due to limited finances. She arranged to speak at a monthly meeting of a local business organization. In this brief talk she highlighted the goals of the CSP, and shared several inspiring stories of consumer achievements, which included ways in which they were becoming valuable contributors to the community through projects such as park beautification and volunteer work at the local senior center. She shared the need the program was experiencing in the mission to assist persons with mental illness live in the least restrictive setting possible. As a consequence of her efforts, the organization agreed to provide refrigerators and stoves for each consumer who was placed in an independent apartment.

This illustrates what can happen when case managers approach potential resource providers armed with knowledge, confidence, and positive expectations. At times, however, advocacy overtures fall on deaf ears. If such outcomes reflect discrimination, or less than full compliance with legislative initiatives designed to promote accessibility for the handicapped, case managers must be prepared to, and receive agency sanction for, efforts to influence systems through more confrontational approaches.

Coercive power refers to the ability to influence another by engaging in activities viewed by the resource gatekeeper as undesirable. The use of such negative sanctions is suggested as a last resort to be considered only when more positive, collaborative efforts have not been successful. One must plan these strategies carefully. There is always the possibility of unintended consequences for both consumers and case managers. Therefore, coercive strategies relating to a specific consumer situation are undertaken only when the consumer has been fully informed and consent is documented on the treatment plan. In addition, the support of the treatment team and program administration should be solicited. The following case example describes one case manager's persistence in advocating the needs of a consumer using strategies ranging from positive to more coercive.

> A case manager was working with a thirty-one-year-old woman diagnosed as schizophrenic. She also was afflicted with multiple sclerosis and could only walk with assistance. The special services van was used by the consumer to get to the aftercare program and medication clinic at the CSP. The building, however, did not have a wheelchair ramp. Therefore, the consumer had to get out of her chair and drag herself backwards up a series of steps to get into the center. The case manager shared her concerns about this situation with the consumer, who agreed that she would like to have access to the program without "having to crawl on my butt." The case manager first approached the CSP director and reminded her of section 504 of the Federal Rehabilitation Act of 1973, which mandates accessibility to all programs or services receiving public funds. The supervisor agreed that something needed to be done, and promised to take the matter up with the executive director. In a few

weeks the director stated that no ramp could be built due to inadequate footage to comply with building codes. They were, however, exploring the possibility of moving the program to a building that was accessible; but there were no plans regarding when this move would take place. Several months passed. With the onset of colder weather the case manager approached the supervisor once again, and suggested that she was thinking about calling a friend at the local paper to see if he would be interested in doing a story (with pictures) of this woman's plight. In less than two weeks, plans were in place to move the program to an accessible building.

Successful advocacy/linkage efforts are intended to assist consumers in gaining a needed resource such as a place to live, or to become involved in a community situation where their interests and skills may be expressed. Experienced case managers know that sometimes helping consumers get what they want is not the most difficult part of their job—it is working with them and other support people to help consumers maintain these achievements. The range of helping activities inherent in this function are connected to the monitoring function.

Monitoring: Collective and Continuous Review of the Helping Process

Monitoring, in the most general sense, refers to the process of evaluating the progress that has been made toward some clearly established treatment outcome. Typically, monitoring is done through progress notes or quarterly reviews completed by the professional. In the strengths-oriented case management approach, however, the monitoring function becomes a shared focus of each helping meeting. By making the goal planning process the empirical focus of the work, consumer gains in terms of successful activities are recognized and reinforced. Additionally, activities that have not been completed are discussed and modifications in the plan are developed.

The overarching purpose of monitoring is to empower consumers to assume their own monitoring functions to assist them in recognizing the control they can exert over their own lives, health, satisfaction, and well-being. Recognizing this allows consumers to feel more confident in developing their own plans and in using their own capabilities or the assistance of others to get what they want in a more independent fashion. One consumer commented upon this process:

> I learned honesty. That I can deal with my problems, that it is better to face my problems than to keep them bottled up inside of me, or go off on anybody. She (CM) taught me that I don't always have to depend on other people, that I can do things for myself, and she had patience with me. My mom did my laundry before I met my case manager, and she asked me, "Why don't you do it yourself?" and I never thought of doing it that way, and I thought, maybe she's got a point, I mean, I knew what to do, I even knew how to do it, and I did. She taught me a lot about me that I didn't even know.

Another consumer commented:

> Case management has been helpful. I've gotten some more of my independence back. It takes time for me to get back the things I have lost. I've gotten to the point where I can

> experiment with things. I used to think everything was rock cement, but now I know that just isn't true. I can try something, and if it doesn't work then it's O.K. The important thing is that I try.

As the helping process evolves, consumers may experience a renewed sense of stability in terms of financial circumstances, involvement with vocational/volunteer or leisure time activities, and ability to recognize and manage symptoms of their illness. When this becomes evident, there may be a notable shift in the delivery of helping functions from assessment, planning/implementation, and advocacy to monitoring. At this stage, graduated disengagement with consumers may begin.

Graduated Disengagement: Promoting Normative Interdependence

Graduated disengagement refers to the purposeful activities designed to increase consumers' contact with other providers and naturally occurring helpers in the community. Consequently, the frequency and intensity of case management contacts may diminish. This function is designed to prevent total dependence on the case manager, and to promote consumer empowerment, personal decision-making, and autonomy. It is not suggested that a prescriptive, linear strategy be employed with consumers during the graduated disengagement phase. Each person is different, and each will respond in her own way to the lessening of contact with the case manager. The following questions, however, may serve as a guide in determining how and when this function will be employed:

> Does the consumer have entitlements in place, such as SSI, SSDI, Medicaid, food stamps, Section Eight housing, etc.?
>
> Has the consumer consistently demonstrated the desire to remain in a particular living situation by cooperating with the expectations of the landlord and paying utility bills on time?
>
> Has the consumer been able to maintain functioning while experiencing tolerable levels of positive symptoms of the illness for a period of six months to one year?
>
> Has the consumer consistently demonstrated the desire to engage in daily activities such as cooking, attending medication clinic, and participating in social/recreational activities either alone or with others?
>
> Have you begun to question the need for your involvement with a consumer on an intensive or weekly level?
>
> Are there currently more people available to assist the consumer, both professional and social, with activities that you as the case manager have been performing, such as helping with grocery shopping, or dropping in once a week to see how things are going?

Have you discussed the idea of reducing the amount of contact with the consumer? This activity is essential and cannot be taken for granted. It allows each consumer to respond to this proposed shift in the nature of your work together in her own way.

The critical element of the graduated disengagement function in the strengths model is that the relationship will be changing and not terminating. Consumers are informed that the case manager will remain available, especially during distressing times, to renew more intensive involvement if this is wanted and needed.

PARTNERSHIP IN PROCESS

This chapter has focused upon the beliefs and functions that converge in the strengths model of case management. Working with people who struggle with persistent mental illness has engendered changes in the way we view and provide mental health services. The nature of the relationship has become less prescriptive and more collaborative. Professionals are making the effort to be flexible in where, how, and what activities they are willing to include in the helping process. In a very real way, working with persons with mental illness in the era of de-institutionalization has fused both mental health and social action strategies. As this more holistic vision of social health emerges, conflicts in terms of philosophy and approach are likely to continue. If the well-being of consumers remains as the basis for such dialogue, the outcomes for both consumers and professionals will be enhanced. The poem and song that follow illustrate the joys (and frustrations) of working with people from a strengths vantage point.

IF YOU REALLY WANT TO HELP ME*

If you really want to help me take it slow.
Feel my words, and understand the world I know.
Be there for me in the bad times and the good,
Help me do the things I dream of, not what you think I should.
If you really want to help me show you care.
In your eyes I'll see if you're really there.
Take the time to discover what sets me apart.
Know me with your head, and with your heart.
The road I've traveled has been rough,
I struggle in my mind each passing day.
I pray my strength will be enough,
To keep me going on my way.
If you really want to help me take my hand.
Walk with me as I find joy within the strife.
Seek less to explain, than to understand.
And know that you will truly touch my life.

---

* Inspired by interviews with people with persistent mental illness.

THE CASE MANAGEMENT BLUES*

They say ya got to get the clients to take their medication.
And keep the landlord happy to prevent their eviction.
Well I went to my supervisor, while I was on the run,
But the boss said "No time now . . . are those progress notes done?"
Sometimes I wonder why I do what I do,
Well there ain't no cure for case management blues.
I know for sure I ain't in it for the money.
Or all the problems clients have that keep me hoppin' like a bunny.
Well I went to the director, said "My head's all a-spin,"
and she said, "Gee, that's too bad . . . are your billing forms in?"
Sometimes I wonder why I do what I do,
Well there ain't no cure for case management blues.
Gonna take two weeks and head south for a vacation.
Gonna take my problem to the mental health association.
Well I went to the commissioner, who was runnin' late,
And he said, "Oh, by the way, what's your hospitalization rate?"
Sometimes I wonder why I do what I do,
Well there ain't no cure for case management blues.
Well there must be something that gives my job some meaning.
Something more for me than helping clients with their cleaning.
I went to a consumer, who was smiling warmly at me,
and he said, "If it weren't for you . . . I don't know where I'd be."
At times like this I know why I do what I do,
Well there is a cure for case management blues.

---

* Sung to the tune of "Summertime Blues."

REFERENCES

Alinsky, S. (1972). *Rules for radicals*. New York: Vintage.

Allport, G. W. (1955). *Becoming*. New Haven: Yale University Press.

Bandura, A. (1977). Self-Efficacy: Toward a unifying theory of behavioral change. *Psychological Review, 84,* 191–215.

Bond, G. R., Miller, L. D., Krumwied, R. D., and Ward, R. S. (1988). Assertive case management in three CMHCs: A controlled study. *Hospital and Community Psychiatry, 39,* 411–417.

Claus, K. E. and Bailey, J. T. (1977). *Power and influence in health care: A new approach to leadership*. St. Louis: C. V. Mosby.

Deitchman, W. S. (1980). How many case managers does it take to screw in a light bulb? *Hospital and Community Psychiatry, 31,* 788–789.

Dubos, R. (1965). *Man adapting*. New Haven: Yale University Press.

Epstein, L. (1980). *Helping people: The task-centered approach*. St. Louis: C. V. Mosby.

Etzioni, A. (1970). Power as a societal force. In M. Olsen, ed., *Power in societies*. New York: Macmillan.

French, J. R. P. and Raven, B. (1960). The bases of social power. In D. Cartwright and A. F. Zander, eds., *Group dynamics*. Evanston, IL: Row Patterson.

Goering, P. N., Wasylenki, D. A., Farkas, M., Lancee, W. J., and Ballantyne, R. (1988). What difference does case management make? *Hospital and Community Psychiatry, 39*(3), 272–276.

Gordon, W. E. (1969). Basic constructs for an integrative and generative conception of social work. In Gordon Hearn, ed., *The general systems approach: Contributions toward an holistic conception of social work*. New York: Council on Social Work Education.

Houts, P. S. and Scott, R. A. (1975). Goal planning in mental health rehabilitation. *Goal Attainment Review, 2,* 33–51.

Kisthardt, W. E. and Rapp, C. A. (1989). *Bridging the gap between principles and practice: Implementing a strengths perspective in case management*. Lawrence: University of Kansas School of Social Welfare.

Kisthardt, W. E. (1990). *The impact of the strengths model of case management from the consumer perspective*. Unpublished doctoral dissertation. Lawrence: University of Kansas School of Social Welfare.

Maluccio, A. N. (1981). *Promoting competence in clients*. New York: Free Press.

Modrcin, M., Rapp, C. A., and Chamberlain, R. (1985). *Case management with psychiatrically disabled individuals: Curriculum and training program*. Lawrence: University of Kansas School of Social Welfare.

Rapp, C. A. and Chamberlain, R. (1985). Case management services for the chronically mentally ill. *Social Work, 26,* 417–422.

Rapp, C. A., and Wintersteen, R. (July 1989). The strengths model of case management: Results for twelve demonstrations. *Journal of Psychosocial Rehabilitation, 13*(1), 23–32.

Reynolds, B. C. (1964). The social casework of an uncharted journey. *Social Work, 9,* 13–17.

Richmond, M. (1922). *What is social casework?* New York: Russell Sage.

Roberts-DeGennaro, M. (1987). Developing case management as a practice model. *Social Casework, 68,* 466–470.

Rose, S. (1985). *Advocacy and empowerment: Mental health care in the community*. Boston: Routledge and Kegan Paul.

Schwartz, S. R., Goldman, H. H., and Churgin, S. (1982). Case management for the chronically mentally ill: Models and dimensions. *Hospital and Community Psychiatry, 33*(12), 1006–1009.

Stein, L. I. and Test, M. (1980). Alternatives to mental hospital treatment. *Archives of General Psychiatry, 37,* 392–397.

Weick, A. (November, 1986). The philosophical context of a health model of social work. *Social Casework, 66,* 551–559.

Weick, A., Rapp, C. A., Sullivan, W., and Kisthardt, W. E. (July, 1989). A strengths perspective for social work practice. *Social Work, 34,* 350–354.

White, R. W. (1963). *Ego and reality in psychoanalytic theory*. New York: International Universities Press.

CHAPTER 7

Mutual Help Mechanisms in the Empowerment of Former Mental Patients

Julian Rappaport, Thomas M. Reischl, and Marc A. Zimmerman

When helping professionals take seriously a strengths approach to problems in living we encounter nontrivial implications for the practice of our disciplines. If one believes that all people, regardless of their problems in living, have strengths and skills that can serve them and others well, the traditional relationship between helper and helpee is called into question. Why would people be placed in role relationships that force them to be (and see themselves as) service recipients? In this view, placing people in the role of service recipient as a means to help them overcome their "deficits" is more a result of historical and socioeconomic forces than a rational decision.

If we were to design a human service system with no presumptions as to what form helping would take, and with more regard for the people of concern than for the convenience, prestige, and power of the designers of the system, it is unlikely that we would create a plan in which individual people with problems in living would be expected to find their way into individual offices for an hour or so each week in order to get advice about their problems in living from people who are highly paid, often from a different social class, and who have no personal experience with the problems presented. It is also unlikely that we would isolate people in hospitals and expect them to figure out how to return to their community, spend large amounts of time naming their "disorders," and offer "treatments" that are approximately the same regardless of the name we have given the problem. Unfortunately, social work and psychology, like psychiatry, have followed a format developed by physicians as the means to professionalize practice. Helping role relationships have taken their form from the expert-patient-diagnosis-treatment model that made medicine a lucrative and highly prestigious occupation. Other disciplines seek similar "professionalization" and its rewards.

Copyright © 1992 by Longman Publishing Group.

The culture of the helping professions is paternalistic. It tends to develop parent–child-like relationships. It tends to meta-communicate to those who seek or accept services the expectation that they are, by virtue of their need for help, incompetent. In the expert–client role relationship one person is expected to give help, the other is expected to receive it. Other sections of this volume provide alternative conceptual frameworks designed to avoid some of the unintended effects of a professionalized helping culture, and particularly its emphasis on client weaknesses. Here we provide one example of a practical alternative: mutual help groups and organizations.

The mutual help alternative is based on the assumption that all people can be helpers as well as helpees. Rather than viewing help as a scarce and costly resource, this approach assumes that help is infinite, in that each person who is in need is also a provider of help for others. This paper will not review the literature on self- and mutual help, nor will it explicate the details of a theoretical-conceptual perspective. Rather, it will provide concrete examples of how the mutual help alternative can empower people who have serious problems in living. The examples provided here are based on a research project that gave us the opportunity for long-term observation of one large organization for people with a history of serious problems in living, many of whom have been hospitalized on multiple occasions. (See Rappaport et al., 1985; and Salem, Seidman, and Rappaport, 1988, for a more detailed description of the research project and the organization.) We will not offer a systematic justification of our critique of the helping professions or a defense of the strengths approach. However, it is important to understand that what follows is based on an empowerment view, rather than a treatment or a prevention of mental illness view, of human services.

EMPOWERMENT AND THE STRENGTHS APPROACH

Many of the same implications that follow from a strengths perspective are consistent with what has been called "empowerment" (see for example Rappaport, 1981, 1985, 1987, 1990; Zimmerman, 1990a). The idea of empowerment is developed in detail in the papers referred to above. Much of the discussion in those papers is conceptual and theoretical, providing what we consider the necessary background for our thinking about what in this volume is called a strengths approach. Indeed, a strengths approach held by the professional community is an important component of the empowerment social agenda. Some empirical work is reported in Rappaport, Swift, and Hess (1984), and in Zimmerman and Rappaport (1988). Related research and commentary may be found in a series of papers by Wandersman and his colleagues (Florin and Wandersman, 1990) and in the work of Dunst (Dunst, Trivette, and Deal, 1988; Dunst, Trivette, and Thompson, 1990) and in Gallant, Cohen, and Wolff (1985). For continuing dialogue concerning empowerment see also the work of the Cornell University Empowerment Group (1989). Here we accept their definition of empowerment:

> . . . an intentional, ongoing process centered in the local community, involving mutual respect, critical reflection, caring, and group participation, through which people lacking an equal share of valued resources gain greater access to and control over those resources (p. 2).

That definition was written to be used by people working with low-income families in the United States and other countries. It is, however, applicable to many different contexts. Here it suggests access to and control over psychological resources. Control may be understood as either instrumental or as a gain in identity and meaning that enables one to understand one's place in the world. It can be an enhancement of collective as well as individual control (van Uchelen, 1989). Regardless of the form that empowerment takes, there is an emerging consensus in the papers cited above that empowerment involves a process of gaining power or control by acquiring new resources or competencies. Process is the key to understanding empowerment. An individual or a collective is not empowered simply because they are powerful or they exert control in their environment. They are empowered because the result of their interactions with the environment has been a gain in access and control of resources. The difference is not trivial. If our studies primarily focus on those who possess power, personal or otherwise, we risk not attending to the interactive mechanisms that lead to empowerment. We also risk overlooking individuals or collectives who on a relative standard are not powerful, but are involved in the process of gaining control over their lives, and of helping others to do so.

This paper concentrates on concrete, descriptive examples of the process of empowerment in a particular context: where persons with a history of serious problems in living, who have been designated as "mental patients," have found their way to a mutual help organization that functions without the benefit (or the curse) of control by mental health professionals. It is a context in which people are encouraged to become givers, as well as receivers of help, regardless of how needy they may appear to be.

A Setting for Mutual Help

The growing literature on human helplessness suggests that loss of power may play an etiological role in the onset of depression (Garber and Seligman, 1980). Several studies have demonstrated that persons with external locus of control expectancies may be more vulnerable to the harmful effects of psychosocial stress (Johnson and Sarason, 1978; Kobasa; 1979; Sandler and Lakey, 1982). More unsettling is the possibility that psychiatric treatment may unwittingly encourage the adoption of a patient identity and the surrender of personal responsibility for recovery (Scheff, 1966; Thoits, 1985). While various researchers continue their examination of powerlessness, there has been a notable lack of attention to the other side of the coin: the processes and effects of empowerment, or gaining access and control over needed resources (but see Zimmerman, 1990b). One context in which people may have the opportunity to gain such access is in mutual help organizations.

The observations reported here were garnered in the course of a longitudinal study of a mutual help organization called GROW, founded in Australia in the 1950s and transplanted to a variety of countries around the world. There are now some five hundred GROW groups (over one hundred in the United States). GROW first came to this country in 1978, and we have been following its development since then. Though open to anyone, the organization focuses on persons with a history of mental illness. It was initially influenced by the experience of its founders in Alcoholics Anonymous, and is a "twelve step" organization. However, GROW has its own literature, written by the members themselves. They have organized a set of principles for mental health into what is known as the Blue Book, which members carry and quote from regularly.

Individual groups have between three and fifteen members, meet weekly for about two hours, and follow a structured group method. Each group has an elected organizer who keeps the group on task and selects a participant leader to run each meeting. Many members have the opportunity to become involved in leaders' meetings and to take on responsibility for expansion of the groups into new locations. Some members eventually become paid fieldworkers who take on a high level of organizational responsibility. GROW also sponsors regular social events and training functions. They operate drop-in centers and emphasize the development of friendships among members. People are encouraged to take increasing responsibility as they become involved in what they call a "caring and sharing community" where the aim is to do things with rather than to or for one another.

One important aspect of the organization is its particular model for help. Each person is explicitly encouraged to provide help for others from the very beginning of membership. That expectation runs counter to the previous experience of most GROW members. A common experience for these citizens is a history of alienation, loss of control over their own lives, and a lack of connection to sources of social influence. Such people have heretofore been unable to mobilize personal resources for their own benefit or the benefit of others.

The mutual help context represents an interesting setting for exploring the mechanisms of empowerment because it offers opportunities for acquiring new competencies at several levels of functioning. This is different from other interventions for the mentally ill, such as psychotherapy, where clients are offered the opportunity to enhance their control only in their own lives. One-to-one therapy does not offer direct opportunities to influence others or the larger community. Even group therapy is limited because the interactions are ultimately controlled by the therapist who occupies an expert role in the group. In a mutual help organization, a large subset of members develop a sense of responsibility to other persons and to the organization which seeks to have social influence.

This operationalization of what Frank Reissman (1965) called the "helper therapy principle" has been theorized to be an important mechanism in the mutual help context for some time. As a part of our empirical study of the GROW organization, we followed 85 members in a longitudinal study of giving and receiving help. We found that members who provided more helping behaviors to others in the group meetings (assessed by detailed behavioral observations) showed both higher rates of attendance and greater improvement in social adjustment over time (Roberts, 1989). Below we describe the experiences of some of these people. We have observed a continuum of empowering experiences. At one end are those who simply attend meetings and social functions as a source of maintaining themselves in the community. Others begin to provide social and interpersonal comfort and support to peers as well as receive help. Still others take on formal roles in the organization and develop a sense of efficacy that extends to a small group. Some members move toward even larger responsibilities of internal organizational development and acquire the ability to act in the larger context of social influence as the organization expands and seeks new resources.

EMPOWERING MECHANISMS

Underpopulation

Chief among the empowering mechanisms in GROW is an organizational strategy of deliberate underpopulation. This term refers to the creation of settings in which there are more roles available than there are people to fill the roles, and in which there are more tasks to be performed than people available to perform them. Creating underpopulated settings (Barker, 1960; Wicker, 1979) appears to initiate empowerment processes for many members.* For example, GROW routinely establishes groups before enough members have been recruited. Expansions into new communities occur before the organization has enough leaders to assume the duties of fund raising, locating meeting space, recruiting members, and caring for others (Zimmerman et al., 1991). Underpopulated settings are vacuums of responsibility that force the organization to find members to assume these responsibilities. Many members agree to assume responsible roles because they feel genuinely needed and the role responsibilities are meaningful.

Formal roles vary in responsibility, ensuring an opportunity for every member regardless of level of functioning. At weekly group meetings two persons occupy the stable leadership roles of *organizer* and *recorder*. The recorder's primary responsibility is to administer a survey of questions aloud to the group to check the group's functioning. The organizer assumes the major responsibilities of encouraging the group to follow GROW's structured meeting schedule, keeping the keys for the meeting rooms, and selecting the leader for each meeting. The *leader* is directly responsible for guiding the group through the meeting's structured agenda. The members rotate other roles as well; each week someone tells a story of personal growth since joining GROW, and someone else is asked to prepare refreshments. Within the organization there are volunteer roles for persons willing to serve on committees such as the *program team* and the *management team*. These committees regularly monitor and plan organizational activities for the groups. GROW also maintains a small staff of paid *fieldworkers* who start and monitor groups, publicize meetings, recruit members, and perform other training and fund raising duties.

Since the groups and the organization have more roles than people to fill them, members are encouraged to assume responsibilities before they or others feel they are ready to do so. Unlike most professional mental health services, the operation of GROW meetings and the accomplishment of responsibilities depends on members rather than experts taking on these tasks. Deliberate underpopulation, then, provides meaningful opportunities to develop new competencies and to promote gains in personal power and control.

Support Structures

This strategy of underpopulation and encouraging members to assume greater responsibility occurs within an organizational culture of acceptance and support. If it were oth-

---

* We prefer the term *underpopulated* to *undermanned*, the original term used by Barker before its sexist nature was obvious.

erwise, underpopulation would likely backfire by placing individuals in positions of inevitable failure. Instead, GROW provides settings with the intended purpose of supporting individuals who have taken on new challenges in the organization. In addition to the group meetings where Growers praise each other for taking action addressing personal problems, members also agree to contact each other between meetings, either by phone or for social activities such as meeting for coffee. Groups in each area take turns hosting a monthly social event. Each month the organization also holds afternoon-long meetings for group leaders. One month the meeting will be devoted to discussing papers on mental health written by Growers (leadership meetings) and the next month they will focus on group problems (organizer and recorder meetings).

Construal of Problems as Opportunities

GROW also emphasizes a way of construing problems associated with new challenges that promotes self-acceptance and the acquisition of competencies. Several quotations from GROW's Blue Book, its pocket manual for living, poetically illustrate these construals. First, problems are viewed not as hurdles but as opportunities:

> Mostly, when things go wrong,
> They're meant to go wrong—
> So we can outgrow
> What we have to outgrow
> You've got a problem? That's *good!*

Second, members should not expect themselves to act flawlessly:

> Settle for disorder in lesser things for the sake of order in greater things; and therefore be
>   content to be discontent in many things.
> If the rough road gets you there and the smooth one doesn't which are you going to choose?
> Have the courage to make mistakes.

Third, members should disregard excessive self-doubts and unreasonable criticism from others while affirming their own personal esteem:

> I am more durable than vulnerable.
> Say something nice about yourself—without adding "but"
> Those who matter, don't mind.
> Those who mind, don't matter.

Finally, taking responsibility for one's own recovery and for helping others is accomplished with the support of others:

> If you need help, help others.
> To help others best, let them help you.
> Mental health can't be taught—it has to be learned together.
> You alone can do it, but you can't do it alone.

> May the spirit of friendship make us free and whole persons and gentle builders of a free and whole community.

Growers are encouraged to memorize these sayings and to recite them when problem solving or helping others, and to use them to guide actions.

What follows are several case descriptions of persons who were empowered as a result of their involvement in this underpopulated and supportive organization. The cases represent a sampling of success stories at several levels of involvement: being helped, helping others, group leadership, and organizational leadership. In describing each case, we focus on the organizational mechanisms which created opportunities for the empowerment of these individuals. The data for each case was gathered from multiple interviews, group observations, hospital records, and field notes.

CASE EXAMPLES OF EMPOWERMENT

EMPOWERMENT THROUGH BEING HELPED

The first case is an example of a person with persistent psychological problems who finds acceptance and support at GROW. Consistent attendance and participation in the meetings and social events represent initial steps toward taking responsibility for recovery. Dave attended his first GROW meeting on his mother's advice. He hoped to meet friends and to receive help for physical pains, which he believed were caused by Satan. He was thirty-four years old, unmarried, unemployed, and dependent on federal disability benefits to pay rent at a private, supervised board and care home. Up until three months before joining GROW, Dave had lived in nursing homes. Dave reported eleven psychiatric hospitalizations over a period of five years including three stays of ten months or more. His hospitalization records reveal his DSM-III primary diagnoses at several admissions was paranoid schizophrenia. He reported that his mental problems were due in part to recreational drug use in the past. He had avoided further hospitalizations with the help of a day treatment program, a community crisis team, and antipsychotic medications.

A consistent attender at GROW meetings during his first year, Dave successfully developed a supportive network of friends in the group. By the end of the first year he reported that he considered ten Growers among his closest friends and had hosted two group social events at his parents' nearby farm. He was particularly close to the two group leaders who took an active interest in helping him at the meetings and in keeping contact between meetings. Dave's interviewer felt these two group leaders kept Dave out of potentially troublesome situations as he adjusted to more independent living conditions. At the meetings he spoke often of his physical pains and of daily events that would upset him such as a housemate accusing him of stealing, dead insects on car windshields, and thinking Satan was attacking him. The group provided support, urged self-acceptance, and offered practical suggestions to address these issues. More importantly, Dave often followed through on the suggestions of the group and this self-activation may have facilitated his strides toward more independence. Not only had he avoided hospitalization during his tenure in GROW, but he eventually moved to and adjusted to an unsupervised, independent apartment. His psychiatrist also decided to reduce his medication prescription by 33 percent.

Dave's improvement took the form of active help seeking in his group. He talked about his adjustment problems and took active steps to develop and utilize a network of supportive friends. Dave never assumed an active helping role in his group, but, as some other cases illustrate, other Growers with severe problems did take advantage of opportunities to help.

EMPOWERMENT THROUGH HELPING OTHERS

The second case illustrates how empowerment may be promoted as the group encourages members to look beyond their own problems and help others. Bill joined GROW three months after his divorce on the recommendation of a woman at an Al-Anon meeting. He attended the group regularly from the start despite living forty minutes away. At first Bill spoke very little at the meetings. He rarely talked about himself and only listened while others discussed problems. After a few months, Bill told the group he felt self-conscious about his noticeable stutter and he apologized for not speaking more. During his first interview, Bill revealed that he was unsure if he really belonged in GROW because the other Growers' problems were more severe than his.

His marital breakup aside, Bill's life did appear comparably more stable than some of the other members'. He was forty-four years old and a long-time production worker at a small plant. Other than two months of marital counseling, he had had no experience with mental health services. He served on the board of elders at his church and enjoyed his weekly bowling league. His interview revealed several close friends at work, at church, and on the bowling team. Bill also reported, however, that he felt estranged from his twenty-year-old son and that he was lonesome since his divorce. He felt some coworkers took advantage of his personal weaknesses. His interest in GROW stemmed from his desire to become more skilled at sharing feelings with others, to grow closer to God, and to have peace of mind by controlling his emotions and thoughts.

Several members of Bill's group, including the organizer, asked Bill to provide helpful suggestions after the group had exhausted several possibilities. While he was a man of few words, his ideas were praised and valued by the group and the person being helped. By the end of his first year in GROW, Bill had taken a more active role in the meetings, although from the start he spent much more time helping others than he did receiving help for his problems. He did, however, consult with the group several times about how to become closer to his son. Well into his second year, Bill became one of the group's more active and perceptive helpers, saying not only supportive comments but also helping others think differently about their problems and suggesting reasonable practical tasks. Group observer ratings of Bill's helpfulness noticeably increased after his first year. He was also spending more time with Growers outside the meetings including group picnic excursions to his trailer on a nearby lake.

There were also strides in Bill's personal life: his relationship with his son improved, he felt more assertive in seeking out friends, he decided to think more for himself rather than let others control him, and he began running four miles daily. Bill attributed much of his progress to his increased involvement in GROW: "Knowing I can help others has given me more self-confidence. . . . GROW has also helped me with my speech. It has helped me relax and I stutter less."

While Bill never assumed any formal leadership position in GROW, he became one of his group's most consistent and effective helpers and grew more involved with organizational leadership meetings. He was frequently called upon to tell his story of personal growth through GROW as a showcase for how GROW can help others. He felt that helping others facilitated his communication skills to the point where he felt more comfortable speaking at church meetings and he wrote and presented a paper on anxiety for one of

GROW's leadership meetings. His overall improvement in self-esteem and personal efficacy may have helped facilitate a major transition: he started dating a woman he met in GROW. This was his first romance since his divorce and he eventually decided he wanted to remarry. Both he and his fiancée felt confident that from GROW they had a solid foundation of understanding for a marriage.

EMPOWERMENT THROUGH GROUP LEADERSHIP

Steve's story illustrates how deliberate underpopulation creates opportunities for taking on additional responsibility and competence building. In Steve's case, taking on leadership responsibilities in a new group facilitated his acquisition of greater functional control in his own life. Steve reported his psychological troubles began in college and, in the following ten years, he had been hospitalized in psychiatric facilities eleven times. State facility records indicate six extended stays between two and eight months during this period. His DSM-III diagnosis at his most recent admission was chronic paranoid schizophrenia. At the age of twenty-nine Steve joined GROW two weeks after his release from a state hospital. His father had gone to several meetings before urging Steve to attend. Steve attended the meetings with his father consistently for over a year until GROW decided to establish a new group in the same community. Steve joined this new group and was promptly elected to fill the new group recorder position and, after seven months, became the group's organizer.

Taking responsibility for his group's operation was a major step for someone who had been unwilling or unable to function outside a hospital ward in the last ten years. Even more remarkable is that he became, in our observer's words, "an effective and competent leader." He frequently challenged other members to take action to address their problems. Another group leader adopted a more emotionally supportive helping style providing a nice complement to Steve's practical approach. The observer noted that Steve's psychiatric history was difficult to believe given how rationally and skillfully he organized the meetings. Members of the group also indicated a high level of respect for Steve since he had overcome so much since joining GROW. He also took an interest in helping other group leaders at the organizers' and recorders' meetings and at leadership meetings where he gave presentations on his thoughts about mental health.

Steve's interviews over the next two years further document his strides toward greater functional control in his life. He progressively secured jobs with greater responsibility, from being a grass cutter to a part-time delivery person to a full-time patient transporter at a local hospital, where he supervised students and government-supported employment trainees. After successfully completing a college English course, he entered a radiology school and completed his first year as a full-time student while working part-time at the hospital and maintaining his organizer position in GROW. Over the four years he was involved in GROW he not only avoided further hospitalization, but he and his psychiatrist eventually terminated his counseling sessions and changed his medication from bimonthly prolixin shots to daily stelazine pills, which were subsequently reduced by 60 percent.

Beth's story is another example illustrating how underpopulation promotes empowerment, and also the importance of organizational support and patience. Beth was literally dragged to her first meeting by a GROW fieldworker. In the preceding four years she had been hospitalized six times (including an eleven-month stay at a state psychiatric facility) and had been diagnosed as having a schizoaffective disorder. A former elementary school teacher, Beth was thirty-nine years old, recently divorced, unemployed, and living on federal disability benefits.

She was an unlikely candidate for group organizer as her attendance during the first year was irregular and dependent on whether the fieldworker would pick her up for the meeting. She rarely spoke at meetings unless directly addressed. This group, however, had struggled for over a year without a willing group organizer when the fieldworker asked Beth to assume this role. She agreed, but for a long time exerted little leadership in the meetings. In fact, during her first year as organizer she was hospitalized twice and took extended leaves from the group. Soon after her last hospitalization, however, Beth began to lead the meetings more effectively. She reported wanting to take the job more seriously. The group observers noted a respective increase in her helping behaviors and in keeping the group on task.

Beth appeared to be making other personal strides at the same time. She took a part-time tutoring position in an elementary school as part of a work training program. She moved to an independent, unsubsidized apartment and reported feeling happier and more expressive. Because the organization is one which is run by and for its own members and because the organization not only provides roles but genuinely needs its members to fill them, these two examples illustrate how personal gains become intimately tied to taking responsibility for others.

EMPOWERMENT THROUGH ORGANIZATIONAL LEADERSHIP

Joan's case parallels many others who rose to paid leadership positions in GROW. Most fieldworkers joined as members and filled other group and organizational leadership positions before becoming fieldworkers. We found most fieldworkers to be highly committed to their work even though some were dealing with their own personal problems and adjustments. They were often asked to live and work in drop-in center houses rented by GROW. When the need arose, fieldworkers were asked to move to other communities to fill similar positions. Because the organization is intentionally structured in an underpopulated fashion, there are always opportunities for members to take leadership. That is, power and control in this organization are not scarce commodities to be hoarded by a small group of people, but viewed as infinite and expanding, limited only by the members' willingness to assume control.

A friend referred Joan to GROW three months after she divorced her husband of twenty-seven years. She was forty-seven and living alone for the first time since marrying and raising four children. At her first meetings, Joan talked about the pain of her marriage and her strained relationships with her children after the divorce. She also discussed feeling lonely, depressed, and worried about money matters. She worked full-time in a mailroom and part-time as a sales clerk to meet expenses. Joan attended GROW every week and despite having immediate problems of her own, group observers consistently noted her skill and willingness to help other Growers.

The member-leaders must have also noticed her skills because within five months of joining, she was asked if she would serve as the group's organizer. She agreed, and before the end of her first year had increased her involvement in GROW several ways, including volunteering to serve on organizational committees and the Board of Directors. On her own initiative, she started and sponsored a special group for college students. This assumption of power and control was not seen as a threat, but as desirable for the organization. Joan's interviews in that first year also note that additions to her social network included twelve Growers who she considered close friends.

The organization's appreciation of Joan seemed to come at a time when it was sorely needed. Before the end of her first year in GROW, her husband remarried, which greatly upset her. Shortly after, her nineteen-year-old daughter died in an automobile accident. Her involvements in GROW provided not only a diversion from these events, but also a means for developing supportive friendships and a new career. At this time, GROW was rapidly expanding into new communities and offered Joan one of the new fieldworker positions.

GROW's interest in hiring Joan was not surprising, given her skills. Joan's acceptance of the job offer, however, seemed remarkable given the number of changes that had already occurred in her life. Her interviews indicated that, taking the lead from GROW's literature, she felt these changes were a means for personal growth, for achieving a fuller understanding of others who suffer, and for a more meaningful participation in her community. Other settings where people seek help may have promoted a similar construal of life changes, but this orientation seems different from therapeutic settings that promote stress management by reducing responsibilities.

The new job presented several new challenges. Since the position was in another community, Joan moved into a GROW center house which housed state clients who needed temporary crisis support. The fieldworker job was different from her mailroom job because she was now responsible for structuring her own work activities. There were groups to attend, but other responsibilities like publicizing, recruiting, and starting groups involved self-initiated efforts. The fieldworkers met monthly to discuss these issues and support each other. As a result of this opportunity and the support, Joan felt she grew more competent in her duties over time. She also continued to seek new challenges as she initiated a large communication and fund raising operation after a national magazine published an article about GROW.

SUMMARY

In all of these cases, we note how this mutual help organization offered meaningful opportunities for gaining a sense of competence, personal influence, and control. These individuals were empowered in terms of their respective levels of functioning. At group meetings Dave, who struggled with persistent delusions and hallucinations, found acceptance and active support and guidance. His empowerment took the form of accepting responsibility for consistent attendance and participation in meetings and social events, which may have facilitated his continuing community adjustment and moves toward independent living. Bill took greater control by looking beyond his own problems and offering support and guidance to other Growers. The opportunity to care for others was important to him. The close relationships Bill developed and his active helping in his group met his nurturance needs, built his self-confidence, and permitted him to become romantically involved with a woman again. Taking on formal leadership roles in the group seemed to promote confidence and competencies for both Steve and Beth. The fact that the organization always has such opportunities built into its structure meant that they were available when needed. Steve appeared to take the responsibility quickly and his own personal development can only be described as dramatic: He not only terminated his pattern of repeated hospitalizations, but he established the grounding for a professional career and an independent life. Beth, while slow to take the responsibility in her group, eventually did assume an effective leadership role and also began to make strides toward functional independence. Finally, Joan, like Bill, found in GROW a place to talk about her divorce and her adjustment problems. GROW took advantage of her natural helping skills and offered opportunities to challenge and develop her competencies in GROW's organizational expansion. Thinking about empowerment as a process facilitated the examination of power gains in each of these people regardless of each person's absolute level of power.

Exploring empowerment processes also focused our attention on the dimension of time. In each case, empowerment could be observed only by noting development and change over time. It may not be an accident that each story spans at least two years. Within this target population there appear to be considerable individual differences. Steve and Joan, for instance, responded quickly to their participation opportunities; Bill and Beth seemed to require more time. Beth's story is particularly intriguing in this regard because the organization allowed her a long period of time to develop her leadership skills. Even subsequent hospitalizations did not deter GROW's faith in her ability to become an effective group organizer.

In this exploration of the mutual help context, it is important to distinguish between the concepts of empowerment and personal adjustment. This definition problem is difficult because these two ecological processes often occur together and are not mutually exclusive. The distinction is subtle but potentially important for delineating policy and program alternatives. We believe that empowerment broadly represents the interactive processes that enhance control and influence over one's life circumstances. Traditionally, adjustment broadly represents the interactive processes that lead to successful maintenance outside the institution. Empowerment suggests one set of metaphors: building competencies, taking control, assuming responsibilities, and being involved. Adjustment suggests another set: remediating deficits, taking care, promoting survival, and being independent. While several cases in this paper suggest empowerment and community adjustment are parallel processes, this may not always be the case. For instance, Beth assumed the responsibilities of organizer in her group at a time when she struggled with living outside the hospital. Policies and social programs designed to facilitate community adjustment may profit by incorporating the type of empowerment mechanisms noted in GROW. Toward this goal, further exploration of the relationship between empowerment and adjustment may be a fruitful area of research (see Dunst, Trivette, and Thompson, 1990).

Despite its inherent problems of internal and external validity, explorations of individual cases provide a rich method for isolating empowerment processes. The cases discussed above dramatically illustrate empowerment in the context of mutual help. In a sense, these stories tell us what is possible when persons have meaningful opportunities to learn new skills and take on new challenges. They also suggest that even persons with chronic and serious psychological disorders can respond to the empowerment mechanisms of mutual help. Underpopulated settings that depend on persons taking responsibility for that setting can and have motivated even the most disturbed persons to assume new responsibilities. We also learned from these stories that a supportive organizational culture with a tolerance for mistakes is probably also necessary if a troubled person is to embark on a path to empowerment.

REFERENCES

Barker, R. G. (1960). Ecology and motivation. In M. R. Jones, ed., *Nebraska Symposium on Motivation*. Lincoln, Nebraska: University of Nebraska Press.

Cornell University Empowerment Group (October, 1989). *Networking Bulletin, 1* (2).

Dunst, C. J., Trivette, C. M., and Deal, A. (1988). *Enabling and empowering families*. Cambridge, MA: Brookline.

Dunst, C. J., Trivette, C. M., and Thompson, R. B. (1990). Supporting and strengthening family functioning: Toward a congruence between principles and practice. *Prevention in Human Services, 9*, 19–43.

Florin, P. and Wandersman, A., eds. (1990). Citizen participation, voluntary organizations and community development: Insights for empowerment through research. *American Journal of Community Psychology, 18*, 41–54.

Gallant, R. V., Cohen, C., and Wolff, T. (1985). Change of older persons' image, impact on public policy result from Highland Valley Empowerment Plan. *Perspective on Aging, 14*, 9–13.

Garber, J. and Seligman, M. E. P., eds. (1980). *Human helplessness: Theory and applications*. New York: Academic Press.

Johnson, J. H. and Sarason, I. G. (1978). Life stress, depression and anxiety: Internal-external control as a moderator variable. *Journal of Psychosomatic Research, 22*, 205–208.

Kobasa, S. C. (1979). Stressful life events, personality, and health: An inquiry into hardiness. *Journal of Personality and Social Psychology, 37*, 1–11.

Rappaport, J. (1981). In praise of paradox: A social policy of empowerment over prevention. *American Journal of Community Psychology, 9*, 1–25.

Rappaport, J. (1985). The power of empowerment language. *Social Policy, 16*, 15–21.

Rappaport, J., Seidman, E., Toro, P. A., McFadden, L. S., Reischl, T. M., Roberts, L. J., Salem, D. A., Stein, C. H., and Zimmerman, M. A. (1985). Collaborative research with a mutual help organization. *Social Policy, 15*, 12–24.

Rappaport, J. (1987). Terms of empowerment/exemplars of prevention: Toward a theory for community psychology. *American Journal of Community Psychology, 15*, 117–148.

Rappaport, J. (1990). Research methods and the empowerment social agenda. In P. Tolan, C. Keys, F. Chertok, and L. Jason, eds., *Researching community psychology*. Washington, DC: American Psychological Association.

Rappaport, J., Swift, C., and Hess, R., eds. (1984). *Studies in empowerment: Steps toward understanding and action*. New York: Haworth Press.

Reissman, F. (1965). The "helper" therapy principle. *Social Work, 10*, 27–32.

Roberts, L. J. (1989). Giving and receiving help: Group behavioral predictors of outcomes for members of a mutual help organization. PhD dissertation, Department of Psychology, University of Illinois, Urbana-Champaign.

Salem, D. A., Seidman, E., and Rappaport, J. (1988). Community treatment of the mentally ill: The promise of mutual help organizations. *Social Work, 33*, 403–408.

Sandler, I. N. and Lakey, B. (1982). Locus of control as a stress moderator: The role of control perceptions and social support. *American Journal of Community Psychology, 10*, 65–80.

Scheff, T. (1966). *Being mentally ill*. Chicago: Aldine.

Thoits, P. A. (1985). Self-labeling processes in mental illness: The role of emotional deviance. *American Journal of Sociology, 91*, 221–249.

van Uchelen, C. (1989). Healing and cognitive control in cross-cultural perspective. Paper presented at the second Biennial Community Psychology Research and Action Conference, East Lansing, MI.

Wicker, A. W. (1979). An introduction to ecological psychology. Monterey, CA: Brooks/Cole.

Zimmerman, M. A., Reischl, T. M., Rappaport, J., Seidman, E., Toro, P. A., and Salem, D. A. (1991). Expansion strategies of a mutual help organization. *American Journal of Community Psychology, 19*, 251–278.

Zimmerman, M. A. (1990a). Taking aim on empowerment research: On the distinction between individual and psychological conceptions. *American Journal of Community Psychology, 18*, 169–177.

Zimmerman, M. A. (1990b). Toward a theory of learned hopefulness: A structure model analysis of participation and empowerment. *Journal of Research in Personality, 24,* 71–86.

Zimmerman, M. A. and Rappaport, J. (1988). Citizen participation, perceived control, and psychological empowerment. *American Journal of Community Psychology, 16,* 725–750.

CHAPTER 8

Aged Adult Protective Services Clients:

People of Unrecognized Potential

Eloise Rathbone-McCuan

This chapter analyzes several trends that influence the social service delivery orientation in the field of aging and characterize current social work practice with elderly people. The practice models used by many social workers, including those recently trained in gerontology concentrations, reflect a preoccupation of older clients as individuals and groups with emotional, social, physical, and resource deficits justifying and legitimizing social work intervention in their lives. The evolution of these current orientations can be interpreted in the context of recent social historical analyses of cultural ageism in America; for example, in the roots of the medical profession's interest in geriatrics. Parallels can be drawn between social work and medicine as each established a "pathology orientation" about old age to legitimize the emerging clinical specialty.

Adult protective services are a growing component of the public social services system and are aimed at high-risk adults and older persons. In some of these programs caseworkers apply traditional "old age as social problem" orientations. However, alternative perspectives are being developed to redirect patterns of worker–client relationships and the larger structural context of service provision. Based on the author's collaboration with adult protective service caseworkers in Tennessee and Vermont to develop alternative frameworks for practice activities related to self-neglect, a schemata compatible with the strengths perspective is outlined. It addresses some practice principles also discussed in other chapters concerned with the chronically mentally ill and emotionally disturbed children. The importance of preparing social workers to evaluate the limitations of the dominant social problem perspective and to recognize the value of applying approaches that focus on human potential is a recommended direction for all practice with older persons.

Copyright © 1992 by Longman Publishing Group.

EVALUATION OF AGEISM IN AMERICAN CULTURE

Only recently have social historians begun to raise questions about the social class and cultural position of old people in America's earlier periods. The motivation for such study was to discover whether the stereotypic, ageist attitudes of today are reflected in the premodern era. Some of the questions about cultural ageism and its role in our society's development include: Were older citizens honored or devalued? Did they command community influence based on advanced age or their potential to pass on economic and social status to younger generations? Were old persons safeguarded in the bosom of family life regardless of the burdens placed on the kin unit, or were there options for the family to transfer caregiving responsibility to other sources? What were the individual and community norms that sanctioned or prohibited certain patterns of attention to older persons' welfare?

Without much reflection on these questions, gerontologists have assumed that the quality of life for aged persons, as a category in the population, quickly and dramatically declined with the advent of industrialization and urbanization. This interpretation has been supported by modernization theory that explains the history of the aging in terms of the structural differences between traditional and modern societies and between earlier and later periods of development in capitalist nations.

The "new history of old age," the recent work of a small group of social historians interested in the study of old age, does not support the idea of the universality of previous community beneficence and family loyalty toward old people. But there are many myths that have been sustained by a false perception of history, and it seems clearer now that our beliefs about the elderly ("ageism") transcend social and economic changes.

Gratton (1986) summarized the alternative view of the social condition of the aged as revealed in recent social historical studies:

> One would fully expect that an economic transition of the magnitude of industrialization, which undermined the previous economic system and its contingent age relations, would have a most direct effect on the place of the aged in society. But the most powerful new histories of aging in America explicitly reject this logic: they see the structural change from farm to factory as of little consequence. The declines in the elderly's status is connected to an independent force, ageism. Cultural attitude is found to have more importance than structure. It is on this presumption that the new history of the American aged has been written (p. 6).

Butler (1975) was among the first gerontologists to suggest that prejudice against old people, or ageism, was no mere epiphenomenon, no simple set of misperceptions that can be corrected by image makers or social engineers. What social historical analyses suggest is that there were many cultural conditions that reinforced ageism; for example, the legacy of certain popular moralities that dominated in the 1800s.

Cole (1986) has noted that many of the influences of Victorian morality (and ideology) associated with the decline of household economic productiveness and growth of a marketplace have perpetuated the presence of restrictive norms and negative stereotypes toward the old. He attributed the origins of ageism in eighteenth-century America, in some measure, to the fact that old age was an embarrassment to the new morality of self-control:

> The primary virtues of civilized morality—independence, health, success—required constant control over one's body and physical energies. The decaying body in old age, a constant reminder of the limits of physical self-control, came to signify dependence, disease, failure and sin (p. 61).

Another important historical analysis was conducted by Fox (1978), who studied institutionalization for insanity between 1870 and 1930 in California. From the primary analysis of Fox and secondary analysis of his work by Dowd (1984) some relevant perspectives can be added to the assessment of current cultural conditions that surround many elderly who are reported by the community to be self-neglecting. From the late 1800s to the start of the Great Depression, Fox found that aged women were especially likely to be committed to institutions. Demonstration of senility was determined quickly on the bases of many of the normal processes of aging, such as slowed reflexes or bothersome personality qualities and traits. Inability to contribute to family productivity was yet another motive for finding ways to remove aged persons, who also were seen as a source of community stigmatization. The contemporary community norms that support "protection of the old against themselves" have, like these discussed by Fox, the dangerous potential to legitimize current practices of commitment into institutional settings where the old, especially very old impoverished women, can be "cared for." Diagnostic judgments of incompetencies and self-harming motivations can serve as a powerful social control mechanism over the fate of some aged Americans.

There is little published literature documenting how the profession of social work progressed toward the service roles assumed with aged groups by the mid-twentieth century. Lowry (1985) considers that little interest in social work practice with the aged was evidenced prior to 1945. After the end of the Second World War, research societies such as the Gerontological Society of America were founded and clinical social workers began to present papers about the need of social work services to be extended to old people. The first White House Conference on Aging in 1961 included social work representation and by the early 1970s there were active efforts to make casework, group services, and community organization efforts available to the older population. Hashimi (1988) has suggested that social policies and practices applied to the chronic mentally ill elderly in the late nineteenth and early twentieth centuries involved psychiatric agents who were sanctioned to remove persons of unwanted status from the community. On the assumption that much of the evolution of medical and psychiatric social work practice was influenced by the attitudes and dispositions of physicians, there are some parallels in the evolution of geriatrics as a medical specialty that may help to elucidate the progression of geriatrics as a social work specialty.

In 1909, I. L. Nascher began the process of attempting to interest physicians in what he called "geriatrics," but there was no rush from medical colleagues to meet his appeal. Haber (1986) states:

> The present-day reluctance to specialize in this field can be linked to the original model on which it was based. From the start, physicians [such as Nascher] who saw a

need to treat the old as a separate group characterized their prospective patients as highly undesirable and incurable (p. 67).

Some of the more contemporary medical literature, especially that which describes elderly patients with a combination of biopsychological symptoms, remains negatively stereotypic. Social workers also stereotype the aged (Ford and Sbordone, 1980; Kosberg and Harris, 1978). Elderly people with lifestyles that do not conform to middle class standards are quick victims of the professional interpretation of "pathology" that can lead to their removal from the community into age- and disability-segregated settings.

Clark, Mankikar, and Gray (1975) published a clinical study of thirty elderly patients, fourteen men and sixteen women, whom they labeled as suffering from the Diogenes syndrome (a clinical condition of gross neglect in old age). Medical and psychiatric authority and judgment were applied as the rationale for institutional care. They described the patients this way:

> All had dirty, untidy homes and a filthy personal appearance about which they had no shame. Hoarding of rubbish (syllogomania) was sometimes seen. All except two lived alone, but poverty and poor housing standards were not a serious problem. All were known to the social services department, and a third had persistently refused offers of help. An acute presentation with falls or collapse was common, and several physical diagnoses could be made . . . the mortality, especially for women was high; most of the survivors responded well and were discharged. Half showed no evidence of psychiatric disorder and possessed higher than average intelligence. Many had led successful professional and business lives, with good family backgrounds and upbringings. Personality characteristics showed them to tend to be aloof, suspicious, emotionally labile, aggressive, group-dependent, and reality-distorting individuals. It is suggested that this syndrome may be a reaction late in life to stress in a certain type of personality (p. 366).

This description is representative of the pathological definitions that may be found in clinical geriatrics.

Some of the professional practice with and treatment of aged persons shows continuity between the past and present. Norms and values of cultural ageism affected the older population in ways that allowed professional and legal definitions to manage elderly persons in a manner satisfactory to the community if their presence was a menace. These definitions can still be applied to thwart an aged individual's potential to remain an active and contributing member of society.

PROBLEM DEFINITIONS APPLIED TO AGED PERSONS

The social work profession, perhaps as much as the medical profession, remains oblivious to or minimizes the social and environmental dimensions of aged persons' health and has applied the problem-by-definition mentality to aged persons. It seems that much of conventional social work theory, applied by academics and practitioners, equates individual need to pathological problems. On the whole, we are giving too little attention to the context of human need that looms behind so much of what gets identified as personal/individual problems.

Minkler (1984) urged the necessity of all disciplines and professions in gerontology to rethink the aging problem.

> By rejecting the notion that aging or any other social problem can be viewed and understood in isolation from larger political, social, and economic issues, the political economy perspective [as well as the strengths perspective and the feminist practice perspective] requires us to take seriously the "problems behind the problem" (p. 10).

Navarro (1984) noted that a particular problem lies in the dominant notion that the main criteria dividing our society into differentially powerful groups are race, sex, and age. The large scale neglect of social class as a criterion—indeed as the primary criterion for how power is distributed in the United States—contributes to false notions of the relatively "classless" nature of our society, obscuring a critical link between the majority of members of different ethnic, sex, and age groups.

Among the increasing number of social scientists who are challenging the perpetuation of the labeling process (it is based on power inequalities between labeler and labeled) as the framework for understanding individual and collective needs of the aged, Minkler and Estes (1984) offer cautions applicable to the conceptualizations of many human experiences that undergird the provision of social services. The profession of social work has yet to confront the social construction of reality concerning aging and old age that supports and reinforces public policies and institutional arrangements to manage and sequester the elderly. We as practitioners seem unaware of the social creation of the dependent status of the aged and the management of that dependency through public health and social service policies.

Goldstein (chapter 3) critically analyzes how current social constructions, so pervaded with pathological assumptions and interpretations, have prevailed in social work practice theory and its application. Much of the knowledge gathered through social work research has not contributed to our ability and willingness to enter the client's metaphoric and moral world. If social work research is a form of practice subject to the ethics of the profession and if those ethics are as important as the standards of "good science," then we must scrutinize the "whats and whys" of how we contribute to the prevailing social constructions about various groups. The experiences of very old persons trying to survive in the community illustrate his points very dramatically.

As a foundation for creating a strengths model for social work practice with the aged, it is essential that some knowledge be gathered through qualitative study. As stated by Rowles and Reinharz (1988):

> Qualitative gerontology is concerned with describing the patterns of behavior and processes of interaction, as well as revealing the meanings, values, and intentionalities that pervade elderly people's experiences or the experience of others in relation to old age. . . . The process of gathering data for qualitative research usually requires personal interaction with the individuals and context under study so that the researcher can hear people's language and observe behavior in situations (p. 6).

While some qualitative research has the same epistemological limitations of quantitative research, it also demands that the process of inquiry place the researcher directly into the more intimate context of peoples' lives and experience. This does not ensure that the interpretation of knowledge is equal to the weight and shape of the realities as experienced by the person who shares it. However, it is potentially a better match than those approaches that demand and validate the separation of definitions of reality between those who study and those who are studied. The application of qualitative analysis has been useful to the author in the study of self-neglect adult protective services.

ADULT PROTECTIVE SERVICES AS A SYSTEM OF DELIVERY

There is no specific practice theory of adult protective services, but a set of principles for defining the protective services practice context was set forth by the Center for Research and Advanced Study at the University of Southern Maine (1982). That framework is broadly applicable to many of the groups discussed in this paper because social workers usually investigate all cases reported to determine the presence of abuse, neglect, and exploitation in adult clientele. The agenda of adult protective services is one that attempts to preserve the autonomy of clients:

> When interests compete, the adult client is the only person you are charged to serve; not the community concerned about safety, the landlords concerned about property, citizens concerned about crime or mortality, families concerned about their own health or finances.
>
> When interests compete, the adult client is in charge of decision-making until she/he delegates responsibility voluntarily to another or the court grants responsibility to another.
>
> Freedom is more important than safety; that is, the person can choose to live in harm or even self-destructively provided she/he is competent to choose, does not harm others and commits no crimes.
>
> In the ideal case, protection of adults seeks to achieve simultaneously and in order of importance: freedom, safety, least disruption of lifestyle, and least restrictive care alternatives (p. 5).

These are practice principles based on a philosophy and a vision of the rights of people compatible with any social work practice role assumed with aged clients. Furthermore, the interpretation and application of these principles in protective services practice with self-neglecting clients clearly demonstrates a strengths perspective in action.

CONCEPTUALIZATION OF ADULT SELF-NEGLECT

The focus of the author's work is to understand individual behavior and experience among those aged persons referred to protective services and determined to be self-neglecting. Given the content and structure of adult protective legislation throughout the country, it is necessary for the caseworker to investigate reported cases and to make a determination of founded/unfounded risks. The determination of founded risk must then be "categorized" in order to separate abuse (other or self), neglect (other or self), and exploitation.

The process of case investigation requires caseworkers to engage in a labeling process even though legal status and civil liberties require that workers do not abuse adult rights. There is resistance to understanding this case investigation responsibility for what it is—the defining of an old person as abused, neglected, or self-neglecting is the assigning of a negative label. Like other negative labels, but it reflects and legitimizes the marginal and powerless position of the old person (Dowd, 1984).

Within the interactional social exchange process between caseworker and adult protective services client, how does one assess the experiences, activities, efforts, priorities, and resources of an aged person who is to be "investigated?" There appear to be four behaviors that must be considered in self-neglect. *Self-care* refers to actions initiated or tasks performed by the adult as part of the daily routine. *Personal care* is a particular aspect of a person's daily routine related to physical maintenance, such as bathing or food preparation. The person's irregular, incomplete, or ineffective performance of activities in the daily routine, especially personal care tasks, may reduce *well-being*. *Self-interest* is the motivation that keeps an older person trying to perform personal care tasks and complete other more general maintenance activities.

Self-care behavior is the central focus in the traditional assessing of the degree of dependence experienced by an old person. These capacities, or their lack, are what lead social workers to judge the "functional capacity" of an aged person as well as to make judgments about self-neglecting behaviors. As these assessments are applied, they frequently contribute to a social construction of a reality of dependency (and pathology) among the elderly.

On the other hand, assessment can be done from a strengths perspective by reconceptualizing what is to be accomplished by the caseworker in assessment. This means accounting for what old people can and do undertake to secure their well-being. Assessment can afford the worker the opportunity to enter the reality of the aged person, understand how she experiences daily life, and what successes she finds in the daily routine of life. We forget too easily that old people with cognitive and physical changes have strengths. Even in the settings that offer the best rehabilitative and preventive services to older persons, the approach is to compensate for what people cannot do rather than to enhance what they can do.

OLLIE MAE

Ollie Mae was a sixty-eight-year-old black female who suffered from several physical disabilities. She had heart disease, a seizure disorder requiring medication, and hypertension. She also had double below the knee amputations requiring prostheses on both legs. She had very little education, having been raised in a poor rural Arkansas community. At the time the protective service worker met her, Ollie Mae was living with a niece and granddaughter because her doctor decided she could not live alone following her battle with pneumonia. Medical personnel had defined Ollie Mae in terms of her physical deficits.

However, as the caseworker came to know Ollie Mae, he realized that she possessed many strengths. To begin with, she had learned to walk on two prostheses, a significant accomplishment at any age, but even more notable in an older individual due to the muscle coordination and strength required. She also handled her finances well on her own until living with her niece and granddaughter who were misusing her funds to support their drug use. The caseworker helped her move back to her home, which needed certain repairs such as new water pipes. Following these repairs, Ollie Mae moved back home where she stayed without incident for four more years. Due to a change in assessment forms the worker had to ask Ollie Mae if she used a wheelchair ever as he had never seen her use one; she had always used her prostheses. Ollie Mae replied that she used her wheelchair in the springtime only to plant her garden because this required the use of both hands. She died of cancer in her own home, active until her last days.

In view of the conventional social construction of dependency as inherent in old age and given that most of our professional practice is grounded in that construction, social work needs to challenge such definitions and shift approaches to practice with so-called dependent groups. That altered construction is readily available to use by looking at the lives of millions of old people.

Visions of independence in old age can be realized in the lives of the poor, minority, old women. While it is typical to read researcher and practitioner descriptions of the status of old, poor, minority women as one of "fourfold jeopardy," their personal reality does not reflect such definitions. Despite the powerful and oppressive forces of racism, sexism, and poverty, their private lives are examples of countless strengths that help them survive and cope, and experience quality in their lives. While many older black women articulate the impact of poverty, sexism, and racism in their lives, the majority do not describe their lives as filled with deprivation.

JEWELL

Jewell was an eighty-eight-year-old black female who lived with her ninety-year-old husband, Rush. He was blind and required a lot of Jewell's attention. They had a picture of John Kennedy in their living room and talked with fondness about the 1960s when the Civil Rights Act was passed. Eventually Rush had to be placed in a nursing home, which Jewell understood. She visited him daily. Later Jewell had to be placed in a boarding home herself as her cognitive abilities began to slip; however, she recognized this and asked the caseworker for help with the process. Although she had faced the difficulties of racial and sexual discrimination and then the difficulties of aging, Jewell did not feel badly about her life or the kinds of care and the resulting restrictions placed on her. She maintained a positive attitude, in part because she recognized all she and Rush had been through and survived in their lives.

Most old persons act to protect themselves against diverse forms of vulnerability associated with crises and loss. If these cannot be prevented, they find ways to maintain themselves in the face of altered conditions and circumstances. Among the elderly in our communities there are many who have lost some degree of physical or mental capacity necessary to perform personal care and more general self-care functions. Most are acutely aware of the personal meaning and reality of these lost capacities, but too often social workers ignore the personal meaning and interpretations of their old clients. Caseworkers readily superimpose their own definitions of the client's reality without thought that definitions of the situation might vary; that worker and client may define reality very differently.

Practitioners need a framework that not only helps them to understand the realities of the client, but forces them to respect those realities. One of the ways this transformation of practitioner thinking can take place is to encourage and expect practitioners to understand more about the major experiences in the lives of their clients. Providing them with a framework to understand their clients' experiences will, hopefully, promote less misunderstanding, avoid superimposing definitions of reality onto the clients, and help dispel stereotypes associated with sex, color, class, and disability.

"PORCH LADIES"

These two sisters moved into a house in a southern city following their brother's death. The home was strewn with trash and unlivable inside. However, the two sisters lived out on a porch, thereby gaining the nickname from social service providers of "Porch Ladies." The caseworker received much pressure from the community to file for guardianships, but consistently refused as these women were happy living as they were. In fact, they had been homeless in New York and felt quite fortunate now. However, the caseworker did manage to get the women to agree to home repairs to prevent the neighbors from taking environmental action against them. In time, the "Porch Ladies" moved inside their repaired home and wanted to open their home to other elderly homeless individuals. They did this as a matter of choice, not as an accession to others' demands.

Direct practice models taught as a foundation for working with the aged rarely address a strengths perspective in a direct presentation of its importance to worker roles. In order to determine if an alternative framework has the potential to change practitioner thinking and behavior, workers need to be trained with a strengths framework. Adaptive compensation involves at least six dimensions (there may be many more) and can help practitioners gain greater understanding of the experiences of old people who have disability or social and emotional trauma that challenges their functional ability.

As applied in adult protective services case work, each dimension of adaptive compensation must reflect the worker's awareness of the need to preserve capacity, freedom, and dignity; a central goal of all aspects of social work practice with aged clients and a central focus in the provision of emergency services such as temporary shelter or care, social supports from formal and informal sources, home supports and housing, medical and personal care, and legal and financial assistance. Steps taken in work with the client involve determining needs within the definition that is part of the aged person's adaptation and compensation as life moves and shifts.

Presented in the list below are important dimensions of the individual experience of adaptive compensation. These dimensions are used as a focus for training new social workers to prepare for their jobs as social co-counselors when employed by the Tennessee Department of Human Services (Rathbone-McCuan and Bricker-Jenkins, 1989).

Dimensions of the Adaptive Compensation Process for Self-Care

Sense of Self	Who am I and what do I need?
Sense of Will	What is my motivation to care for myself and be independent?
Awareness of Capacity	Can I perform tasks and obtain the resources to meet my needs?
Awareness of Potential	Can I learn a new skill or modify the skills I now retain?
Options in the Environment	Are there resources in my environment that can offer me help?
Acceptance of Assistance	What actions and activities will I allow others to perform for me?

Each dimension represents a factor that may be relevant to an aged person confronted with a major loss of ability and need to make some adaptive compensations. Any major loss has the potential of having an impact on self-perceptions, or the sense of self, because something about the individual and/or their environment has changed to create one or more issues of self-care process that either she cannot accomplish or must make some adaptation to accomplish.

The first dimension indicates that an aged person questions or reconsiders his/her sense of self when confronted with a loss. The person defines that loss as having some impact on personal identity. That impact on identity is the client's reality and it must remain central throughout all of the interactions between the client and worker. The worker should not guess about that reality, but rather engage in a participatory and dignified exploration of the meaning of the client's altered sense of self. Not all aged persons find that the same loss alters or decreases self-esteem. Some encounter little change in the face of dramatic physical and social changes.

The second and third dimensions refer to the client's own cognitive and emotional exploration of the loss and the ways to manage its impact and consequences. Motivation plays an important role as an aged person weighs what compensations might be necessary. Again, the worker does not superimpose her notions of what will motivate a person to compensate, but tries to understand that incentive from the client's perspective or what may foster and sustain the motivation.

The awareness of capacity dimension involves the older person's understanding and knowledge of self-care, especially daily personal maintenance tasks. Some clients are clear and accurate about what resources they need to help them complete self-care tasks. But if one believes in the old casework principle "Start where the client is," then the client's judgment of what resources are needed becomes the first step in resource exploration. It is necessary for the worker to explore the resources defined by the client as well as those that she believes to be of value. There may be differences of opinion between the worker and client about what would be helpful to the older woman. A worker can disagree with a client, but in doing so has the responsibility to state that difference in a clear and respectful manner and avoid giving a confrontational and disrespectful response. The service requests from clients may seem foolish or unrealistic, but clients have the right to make their requests known. Sometimes the worker fears there will be conflict with the older client, but some degree of conflict can be valuable if handled appropriately, and may lead to more appropriate service provision.

Awareness of potential, the fourth dimension, identifies the importance of an aged person's confidence that she can learn new skills and/or modify old behavior associated with self-care. Cognitive and physical impairments may quickly and drastically disrupt the person's ability to perform self-care functions. This situation may lead to feelings of despair and depression that can be ameliorated if assistance is made available through informal networks of relationships and/or community services. Older individuals gain much satisfaction and a sense of pride when they perfect new techniques or develop positive attitudes to promote better self-care. The responsibility is on the worker to know what formal resources are available before suggesting them and to take the time to evaluate the existence and potential accessibility of informal resources. Above all else the caseworker must avoid making assumptions about the client's potential to accomplish gains she sees as desirable or feasible. If this occurs it may actually lower the client's potential by defeating efforts to consider services before they are sought.

HELEN

Helen was an eighty-two-year-old black female referred to Protective Services because she was living with a niece who was financially exploiting her. She had one above-the-knee amputation and walked with a prosthesis and a walker. She also suffered from diabetes, which was sometimes out of control as her niece would not always buy her the right groceries. The daycare center and the doctor felt that Helen needed a boarding home facility, but Helen felt that she could live in a senior citizens apartment. The caseworker initially took her around to several boarding homes, realized that she was capable of much more as he saw her walk around in snow with her prosthesis in spite of her near blindness. The caseworker reassessed his recommendation to Helen about her living arrangement. They agreed that she would try living in a senior citizens apartment if she would agree to a boarding home situation if senior housing did not work out. She lived in her apartment for the three years with much independence until a stroke rendered her incapable of that degree of self-care.

The options in the environment dimension suggests that it is important to consider fully what resources are available in the personal network as well as from formal community resources. It is different than the fourth dimension because it considers existing resources that can be used to assist the person. Aged persons who are in crisis or suffering from depression often have difficulty believing that some assistance is available to make daily life better or safer. They may have lost hope. The caseworker must be sensitive to the individual's attitudes and feelings, must identify and mobilize the needed supports, and must engage the client in that exploration. Mobilizing naturally occurring options in the environment through the partnership of worker and client is a very important aspect of case management.

BERNICE

Bernice is a sixty-eight-year-old female who is quite obese. She also has a reputation among social service agencies of calling with many demands and angry accusations of inattention to her health. A caseworker listened to her anger and then helped her reach beyond this to her depression. After Bernice cried about her situation, which revolved around her obesity and consequent disability (she had arthritic knees, but the doctor would not operate unless she lost weight), Bernice was able to engage in a plan of dieting and assisted exercise supervised by visiting nurses with the help of a dietitian. As she began to lose weight, Bernice started to experience an elevation of her self-esteem as well as positive reinforcement from the nurses. With this extra attention to her health and the boost in her image, Bernice no longer felt the need to vent her frustration on social agency personnel.

The last dimension suggests that acceptance of assistance is a vital part of adaptive compensation. If an older person perceives that assistance will help to compensate for a loss of functional ability, getting him or her to make use of the resource may not be a major problem. However, many times convincing a client of some potential benefit is difficult because prior experiences with the formal system and/or reliance on an informal resource that has broken down sets up an expectation of no benefit.

There is yet little agreement about what system of practice is most appropriate for adult protective services. If the rationale for offering assistance to older persons includes an awareness of the strengths and potentialities that they have in their own lives, then it is paramount to develop a practice model that involves clients in problem resolution through their participation in meeting the areas of self-defined need. The system of practice must legitimize and support the application of resources in the client's own personal environmental network, elicit prompt and appropriate resources from the formal resource networks, and attend to the safeguarding of all the social, economic, emotional, and physical resources that the client has within her personal domain. In face of the many biological, social, emotional, and economic changes associated with the aging process, behavioral, intellectual, physical, experiential, and spiritual strengths must be recognized and incorporated into practice.

CONCLUSION

This chapter has reviewed current historical works that provide new direction to understanding the historical context of old age in America. It is an informative area of research because it helps us to understand the cultural progression of attitudes toward aging and treatment of the elderly. There are many limitations to the current social construction of old age as a social problem. Such a construction touches on all aspects of social work practice with older persons. Pursuit of new frameworks for understanding the experiences of older people is long overdue and must be undertaken as a fundamental task of clinical social work practice with older persons.

Issues of self-neglect in the elderly arise in almost every aspect of gerontological practice, including medical and mental health contexts. Adult protective services is only one of many service delivery systems where exploration and change in approach is needed. The model of adaptive compensation and the ways that it might be applied by social workers is still a preliminary attempt to describe an alternative framework to practice. It should, therefore, be subject to field-tested applications in different systems, and rigorous evaluation.

REFERENCES

Butler, R. N. (1975). *Why survive? Being old in America.* New York: Harper & Row.

Center for Research and Advanced Study (1982). *Improving protective services for older Americans.* Portland: University of Southern Maine.

Clark, A. N. G., Mankikar, G. D., and Gray, I. (1975). Diogenes syndrome: A clinical study of gross neglect. *Lancet, 1,* 366–368.

Cole, T. R. (1986). Putting off the old. In D. Van Tassel and P. N. Sterns, eds., *Old age in a bureaucratic society,* pp. 49–65. Westport, CT: Greenwood Press.

Dowd, J. J. (1984). Mental illness and the aged stranger. In M. Minkler and C. L. Estes, eds., *Readings in the political economy of aging,* pp. 94–113. Farmingdale: Baywood.

Ford, C. V. and Sbordone, R. J. (1980). Attitudes of psychiatrists toward elderly patients. *American Journal of Psychiatry, 137,* 571–575.

Fox, R. W. (1978). *So disordered in mind: Insanity in California 1870–1930.* Berkeley: University of California Press.

Gratton, B. (1986). The new history of the aged: A critique. In D. Van Tassel and P. N. Sterns, eds., *Old age in a bureaucratic society,* pp. 3–29. Westport, CT: Greenwood Press.

Kosberg, J. and Harris, A. (1978). Attitudes toward elderly clients. *Health and Social Work, 3,* 68–90.

Haber, C. (1986). Geriatrics: A specialty in search of specialists. In D. Van Tassel and P. N. Sterns, eds., *Old age in a bureaucratic society,* pp. 66–84. Westport, CT: Greenwood Press.

Hashimi, J. (1988). United States elders with chronic mental disorders. In E. Rathbone-McCuan and B. Havens, eds., *North America elders,* pp. 123–138. Westport, CT: Greenwood Press.

Lowry, L. (1985). *Social work with the aging.* New York: Longman.

Minkler, M. (1984). Introduction. In M. Minkler and C. L. Estes, eds., *Readings in the political economy of aging,* pp. 10–22. Farmingdale: Baywood.

Navarro, N. (1984). The political economy of government cuts for the elderly. In M. Minkler & C. L. Estes, eds., *Readings in the political economy of aging,* pp. 37–46. Farmingdale: Baywood.

Rathbone-McCuan, E. and Bricker-Jenkins, M. (1989). Self-neglect and adult protective services. In M. Bricker-Jenkins, ed., *Resource handbook assessment,* pp. 297–341. Knoxville: University of Tennessee College of Social Work, Office of Research and Public Service.

Rowles, G. D. and Reinharz, S. (1988). Qualitative gerontology: Themes and challenges. In S. Reinharz and G. D. Rowles, eds., *Qualitative gerontology,* pp. 3–33. New York: Springer.

CHAPTER 9

A Strengths Approach to Children with Emotional Disabilities

John Poertner and John Ronnau

In the quest for conceptual clarity, the impact of a problem's definition upon those whose problems are being defined is too often overlooked. Once a label such as severely emotionally disturbed has been assigned to a child or an adolescent, "there follows inexorably a chain of actions bent to institutional forms, actions that may be less related to the primary data of behavior than to the social arrangements that have been made to care for generic types of children" (Hobbs, 1982, p. 25). Those structures then tend to validate the established definitions by evoking the expected behaviors on the part of the people served. The adolescent admitted to the state hospital because his parents can no longer "put up with his behavior" soon begins to play the part of a state hospital patient. He adapts to the behavior expected of him in order to emotionally survive the experience. He begins to own the "crazy" label.

The standard mental health terminology used to describe the problems experienced by adolescents and children with emotional disabilities include psychosis, severe depression, major difficulties at school or work, and severe impairment in forming and maintaining relationships. Overlaying these symptoms are patterns of chronicity, recurrence, and stressful family situations (Lourie and Katz-Leavy, 1986; Strauss, Downey, and Sledge, 1979). The DSM-III diagnoses most commonly assigned to children and adolescents with severe emotional problems include conduct disorders (unsocialized or aggressive types), anxiety disorders, schizoid disorders, major depressive disorders, developmental disorders, and schizophrenia (Norman, 1987).

In this paper a disability model will be developed for working with children and youth with severe emotional problems. It is a less-stigmatizing approach to children and it includes an emphasis on their strengths. The idea of disability does not engender the sense of hopelessness that accompanies standard diagnoses of mental illness. The pub-

Copyright © 1992 by Longman Publishing Group.

lic has come to understand that a disability can be compensated for, if not altogether overcome. The notion of coping with a disability carries with it the understanding that the individual can, with adequate support, learn to make the most of his strengths and live successfully in the community.

In 1984, the National Institute of Mental Health established the Child and Adolescent Service System Program (CASSP) to specifically address the needs of severely disturbed children. The CASSP definition of severely emotionally disturbed children and adolescents includes five broad categories: (1) chronological age, (2) the nature of the disability, (3) a need for multi-agency response, (4) a diagnosis of mental illness, and (5) duration (Lourie and Katz-Leavy, 1986). The CASSP definition has provided a model for departments of social services in many states.

EXTENT OF THE PROBLEM

There is a lack of agreement, confusion, and probable error in the national data on the extent of the problem (Lourie and Katz-Leavy, 1986). Hobbs (1982) contends that "no one knows how many emotionally disturbed or mentally ill children there are in the United States" (p. ix). The consequence of this imprecision is that data pertaining to this population are often overlapping and confusing (Shore, 1983). Despite the imprecision, the number of children and adolescents experiencing severe emotional disturbance justifies cause for concern and attention to this population. Lourie and Katz-Leavy (1986) used an estimate of seventy thousand chronically mentally ill children and adolescents for purposes of developing a service model. Knitzer's (1982) study reported 3 million severely mentally disturbed children and adolescents in the United States. In 1984 the U.S. Department of Education figures indicated a 25 percent increase from 1977 in the number of emotionally disturbed children identified in the public school system (1986). Lourie and Katz-Leavy (1986) contend that 11.8 percent of the population under 18 is the most appropriate figure for determining the need for mental health services among children and adolescents. Applying this figure to the 1980 U.S. Census results in an estimate of 7.5 million individuals under the age of 18 in need of mental health services. The President's Commission on Mental Health estimated that 5–15 percent of the 3–15-year-old age group require mental health services (Lourie and Katz-Leavy, 1986).

Dominant Theories of Intervention

Intervention or treatment models are derived from the definition of the problem. The problem is labeled, the consequences of the problem to the individual and society are identified, and those factors said to contribute, cause, or maintain the problem are specified. Interventions then are designed to change or alter one or more contributing factors. In the case of children with severe emotional disturbances, the definitions used provide little direction or assistance in developing models of intervention. Most of the definitions contain four components: age, duration, need for multiple services, and some vague conception of mental illness or behavioral disability. Most of us who survived our youth and adolescence would quickly admit that various periods of extended duration from birth to independence are problematic. Given our relatively weak helping methods and techniques it is also not uncommon for any child who is referred for social work services to be identified as needing a range of largely unavailable services. And given the vagueness of the idea of mental illness or behavior disorder, it is all too common for a youth who doesn't quickly respond to professional treatment to receive a stigmatizing label such as unsocialized conduct disorder.

It may be that the only reliable characteristic of these youth is that they have failed in all of the service systems. These children have failed in the education system, frequently not in the sense of poor grades but by being unable to take advantage of education as it is delivered in our communities. In an earlier time they may have just disappeared. Under the constraints of the Education of All Handicapped Children Act (P.L. 94-142) they are labeled behavior disordered.

Those children have also failed in the child welfare system. While they may initially enter this system as victims of abuse or neglect, their "failure to adjust" to foster families or group homes puts them in jeopardy of being placed in the most restrictive institutional setting. Rejection by the child welfare system because they do not fit the normative requirements of that system makes it likely that they will be labeled "a mental health problem."

As a last resort these children often find themselves in either a juvenile correction setting or a mental hospital. These facilities can, if nothing else, provide care, custody, and control. It is our position that these youth have not failed society as much as society has failed them. This failure stems largely from the models of intervention we use to work with them. There are three dominant treatment models presently used with this population. One identifies the youth as mentally ill, the second views the youth's problem as behavior disordered, and the third defines the family as dysfunctional.

The Mentally Ill Child.   Children who exhibit abnormal behavior are likely to be identified as mentally ill. The delivery of mental health services to children is, in fact, a growth industry. Marks (1987), in her study of a local school district and community hospital, found an alarming number of children who left school, spent time in the psychiatric ward of the local private hospital, and disappeared from the community. Petr and Spano (1990) have identified the phenomenon of "transinstitutionalization" of children. While the number of children in homes for dependent and neglected children decreased from over 96,000 in 1950 to 47,600 in 1970, the number of children in mental hospitals and residential treatment more than tripled from 11,000 to 35,000. That is to say, many of these children probably moved from one kind of institution to another.

The mental illness model has no more positive outcomes to offer many of these youth than does the behavior disorder model. The youth released from the psychiatric ward of the local hospital, or released from the state mental hospital, is expected to readjust smoothly to life with family, friends, and teachers. However, even most adults do not have the skills to manage the stigma associated with returning from these institutions (Goffman, 1959). Yet we expect children to function normally upon release from a mental hospital without adequate preparation. Because the label of mental illness is a master status, the youth who carries it will have many behaviors pejoratively defined. A playful preadolescent punch on the arm becomes a sign of aggressive behavior associated with mental illness. The snapping of a bra strap by a male adolescent becomes sexual deviance associated with mental illness. Furthermore, some children are quick to rise to the occasion and fulfill the expectations implicit in this vague but powerful label.

Some caregivers find relief in finally having their child labeled mentally ill: "We now know what it is." Unfortunately, for many, expectations of a cure accompany the label. These hopes are often short-lived as it becomes clear that for some serious mental disorders, cures are out of the question. Children and parents now confront a bleak future on several counts. Not the least of these is the idea inherent in most conceptions of mental illness, that the cause of the illness lies either within the family or within the stricken individual.

The Behavior Disordered Child.   Aberrant, non-normative behavior brings these children to the attention of social workers and other community professionals. It is easy to see the appeal and derivation of this label. Children who constantly fight with peers, attack adults with weapons, run away from home, and set fires are exhibiting behaviors that the community wants stopped. The first line of response in this model is personal control. How many of us as youth heard our parents or teachers say "Stop that!" or "Straighten up!"? How many of us as parents have said these words to our children? We expect youth to be in control of their own behavior. But if the behavior continues and is defined by the larger community as deviant or threatening, then other members of the official community move in and attempt to control it.

We have developed elaborate behavior modification programs to control "deviant" behavior of youth. While certain types of behavior modification programs may be very useful and certain practice principles derived from the theory of behavior modification are effective, the way in which behavior modification programs are applied frequently becomes part of the problem. For example, behavior modification programs for youth frequently assume that children lack certain knowledge and skills. Take basic communication skills as an example. Programs designed to improve such skills often assume that rewards provided contingent to normal behavior and applied consistently over a period of time will develop the necessary complex of behaviors that generalizes across situations and environments. These assumptions do hold for some children. However, neither one holds for Mary, when she hears voices saying that she must set her bedroom on fire; or for Joe, who has communication skills but cannot talk about being raped by his brother at age ten; or for Jerry, who cannot talk about what contributed to his suicide attempt or the consequences of the attempt.

Children who find themselves in behavioral programs frequently have control of their behavior most of the time. Many of these children do have the required communication skills. Their difficulty arises when needing to control a specific behavior at a specific time, or when needing to use their communication skills regarding specific difficulties with particular individuals. Programs aimed at increasing behaviors or controlling behaviors must recognize that (1) the problems of these youth are usually situation-specific, not general; and (2) programs based on punitive or negative reinforcement techniques can, if inappropriately applied, increase problematic behaviors.

The Dysfunctional Family.   American society regards children as the property of their parents. Consequently, parents are assumed to be responsible for the care, custody, and control of their children. In playing out this dominant ideology, it is not at all unreasonable to credit parents for youth who excel and blame parents for youth who experience problems. If a child is "acting out," parents did not provide the supervision and structure to instill self-control. If the child is exhibiting bizarre behavior, it is most certainly because of some imbalance in the family system. If a parent should observe that Uncle Joe also had a difficult adolescence, it is most certainly because of some intergenerational malfunction in the family. Family system theories are popular and usually useful and attempt to conceptualize families as the complex entities they are. Yet with such complexity the professional looking for the element of the system which is out of balance will most certainly find one or more. It would be an extraordinary family that would have all subsystems functioning ideally at any point in time.

In addition to being yet another example of blaming the victim (Ryan, 1971), the dysfunctional model is simply not very helpful. The idea that the child as "identified patient" is the carrier and symbol of family disorganization and chaos is currently popular and does have appeal for practitioners. But the family may have become "disorganized" in attempting to cope with, understand, and "normalize" the difficult behavior of a child struggling with a disability. And the family may have done so without the support and understanding of community service providers. Requiring Mr. and Mrs. Jones to map their family tree in the presence of their adopted daughter who is exhibiting bizarre behavior is not useful. Probing the family system for a dysfunction does not help Mrs. Vincent respond to her daughter's auditory hallucinations. Clearly what is needed are other models to help youth and families who continue to have problems in spite of our best professional efforts.

THE CHILD WITH AN EMOTIONAL DISABILITY

This paper has proposed that children now thought of as being severely emotionally disturbed be approached from a particular kind of strengths perspective—the disability model. This model incorporates the following principles:

1. The emotional disability is only one of the youth's characteristics. The individual and the disability are not one and the same.
2. Youth with disabilities also have abilities (strengths).
3. Youth with disabilities can learn and grow.
4. Youth with disabilities are the primary informants on how they experience the disabilities.
5. A youth with a disability should be part of society, not out of the mainstream.
6. Society should make reasonable accommodations for youth with disabilities.
7. Families are the primary caregivers.

Principle 1

The emotional disability is only one of the youth's characteristics. The individual and the disability are not one and the same. The person who is confined to a wheelchair is not generically disabled, but is mobility impaired. The person who cannot hear talking is not disabled but has a hearing impairment. The youth who has periodic episodes of auditory hallucinations is similar. Except for the most severely disturbed youth, the problem behavior accounts for only a small portion of their lives. The rest of the time they are behaving like other children. The point is not that the problems these kids exhibit should be minimized or overlooked—they can cause serious disruptions in their own and others' lives. The point is that the problem becomes the sole basis for the youth's identity. Jeanne and Jeff are not "crazy kids," they may be kids with an emotional disability—a specific and contained emotional impairment, at that.

Principle 2

Youth with disabilities also have abilities (strengths). The same misguided labeling process that dumps kids into the "crazy" category, thus distorting their identities as whole persons, also obscures their talents and strengths. The prejudice operating here is that a "crazy person can't possibly be good at anything." The truth is that youngsters with emotional disabilities can play ball, sing, write, imagine, repair cars, and make friends just like other kids. They may need some special help and support to realize their strengths, but they do have strengths. A case in point is Frank, who one day happened to show his case manager some of his rather well done drawings. The case manager's positive comments were clearly a boon to the youngster's pride. However, the institution in which Frank was living would not allow him to practice his talent because the activity did not fit its elaborate reward system. Mary is another fine example. After the case manager took the time to build a positive working relationship with her, Mary was able to play an active role in charting her plans for independent living. Conversations about what was important to her and how she could reach her goals helped her decide to obtain her GED so she could pursue a beautician's training course. Mary later achieved her goals despite a diagnosis that indicated she was unlikely to reach them.

Principle 3

Youth with disabilities can learn and grow. Individuals with physical disabilities continually fight against the prejudice that a handicap in one aspect of their life renders them incapable in all others. On the contrary, a hearing loss does not preclude an acting career, nor does severe nerve damage to a hand block a successful political career. However, a prejudice operates against youth with emotional disabilities. Once the label is applied, others assume that such a child cannot succeed at school, sports, work, anything. Often this prejudice becomes fact because appropriate educational plans, which could help to ensure the youth's academic success, are lacking. After nine months in the hospital due to a conduct disorder, Randy was placed on trial visit and mainstreamed part-time in public school. He was both excited and anxious about returning to his old school. Unfortunately, while the news about Randy's hospital stay preceded his return, no coordination occurred between the school and the mental health services provided with Randy. Not surprisingly, Randy's new teacher was apprehensive about having the "crazy kid" in class. The school personnel, without sufficient information and staff, were unprepared to help Randy cope with the prejudice, discrimination, and fears of other kids. His parents were similarly unprepared for Randy's return to school. No plan was developed between the parents, the school, and the therapists to monitor and support Randy's academic and social progress or even his attendance. Without the guidance and support he needed, it was not long before Randy began meeting the expectations set for him. He failed both in exhibiting "appropriate" behavior and at his schoolwork. Randy's failure reinforced the idea that he could not "make it." In reality, he simply was not given a fair chance. An adolescent with an emotional disability can learn, grow, and change. But he or she may need consistent long-term support to continue the path to maturity and skill development.

Principle 4

Youth with disabilities are the primary informants on how they experience the disabilities. Even well-meaning service providers are too quick to impose their own views of the world upon their clients. The professional's investment in, and emotional attachment to, their own theory of helping leads them to believe they know what's best. This tendency to exclude the client from all but the most basic steps in the helping process is even more characteristic of those who work with adolescents and children. Professionals are reluctant to ask clients to define problems in their own words. Jack, who gets around town in a wheelchair, gets angry when someone says, "Here, let me help you get across the street." He resents the loss of control and the assumption of total dependence. Likewise, youth who are told what they are experiencing and what they need are not attaining autonomy and independence. In addition, the variance among youth with emotional disabilities is so great that the professional who purports to speak for the child is likely to be wrong much of the time.

Youth with emotional disabilities are the most knowledgeable people about what they experience and how it might be understood. Understanding from their viewpoint the anger, fear, confusion, disappointment, and uncertainty these children may experience is an important first step in helping them. The prescription for understanding this is simple: ask the children. Sam was continually getting into fights at school and complained of loneliness. Through much effort, the case manager helped Sam enroll in a community recreation program so that he might have some positive group experiences. Despite Sam's verbal commitment to the contrary, he failed to attend the first session of the program. The case manager's gentle and sincere questions led Sam to disclose that he was sexually abused as a child and had pervasive social embarrassment and anxiety because of that. With additional support and direct guidance he attended the recreation program and stopped fighting at school. Mary, who periodically experiences auditory hallucinations, can talk about these events as she experiences them and the protection she needs when they occur. Not all youth have Mary's current ability. However, youth with emotional disabilities can learn what Mary has learned. They simply require assistance and encouragement in their learning, and in expressing what they know and what they need to know.

Principle 5

A youth with a disability should be part of society, not out of the mainstream. The ultimate goal of most treatment programs and the professionals who work in them is for the youth with an emotional disability to become a content, secure, productive member of society. While few would argue with the goal, the effect of much of the treatment provided to adolescents and children with emotional disabilities is to cut them off from peers and normal community living. Long-term hospital stays, no matter how competent the treatment, place barriers between youths and their families and community. The best way to learn the skills of independent living is to practice them. The best way to learn to cope in the real world is to live in it.

Fred had been in a hospital since age six. The professionals working with Fred recognized that, at age twelve, he was no longer benefiting from his stay; in fact Fred was becoming "institutionalized." The prognosis for his return to the community seemed bleak. Prior to his return home, the case manager met with Fred's mother, teachers in the school Fred would be attending, and the staff in the community mental health center where he would attend counseling sessions. These meetings clarified the expectations for Fred's behavior for all parties and established support and monitoring systems. The case manager also took Fred to visit the school before his release from the hospital to lessen the shock of returning to the community. Currently this "hopeless" case is doing very well at home in his own community.

Some youths with severe emotional disabilities need occasional hospitalization to help them through an emotional crisis. But these stays should be as infrequent and as short as possible. At least as much effort and money must be put into keeping emotionally disabled youth in a normal environment as is spent on institutional treatment. Family and community are the only places for a young person to learn to be a productive member of society.

Principle 6

Society should make reasonable accommodations for youth with disabilities. Entrance ramps that allow access to buildings for wheelchairs are now commonplace in America. It is now clearly understood in our society that a physical disability does not justify an individual's exclusion from services and cultural events. At times, providing accessibility means making special accommodations, such as entrance ramps. Adolescents or children with emotional disabilities also may need their community to make responsible accommodations to provide access to its services and resources. Education, for example, is an indispensable aspect of a child's development. The socialization and knowledge that school affords are essential if the child is to have any semblance of normal development. Recreation facilities, sports, arts, and entertainment opportunities are necessities all youth have the right to expect. It is the responsibility of society to make reasonable accommodations to allow youth with emotional disabilities to have and to share those experiences and resources. Schools must provide special classes with trained personnel when necessary. Recreational programs should allow for and encourage the participation of these youth with special needs. Youth with emotional disabilities can only learn to behave normally by experiencing normal activities with others. Sarah expressed an interest in learning to play golf, but there was no organized program in her community to meet her special needs. The case manager, working through the special education department of a local university, located a college student willing to give Sarah golf lessons. She greatly benefited from the positive adult interest shown her and enjoyed her new-found recreational opportunity. The next step is to demonstrate to the community of interest that Sarah can function like others. Those people may also need to learn about Sarah's particular disability, how this may occasionally require a unique response to youth like Sarah, and what that response is.

Principle 7

Families are the primary caregivers. Family members play a critical role in caring for individuals with severe emotional problems no matter what their age. Most children are cared for throughout their youth by their families. In most cases where substitute care is provided it is often time-limited and does not constitute a large proportion of the child's youth. The role of family caregivers in the habilitation of adolescents and children with emotional disabilities is indispensable. From many aspects—legal, emotional, developmental—youth are dependent upon their families. These family caregivers must be given the respect and attention commensurate with their roles. Professionals must begin treating them as emotionally disabled youth's primary treatment providers and they should be consistently and integrally involved in youths' treatment from the outset as they are able. Information regarding the needs and strengths of their children must be provided to them on an ongoing basis. Professional help is doomed to failure without the family's involvement, cooperation, and understanding.

CASE STUDY: EXEMPLAR OF PRINCIPLES

We begin our work with youth by developing a relationship as naturally and informally as possible. We establish relationships in ways typical of youth; often, doing things together. Adolescents often are more comfortable in establishing contact through activity as opposed to just talking. Jerry was an adolescent who brought with him a catalogue of diagnoses all suggesting, in the eyes of the "official" mental health system, a very disturbed, occasionally psychotic young man. (In keeping with our policy of case management with youth like Jerry, we rarely refer to diagnoses, never use them in our assessment, and never build case plans around them except to the extent that medication may be a part of the youth's regimen. We only use them to help caregivers, usually parents, to understand some of the elements of a given disorder, and to help them see that the disorder does not encompass the whole of their child's behavior.)

The work with Jerry began with going to the mall and walking around, driving around, or going to the park when he was agitated and upset (the park was where he felt most comfortable). As these activities progressed the case manager would talk with Jerry about how things were going for him in areas of his life such as friendships and making new friends, meeting basic needs, spending leisure time, and school. Where things seemed to be going well, the case manager made sure to find out why Jerry thought things were going well and helped Jerry define his attitudes and behaviors in that area as strengths that he might use elsewhere.

In school, however, things were not going well. The case manager asked what would make things better. Jerry said that when he was transferred to the special school for the behaviorally disordered, he lost all his friends. Now he felt like an outsider, and he was getting into trouble all the time because he hated being there. He wanted to go back to his neighborhood school and be with his friends. The case manager took this as a legitimate request, and acted as if it was possible to fulfill. After assuring that this was something Jerry would like to work on, the case manager and Jerry stopped for soft drinks at a fast food restaurant. They sat in a booth and began to list all the steps that Jerry would have to take to return to his neighborhood school. As Jerry developed the list, the case manager encouraged Jerry to think of as many steps as possible, and clarified ideas and supplied information as needed. For each action listed, they agreed who would do it, and identified a date when it would be done. The case manager made certain that she was not doing all the work and not pre-empting Jerry's own desires and ideas. She also assured herself and Jerry that the tasks were, in fact, doable. The tasks were defined in such a way that they also could serve as opportunities for Jerry to learn daily living skills.

One of the tasks involved asking Jerry's mother to request a copy of his individual educational plan from the school. Jerry was apprehensive about this. There is a certain amount of technical material in such a report, so the case manager agreed to help Jerry and his mother interpret the plan. First, however, the case manager role-played with Jerry so that he would feel more comfortable asking his mother to go to the school and get the report. Another task Jerry wanted to accomplish later was to let people at his neighborhood school know what opportunities, supports, and expectations he needed to be successful. Jerry found it difficult to be specific about this, but he and the case manager worked diligently to manufacture a list. When the time came to present this list to the classroom teacher, the case manager accompanied Jerry and helped him with his presentation, so that he could experience, with support, how a delicate situation with someone in authority could be handled.

As Jerry and the case manager worked through the plan, they both learned. The case manager took every opportunity to remind Jerry of those times when he was exhibiting particular capacities, skills, and resources, a most important kind of learning in the strengths approach. When part of their plan did not work out, they tried to figure out together what happened and revised their plans. They also talked about disappointments, and what can be learned from them that might be useful in the future. The original plan was revised several times, but with each revision the case manager illustrated graphically (on a chart she had developed) how much Jerry had accomplished.

It was difficult, there were fits and starts, but Jerry did return to school and, to this point, has adjusted admirably. The case manager subsequently asked Jerry if he wanted to work on anything else. When Jerry indicated that he probably did not, they reminisced about, and reaffirmed, his recent accomplishments and developed a plan to keep in touch.

Again, while much of what happened here is simply good social work practice, there are some things to keep in mind. None of what happened was based on Jerry's disability (except in the most indirect or contingent way). What Jerry actually accomplished was significant but the more important result was what Jerry learned about his own capacities and skills and how they could be used in a variety of life situations. While the case manager acted as an advocate for Jerry (in getting back to the school, for example), Jerry set his own agenda for work and the case manager was primarily a collaborator with him in realizing these aspirations.

CONCLUSION

The traditional intervention models used with youth who experience severe emotional problems were reviewed in this chapter. Some of the negative consequences of viewing the child as mentally ill, behaviorally disordered, or the product of dysfunctional families were presented. A strengths approach, based upon a disability model, was the alternative proposed. Seven principles of that approach were introduced. We believe using a strengths approach with youth experiencing emotional problems will increase their likelihood of growing up in their own homes and communities, instead of in institutions, and of becoming responsible and productive members of the community, rather than dispirited lifelong users of mental health services.

REFERENCES

Goffman, E. (1959). *The presentation of self in everyday life*. Garden City, NY: Doubleday Anchor.

Hobbs, N. (1982). *The troubled and troubling child*. San Francisco: Jossey-Bass.

Knitzer, J. (1982). *Unclaimed children*. Washington, DC: Children's Defense Fund.

Lourie, I. S. and Katz-Leavy, J. (1986). *Severely emotionally disturbed children and adolescents (report)*. Washington, DC: National Institute of Mental Health.

Marks, J. (1987). Services for children returning to school after brief psychiatric hospitalization. *Social Work in Education, 9*(3), 169–179.

Norman, L., ed. (1987). *Taking charge: A handbook for parents whose children have emotional handicaps*. Portland, OR: Portland State University.

Petr, C. and Spano, R. (1990). Services for emotionally disturbed children: Historical perspectives and contemporary opportunities for social work. *Social Work, 35*, 228–234.

U.S. Department of Education. (1986). Program update—case management. *Update, 2*(2), 10–12.

Ryan, W. (1971). *Blaming the victim*. New York: Vintage Books.

Shore, J. H. (1983). The epidemiology of chronic mental illness. In D. Cutler, ed., *Effective aftercare for the 1980s*, pp. 5–12. San Francisco: Jossey-Bass.

Strauss, J. S., Downey, T. W., and Sledge, W. H. (1979). Intensive psychiatric care for adolescents and young adults. *Hospital and Community Psychiatry, 30*(2), 122–125.

CHAPTER **10**

Building a Strengths Model of Practice in the Public Social Services

Mary Bricker-Jenkins

In January 1964, fresh out of college with a BA in English, I began my social work career as a social investigator with the New York Department of Welfare. At that time we were implementing the 1962 Defined Service Amendments to the Social Security Act. The plan was to "casework" everybody out of poverty—or at least those who were "willing to help themselves." We were to emphasize the social rather than the investigative part of our roles.

Having just completed my mandatory training week, I made an appointment with Matilda Jones for her quarterly recertification visit. Matilda had four children. Two were literally lost in the foster care system. Following agency advice, Matilda had voluntarily placed them during a time of family crisis. Also at our urging, she had not visited them for a long time; the practice wisdom at that time suggested that Matilda should not visit in order to give everyone "time to adjust." Now we were unable to locate the children in the labyrinthine maze of contract agencies to whom we had entrusted their care. Matilda's third child had already been labeled "high risk" at his school—a school he attended when Matilda was able to get him there, which was not very often. Matilda had just brought her newborn home from the hospital; he had several congenital conditions that reflected his heritage of poor prenatal care and marginal obstetrical services.

These were the days before programmatic separation of income maintenance and services, so I went prepared by my training to recertify the family's eligibility for AFDC as well as to proffer social services. I could see Matilda in the window of her tenement as I turned off Broadway and walked cautiously through the rubble of the West Side Urban Renewal District. From her observation post at the front end of her

Copyright © 1992 by Longman Publishing Group.

railroad apartment she signaled to the men hanging out on the street below to give me safe passage. It was 10:00 AM and she was having her breakfast: a piece of toast and a can of beer.

Matilda had learned the system when I was still in grade school. She was ready for me. She had her rent receipt, her electric bill, her clothing inventory, her list of clothing and furniture needs for the baby, and the baby's health department card. She was prepared to discuss the baby's paternity. I made the requisite notes in my little caseworker's book, then closed it and invoked my training. I said, "Mrs. Jones, you know all of this paperwork is very important, but there are other important things we could do together. I really want to work with you on problems and issues and concerns that are important to you. Now I'm going to leave my book closed and I'd really like to talk with you, just talk about stuff together, and things we could do together that'll result in better things happening in your life.

Matilda studied me for a very long moment before she leaned into the space between us and said, "Look, white girl, I wanna tell you something. I got to document my life to you—because I'm poor. I got to show you all my papers, prove I paid my bills, take my baby to your pig doctor, and show you this card that says I take care of my baby—all because I'm poor. I even have to talk about my sex life with you—because I'm poor. I gotta do all that—but I don't have to take none of your social workin'.

"Now I'm gonna tell you three things about your social workin'," she continued. "Number one, it ain't got nothing to do with my life. Number two, I can't eat it. And number three, it don't dull the pain like my Pabst Blue Ribbon. Now you get along, white girl—and you think about that."

I have thought about that for over twenty-five years. For the past four years, I have been able to do something about it. I have been directing the development and implementation of Tennessee's Social Counselor Certification Training Program, a joint effort of the University of Tennessee-Knoxville College of Social Work and the Tennessee Department of Human Services (TDHS). Based on that experience, we designed and have begun a public social services research and development project. This paper traces these efforts to build a strengths-oriented practice in the public social services, identifies some of the conceptual barriers we have encountered, and describes the methods we are using to circumvent those barriers.

A COMPETENCY-BASED APPROACH

The TDHS Certification Program provides ten weeks of mandatory, structured, developmental, competency-based training to all newly hired social counselors in the state. In Tennessee, social counselors are the frontline staff in the public agency and are responsible for service delivery in Adult Protective Services, Child Protective Services, Foster Care, and Adoptions. Job prerequisites include a bachelor's degree, a civil service examination, and an interview with a field-based social services supervisor. About 20 percent of the social counselors hold BSW degrees. Completion of the Certification Program—a combination of centralized residential training and structured on-the-job training—is followed by a rigorous certification examination. A passing grade on this examination and a satisfactory performance evaluation by the supervisor are required for retention as a social counselor.

Similar competency-based worker preparation and certification programs are being established in many state systems as administrators work to improve service effectiveness and meet legal and judicial standards of worker competence. Indeed, several national organizations—including the National Association of Social Workers, the American Public Welfare Association, and the Child Welfare League of America—are advocating the development of a national competency-based training and accreditation program for child protective services workers (National Child Welfare Center, 1988). In so doing, they are extending a strategy that has been pursued vigorously in social work education for over a decade (see, for example, Clark and Arkava, 1979; Gambrill, 1983).

While the competency-based approach provides a rigorous and systematic means of developing curricula and preparing practitioners, we encountered several of its shortcomings in our program development efforts. Some of these present challenges to the development of a strengths perspective. Before describing them, we must first consider the nature of the approach.

What Is Competency-Based Training?

In theory, every position in every workforce can be analyzed for its *function*—what it contributes to the achievement of organizational goals—and its *tasks*—what incumbents must do to perform the desired function. A comprehensive task–function analysis, performed against the backdrop of an organization's mission and goals, is the first requirement for a competency-based staff development effort. The next step is to specify the knowledge, skills, and "expressed" values and attitudes necessary for adequate job performance. These are then analyzed and grouped into discrete, observable "competencies." Ideally, the competencies focus and direct the development of staff development and training programs—and increasingly of supervision, monitoring, and evaluation systems as well (Clark and Arkava, 1979; Teare, 1979, 1981).

Critical to this analytical and developmental process is, of course, the infusion of knowledge and assumptions about the relationship among tasks, functions, and desired outcomes (such as protecting children, achieving permanency in the least restrictive environment, achieving reunification, and the like). The cluster of tasks, functions, and desired outcomes are core elements in a model of practice. Every organization has a preferred model of practice that influences the set of competencies it requires.

There are many models of practice in the field of human services, each with its own knowledge base, assumptions, and prescribed methods. An organization's preferred model may have emerged through conscious choice, through the predispositions and educational backgrounds of its key decision-makers, and through other more serendipitous factors. It may or may not be informed by and consistent with one or more of the models defined in the literature. It is usually eclectic and implicit. But it's there, reflected in what the workers are asked to do, how they are to do it, and—to come full circle—in the training programs designed to ensure that they have the core of competencies needed to implement the model.

Some Limitations of the Competency-Based Approach

The competency-based approach has two inherent limitations. The first involves the technological dimension of practice—what we do (models and methods) and why we do it (practice theory). The second is in the ideological dimension—the overarching purposes, beliefs, and values inherent in any practice system. These dimensions are interrelated, but certain issues are unique to each.

Technological Issues I: On Models, Methods, and Practice Systems.   Competency-based training is grounded primarily on task–function analyses of "what is." It presupposes that we know what we need to do. But do we know that our practice models and methods really work in the lives of Matilda Jones and her sisters?

Most practice models and methods used in public social services programs, practice, and training have been developed in other settings for radically different types of clients. Models developed for populations seeking voluntary services from highly trained social workers with professional credentials do not directly apply to the world of the public agency. To ensure effective public practice, the model must be suitable for work with involuntary clients by largely noncredentialed staff of a bureaucracy perceived as primarily performing a social control function. Obviously, the utility and appropriateness of imported and adapted models and methods must be closely examined with these differences in mind.

We have considerable anecdotal evidence and some research suggesting that much of what works for Matilda Jones and her sisters is not integrated into our practice at all. We know of the power of mutual aid and self-help groups, for example, but few of us teach our workers to find or develop such groups or to work with them effectively (Powell, 1986). We also do not teach them how to create and use such groups within the organization as part of an integrated, coherent practice system. Working for, with, and through mutual aid groups—either those that occur naturally or form around a particular need or interest—is not a part of most competency-based training or education because the needed competencies are not going to surface in a task-function analysis of "what is."

Even when methods and techniques are developed in or successfully adapted for the public social services, we often fail to integrate them into a coherent, internally consistent practice approach. Risk assessment procedures, for example, have become increasingly refined and predictive. To some degree, however, that predictive power is achieved by focusing the assessment narrowly on individual and family dysfunction. After analyzing and thoroughly documenting dysfunction, workers are then expected to refocus and ally themselves with family strengths to achieve case work goals.

Moreover, we use an array of methods and techniques from existing models that are not integrated into an overall practice system. One program in an agency may use a behaviorist approach while another has a psychosocial focus. For work with one family we may contract with an agency that provides home-based services and then supplement that with long-term family therapy provided by an agency whose practice philosophy prohibits home visits. In short, what the family gets is what the worker's got. That, in turn, depends on such things as the practice orientation of the latest demonstration program, the techniques taught at the most recent training road show, or the (usually unarticulated) practice philosophy of the contract agency. What families really need is a coherent, internally consistent, integrated practice system that is infused throughout the service delivery structure.

A well-integrated practice system will also encompass organizational elements. The structure and processes of an organization either support and sustain practice or confound it. What happens at the office invariably affects the client as well as the worker. I agree with the proponents of the functional school of social work who argue that the social service organization itself is an integral part of any practice orientation and system (Smalley, 1965). Unlike the functionalists, however, I believe that an organization must adapt structure and process to the life spaces of clients and workers, not the other way around. Our failure to incorporate the organizational dimension with our practice system profoundly limits our ability to implement even the most appropriate and effective direct practice approaches. Often we are thwarted because the inherent values and assumptions of a given direct practice model are not sustained and supported by the organization's culture, structure, and processes.

Several years ago, for example, we attempted to introduce the task-centered practice model into our public social services system statewide. We trained both workers and supervisors, demonstrating how the methods could be integrated into existing policy and procedures. Training evaluations indicated that both the model and the training were perceived as highly effective. However, the model was soon abandoned in practice. Evaluating this failed attempt, we learned that few supervisors felt comfortable allowing the client to set so much of the agenda—a critical component of the model. They could not reconcile this service imperative with their perceived management directive to control workloads and avoid publicity-generating risk-taking. Moreover, workers who liked the model told us that they wished their supervisors would work with them the way they were expected to work with clients. Their attempts to use the model increased discomfort with their supervision, exacerbating tensions between line staff and supervision. This lack of consonance between the direct practice model and supervision and management models generated conflict and confused workers, and confounded their best practice efforts.

While an integrated practice system must be diverse enough methodologically to respond to the needs and strengths of many kinds of clients and workers, it must have a clearly defined and articulated philosophical core—its operating beliefs and assumptions about human nature, needs, collective responsibilities, and change. Both philosophy and method must be ever open to scrutiny and revision, but uncertainty and change need not be barriers to developing and implementing a system. If, in the interest of an illusory eclecticism and flexibility, we fail to define and align method and philosophy, both staff and clients suffer. To explicate a philosophical core and examine its consonance with an organization's structures and methods are political as well as intellectual undertakings. But what is not clearly articulated cannot be evaluated and changed.

To summarize: We derive competency-based programs from "what is" with scant evidence of what works with our families in our settings. Much, if not most, practice effectiveness research has been done with different kinds of clients in different settings. We tend to exclude from our practice some very powerful methods and techniques that derive from naturally occurring, health-seeking processes in our environments. The direct practice methods and techniques we do employ are loosely organized into a pseu-do-system of practice containing elements that are inconsistent with each other and incongruent with the management and supervision practices intended to sustain and reinforce them. Lastly, the philosophical core to which these practices are inextricably linked is usually unarticulated and therefore unexamined and inconsistent with over-arching beliefs and assumptions.

Before we consider the ideological dimension, there is another technological dimension to be addressed: Much case work failure results not from poor practice but from poor theory. Thus, no amount of training and education, no program redesign, no improvements in management and supervision, and no increases in the numbers of trained workers will be adequate. These are all necessary to build a solid technological base for public welfare practice, but they are insufficient. We need, in addition, new theory about things we have not yet theorized about.

Technological Issues II: On Building Practice Theory.   Our processes of theory-building have often excluded some very important characteristics of our clients and their lives. The excluded characteristics—particularly strengths and environmental as-sets—may be the key to effective helping and healing. Excluding them from the con-ceptual framework of practice theory may be the critical factor in case work failure.

An example illustrates the problem. When I began work on the dynamics of child neglect unit of the Tennessee Certification curriculum, I examined existing training materials and social work course syllabi. Considerable work has been done in this area in the last several years, so it seemed more reasonable and efficient to evaluate existing knowledge and materials than to start from scratch. Yet everywhere I looked I found the shadow of the work of only one man cast upon the literature: Norman Polansky.

Polansky, a capable scholar who cares deeply about practice, published in 1972 his landmark study of the dynamics of child neglect among Appalachian families, *Roots of Futility*. With his associates, he replicated and cross-validated that study in Philadel-phia, reporting the results in *Damaged Parents: An Anatomy of Child Neglect* in 1981. These two works have become so embedded in child welfare curricula that a search through citations led as inexorably to them as rivers to the sea. Indeed, many authors don't even bother with citations; Polansky's profile of the neglectful parent (read mother) has become the unquestioned intellectual currency, the primary medium of exchange among students of the phenomenon.

This does a disservice to Polansky and his associates, who begin their work by citing three approaches to understanding neglect: the economic, the ecological, and the personalistic. They narrow their primary focus to one of these, but caution that "al-though our own work adopts the personalistic approach, we do not believe a family's poverty or its social environment may be discounted" (Polansky et al., 1981).

However, Polansky and associates exacerbate the problem by failing to provide this essential caveat in their conclusion. The message that permeates the current child neglect literature appears in their second work (1981) as follows:

The major findings of the Appalachian study were substantially supported in the Phil-adelphia replication. The mother's maturity or degree of infantilism was again underscored, as was its expression in the forms of apathy-futility or impulsivity. The assumption that, among white low-income families, the mother's personality plays the major role in how well the children are protected proved justified (p. 117).

This important but incomplete piece of information is the centerpiece of virtually all current training and practice models on child neglect. The problem, of course, is that practice based solely on personalistic theory inevitably will be personalistic, focused on changing the individual.

Moreover, when we look at neglect (or any phenomenon) through a lens ground in psychopathological theory, we are surely going to find pathology. Polansky's instruments and conceptual framework constitute a convex pathological lens—one that narrows the focus to the person and filters out most of her nonpathological characteristics. When we view the world of child neglect through this lens, the practice implications are obvious: to save the children, treat the sick mom.

Fortunately, no lens can completely filter out all of the rest of the phenomenological world. In a brief discussion of other findings, Polansky describes as "unexpected strengths" the characteristics of the members of his control group (1981): "A close look at the life histories of our non-neglectful parents reveals us, once again, as a generation short on miracles but not lacking altogether in happy accidents" (p. 158).

What Polansky was seeing may not have been a happy accident at all but the sign of people's innate compelling potential for growth and health converging with opportunities and support for the unfolding of that potential. That is what we must study. If we are to develop practice models that engage the inherent strengths of individuals and families, practice that joins those strengths with opportunities and support for people to satisfy their needs for safety, growth, and health, then our practice theory must be derived from a study and appreciation of those phenomena. We need, for example, to study the members of Polansky's control group. They will give us the material for a theory of strength and growth, and they will tell us how to engage and support the naturally occurring environmental assets on which they rely.

In conclusion, if we are to develop theory for competent and sensitive practice, we must first replace our convex pathological lens—which narrows the focus to problems and risks—with a concave health-oriented lens. This will enable us to focus on strengths and the broad spectrum of environmental opportunities and resources. We might then be able to do strength assessments as rigorously as we do risk assessments. This kind of assessment will inform and direct a practice that engages strengths and operationalizes the concept of empowerment by guiding us in its fundamental process—the creation of choices.

Second, we need to rethink not only what we study, but how we study it. Our world is not static, mechanistic, and linear; rather, it is dynamic, adaptive, evolving, and multidimensional. In the process of studying that world, we change it. Rather than be limited by this, we can use research and theory-building models that capitalize on, rather than control for, this fact. If, as Buckminster Fuller once said, "Truth is a verb," our research must speak in the active rather than the passive voice. There are epistemologies—and their attendant research methods—that enable us to do so (see, for example, Gouldner, 1970; Heineman, 1981; Palmer, 1974, 1987; Weick, 1987). Research, as Julian Rappoport has written (1990), can and must be empowering.

Finally, like life itself, practice theory must be open and organic, tentative and evolving. It must evolve from and support a view of the world that incorporates the enormous adaptive, creative, dynamic, and multidimensional potential of people like Matilda Jones and her workers. That kind of theory will underpin a practice that has those same qualities, a practice that engages clients and workers in a collaborative search for and creation of another set of truths.

To summarize the technological problems in competency-based programs: They derive primarily from an analysis of what we do (models and methods). While it may be possible to rethink and redesign what we do, the effort will (or should) lead us to the brink of enormous chasms on the topography of practice theory. To redesign our practice systems, we need to ask the right questions of the right people in the right way. When we do, we are dealing not only with technological issues, but also with the (usually unexplicated) values, beliefs, and purposes—the ideological core of any practice system.

Ideological Issues in Competency-Based Practice

Again, an illustration from recent work on the development of the Tennessee Social Counselor Certification program will help define the issue. The curriculum has three major components: interpersonal helping skills, assessment, and case planning. A review of the literature conducted during curriculum development revealed notable differences in the approaches researchers and curriculum developers took to these basic components. The differences seemed to fall along a continuum.

In the three curriculum areas, the extremes of the continuum were using interpersonal helping skills to manipulate people versus using techniques that explore meanings and build consensus; assessment models and methods used to categorize and label pathology versus those used to identify strengths and contextualize risk factors; and case planning designed to control versus case planning aimed at mobilizing strengths and resources around mutually derived goals. Where a particular author stood on the continuum was sometimes explicit and stated; more often, it was discernible only through careful scrutiny of the text's language, metaphors, and case examples. Always, the implications for practice directives were enormous.

The literature on interpersonal helping skills and relationships provides a good example. Robert Carkhuff's (1969) well-known matrix of helping skills (Carkhuff and Anthony, 1979) is embedded in a counseling model which presumes that the helper is the more knowing partner who uses skills in a unilateral influence process. Gerald Egan (1986), on the other hand, posits a reciprocal influence process between client and worker through which "in the best cases, positive change occurs in both parties" (p. 24). Notably, both authors build their counseling systems with nearly similar sets of required competencies, differing primarily in how each labels a particular skill. But the nature of the relationships formed and the purposes for which the skills are used are dramatically different in each author's model.

The point is that: similar competencies do not necessarily result in similar practice. Consider two workers trained in the same set of skills derived from the same knowledge base. One manipulates, labels, and controls; the other engages, explores, makes alliances, and empowers. What accounts for the difference?

The easy answer is attitudes and values. Anyone who has attempted to measure attitudes and values in examinations and performance evaluations has confronted one limitation of this explanation. A far more serious one derives from our narrow focus. Many of us have walked away from a case conference mumbling, "That worker has great skills and knowledge, but her attitudes are despicable. Oh well, as long as she doesn't put them on the client and gets the job done." The focus here is on attitudes and values as properties of the worker. What we really need to be looking at is the practice model itself and whether the job can be done through it.

Every practice model has an ideological core. The core contains what we usually refer to as attitudes and values, yet it is more than that. It contains a set of fundamental existential and normative postulates—beliefs and assumptions about "what is" and "what ought to be." These inform not only practice processes, but also the ways in which we develop practice knowledge and the ultimate purposes served by the practice endeavor. In short, ideology is the glue that holds a practice system together and binds it to human conditions, institutions, and practices. And we don't think about it very much.

We also face the intriguing theoretical challenge of incorporating diversity and adaptability into our practice systems. There is, of course, tremendous variation in practice, program, and philosophy from region to region, state to state, county to county. Most attempts to develop and introduce generic practice models and curricula have either ignored this variation or attempted a top-down adaptation; neither approach has tapped the potential of diversity. Practice is ultimately shaped by—not just influenced by—its contexts, and especially its ideological contexts. The conventional competency-based approach to model development and training can only deal with diversity of contexts as overlays or backdrops. We need to use an approach that has at its core an ideology of diversity to create and sustain a practice for diverse ideologies.

Ideologies are not competencies, but they determine the competencies for which we strive. Ideologies are, I believe, the very soul of practice. Matilda Jones was speaking to my soul, not my skills. We need a practice that will respond from that place.

AN ALTERNATIVE APPROACH TO PRACTICE SYSTEM DEVELOPMENT

In Tennessee, the state Department of Human Services and the University of Tennessee College of Social Work's Office of Research and Public Services are collaborating to address two major implications of this analysis. Through our Practice System Development Project we are focusing on (1) the nature of our direct practice model—the core processes by which workers engage with clients daily, and (2) the nature of our practice system—the structures and mechanisms that the state agency uses to install and support practice models.

The project builds on and expands the Social Counselor Certification program, but it is designed to move beyond the competency-based approach by going back to the beginning—the client's experience—and reweaving the practice system around that. Having placed the client at the center, we formulated additional assumptions and design criteria to shape the project and determine its methods.

Specifically, with regard to the direct practice model, we assume the following:

- All models for working with people contain certain propositions and assumptions relating to the purpose and philosophy of practice, to human nature and behavior in the social environment, and to the methods, techniques, and relationships that will be the medium of practice. In order to have an effective practice system, these must be explicit, internally consistent, and reinforcing.
- The model should be grounded in and constructed from the client's experience of what works. Clients are considered the primary experts in this area and are regarded as consultants in all stages of model development and implementation.
- Practice should be culturally contextualized; that is, the culture of the client, the organization, and the community are incorporated as actual components of the practice model. We need to know not only what works, but what works with a particular group of clients in a particular community through a particular agency.
- The purpose of practice is to secure basic human needs, including the need for safety. Public welfare practice in particular should begin with an exploration of the client's basic needs, how she has attempted to meet them for herself and her family, and what opportunities for growth and development she perceives and pursues.
- The model's primary focus and technological base—its requisite knowledge and skills—should relate to strengths and resources, with an emphasis on identifying, engaging, developing, and mobilizing those that already exist in the client's life.

With regard to the practice system, we assume the following:

- We must analyze and attempt to make explicit the value and belief system, as well as the theory base, inherent in each of four major components that contribute to organizational effectiveness (and, therefore, practice effectiveness):
- The policy and design of the programs and services in and through which practice occurs
- The technological base of the organization; that is, the knowledge and skills required to implement the program or service design
- The resources, both material and symbolic, available to enable the organization to achieve its purposes
- The organizational structure and processes
- In order to maximize organizational and practice effectiveness, we must maximize the degree of technical, theoretical, and ideological consistency and integration within and among these four components, which should be regarded as elements in a practice system.

- Given the particular influence of supervision and management on direct practice, a model of supervision and management that is consonant with and reinforces the direct practice model should be developed and installed concurrently. A direct practice model that relies upon collaboration and consensus-building between worker and client will not be sustained for long in a conventional hierarchical and authoritarian agency environment.

- The method for developing supervision and management models should mirror that used to build the direct practice model; that is, the workers and supervisors are the experts on what works for them, their strengths are assumed and sought, and these become the basis for the new supervision/management systems.

Material for constructing the practice model will come from four sources: the existing literature, clients, workers, and administrative judgment. Our primary method is grounded theory, the approach developed by researchers Barney Glaser and Anselm Strauss to build conceptual bridges between dynamic and evolving real world phenomena and substantive theory (Glaser and Strauss, 1967; Glaser, 1978; Strauss, 1986). We will be following a similar approach to develop the adjunct model of supervision and management, identifying behaviors and processes that empower workers to empower clients. Ultimately, we will weave these components into a practice system.

In our review of the existing literature, we are casting a wide net, reading personal journals and poetry, conceptual essays, and exploratory projects as well as well-controlled studies. We are particularly attentive to materials in which the voice of the client can be heard clearly in the dialogue on practice effectiveness (see, for example, Magura, 1982; Mumma, 1989; Poertner, 1986).

Clients are our most expert informants in this study. We will be working with clients like those in Polansky's control group—people who have been clients in our public social services system and have achieved successful outcomes. We will be asking them, "What worked for you?" and building the foundation of the direct practice model from the answers. Because we will be viewing their experience through a concave strengths-focused lens, we expect to find many unrecognized strengths, environmental assets, and naturally occurring growth processes that can be recognized and reinforced through practice.

We have begun observing and analyzing the characteristics, practice processes, and environments of *workers* who have been identified as "effective" by a consensus of administrators, supervisors, coworkers, and clients. These workers provide the measure for what is possible within the existing system. This analysis also provides a fund of knowledge for reality-based training of existing staff and more sharply focused guidelines for selecting new staff.

As suggested earlier, a critical and often unrecognized element in direct practice is administrative judgment about what can be done and what is desirable. Thus, the design of the project calls for a research administration team that includes key administrative staff. The team not only oversees the project, but also participates in the analysis and interpretation of the data. Administrators are, in effect, the guardians of the ideological resources of an organization. When administration is viewed as a normative process (Abels and Murphy, 1981), there is a solid attitudinal foundation for identifying and developing the elements of the organization's ideological core, and integrating them with its technological base. The very existence of the project reveals the value-sensitive nature of administration in this agency.

In all aspects of the project, our primary focus is on what is working well in the system despite constraints of funding, staffing, organizational structure, and conservative legislative and community environments. Rather than attempting to import and adapt a model, we are attempting to identify, nurture, support, and extend what has been occurring naturally, and taking the time and care to observe and analyze it with discipline and rigor.

We are not capitulating in the political struggles for public resources and professional involvement in public social services. Clearly, what we are attempting is a transformation of the organizational culture that will strengthen resolve and capacity in those struggles. The research method we have chosen is itself a tool for doing this.

CASE STUDY: BUILDING A NEW PRACTICE MODEL

This was our first worker observation and I was more nervous than Tim, the worker we were studying. He was doing just what we asked him to do: go on with his work as if we were not there shadowing him and interviewing everybody he works with.

We were on our way to see how Miss Fannie Mae C. was doing, but we had to stop by the Food Bank first to pick up a box for the family. Tim was talking about the way he sets boundaries with his clients so he doesn't get burned out. I really wanted to know about that because everyone we had interviewed said that Tim was "always there" and "accessible."

"I tell the folks what I can do and what I can't," he explained. "Then, after I get to know them a bit, I tell them what I will do and what I won't. I make it a policy never to do anything for clients that they can do for themselves. That's what they teach you in school, but the trick is to figure out what your clients can do and where they really need your help. I make myself really available, then I take my cues from the client about how close to get. They'll let you know what they need you for. But I make it my business to find out from them what they've done for themselves in the past and I look at the changes to see what they can do now. I can get pretty firm and direct. But I also stay very humble and listen very carefully."

At the Food Bank I watched Tim chat with a few of his clients and do two sidewalk consultations with a member of the agency board. Each walked away with some follow-up to do. "I will follow through immediately," Tim said as we drove toward Fannie Mae's. "In this job you never get everything done, so you have to set priorities. Keeping my word, following through on commitments I make to clients and these community agency people—that's something I always do. That's how I build trust. And the agency people will really extend themselves for my clients."

Fannie Mae, age seventy-two, had Alzheimer's disease. Often incontinent and usually bedridden, only intermittently was she able to recognize people and express her needs and wants. She was Medicaid eligible for nursing home placement but her only daughter, Jolene, insisted that she could and would provide the necessary care for her mother. Although Jolene was tender and attentive to her mother, Tim explained, her life was so chaotic that Fannie Mae was at risk.

Two months previously, Jolene, along with her mother and her two boys, aged ten and two, had been evicted from their dilapidated rental house for "creating dangerous and unsanitary conditions." A report was made to DHS on this family, now homeless and out of cash, but with enough property resources in Fannie Mae's name that they were ineligible for cash assistance. Tim had opened a case to provide both Adult Protective Services and Child Protective Services, and he had gone to the churches for help on the family's behalf. Funded by a series of three-day donations, the family had moved from motel to motel until Jolene found one willing to barter a room for cleaning services. The family moved into a dark, leaky room with one double bed.

As Tim was working with the family on housing, entitlements, emergency food, and home health assistance, the father of the ten-year-old had sought and obtained custody of his son through the court. Confused and angry about his brother's sudden disappearance, the toddler had begun to have tantrums. During one of these, he had severely beaten his bedridden grandmother. Tim felt it was necessary to place Fannie Mae in a health care facility, at least temporarily, over Jolene's objections. He had told Jolene of his decision and had initiated the necessary legal proceedings; meanwhile, he was stopping by the motel daily.

"That lady is from the university," Tim explained to Jolene, nodding toward the car. "They are following me around for a research study. They want to know about my job. Yesterday they met some of my clients that always agree with me. You and I have not always agreed and we've had some hard times finding ways to work together. I thought it would be important for them to see that too." Tim explained the consent form, obtained her signature, and asked Jolene if she wanted me to wait outside until the visit was over. Jolene gestured for me to come in.

Tim retrieved the Food Bank box from the car, greeted the toddler, and quietly approached Fannie Mae, who was asleep on the sheetless bed. She had fresh bruises on her face and upper torso. Jolene did not know how she got them. Her son was still having tantrums, but she was watching him carefully. The nurse was coming this afternoon. No, she would not sign to put her mother in the nursing home. "I know you are going to try to get the judge to sign the papers. I'm going to fight you. I have to. She belongs with me." Jolene looked at me. "I'm going to fight him. He's going to do his job, and I understand that, but I'll fight to keep her with me." As we talked about the bleak history of her family with institutional care, Jolene cried in Tim's presence for the first time. He provided a long, gentle silence.

Then, after a discussion on housing plans, the home health services, working with the toddler's anger and anxiety, arranging visitation with the older boy, and finances, Tim reviewed what each had agreed to do next. "And you will be sure that your son isn't alone with her. And you know that I will be seeing our attorney in the morning to get her into the nursing home. I know you don't want me to. I am really sorry that I have to go against you. And I will see about transportation for you to get there every day."

"Yeah, I know what you're going to do, and you know that I'm still going to try to stop you. But I'll think about what you said. And the boy will not be alone with her." She turned to me. "He's just doing his job. He's good."

"What makes him good?"

"His job is to watch out for my momma and the kids, but he cares about me too. He cares about all of us. Look over there. He don't mind bringing the food when he knows I can't get it. But he respects me. He's very honest with me. He always tells me what he's going to do and why. He never goes behind my back. If he disagrees, he just tells me. He visits with me, talks with me. My friends don't come by much anymore because of my momma. He knows about my life. And he's not afraid of it."

REFERENCES

Abels, P. and Murphy, M. (1981). *Administration in the human services: A normative systems approach.* Englewood Cliffs, NJ: Prentice-Hall.

Carkhuff, R. R. (1969). *Helping and human relations* (Vol. 1: Selection and training; Vol. 2: Practice and research). New York: Holt, Rinehart and Winston.

Carkhuff, R. R. and Anthony, W. A. (1979). *The skills of helping: An introduction to counseling.* Amherst, MA: Human Resource Development Press.

Clark, F. W. and Arkava, M., eds. (1979). *The pursuit of competence in social work.* San Francisco: Jossey-Bass.

Egan, G. (1986). *The skilled helper: A systematic approach to effective helping,* 3rd ed. Monterey, CA: Brooks/Cole.

Gambrill, E. (1983). *Casework: A competency-based approach.* Englewood Cliffs, NJ: Prentice-Hall.

Glaser, B. G. (1978). *Theoretical sensitivity: Advances in the methodology of grounded theory.* Mill Valley, CA: The Sociology Press.

Glaser, B. G. and Strauss, A. (1967). *The discovery of grounded theory.* New York: Aldine.

Gouldner, A. W. (1970). *The coming crisis of western sociology.* New York: Basic Books.

Heineman, M. B. (1981). The obsolete scientific imperative in social work research. *Social Service Review, 55,* 371–397.

Magura, S. (1982). Clients view outcomes of child protective services. *Social Casework, 63,* 522–531.

Mumma, E. W. (1989). Reform at the local level: Virginia Beach empowers both clients and workers. *Public Welfare, 47*(2), 15–24.

National Child Welfare Resource Center for Management and Administration. (Summer, 1988). *Training Newsletter, 1*(2).

Palmer, P. J. (1974). *Action research: A new style of politics in education.* Boston: Institute for Responsive Education.

Palmer, P. J. (September–October, 1987). Community, conflict and ways of knowing: Ways to deepen our educational agenda. *Change, 19,* 20–25.

Poertner, J. (1986). The use of client feedback to improve practice: Defining the supervisor's role. *The Clinical Supervisor, 4,* 57–67.

Polansky, N., Chalmers, M., Buttenweiser, E., and Williams, D. (1981). *Damaged parents: An anatomy of child neglect.* Chicago: University of Chicago Press.

Polansky, N., Borgman, R. D., and DeSaix, C. (1972). *Roots of futility.* San Francisco: Jossey-Bass.

Powell, D. R. (March, 1986). Parent education and support programs. *Young Children, 41,* 47–52.

Rappoport, J. (1990). Research methods and the empowerment social agenda. In P. Tolan, C. Keys, F. Chertok, and L. Jason, eds., *Researching community psychology.* Washington, DC: American Psychology Association.

Smalley, R. (1965). *Theory for social work.* New York: Columbia University Press.

Strauss, A. L. (1986). *Qualitative analysis.* Cambridge, England: Cambridge University Press.

Teare, R. J. (1979). A task analysis of public welfare and educational implications. In F. W. Clark and M. L. Arkava, eds., *The pursuit of competence in social work,* pp. 131–145. San Francisco: Jossey-Bass.

Teare, R. J. (1981). *Social work practice in a public welfare setting: An empirical analysis.* New York: Praeger Publishers.

Weick, A. (1987). Reconceptualizing the philosophical perspective of social work. *Social Service Review, 61,* 218–230.

The Strengths Approach to Assessment and Research

PART III

The Strengths Approach to...

Assessment and Research

CHAPTER 11

Assessment of Client Strengths

Charles D. Cowger

The focus of this chapter is the assessment of individual client strengths in social work practice. It is grounded in the belief that social work has been long on philosophy and theory that flaunts a client strength perspective, but short on practice directives, guidelines, and know-how for incorporating strengths into practice. The importance of a strengths perspective in assessment is first discussed, followed by the presentation of an assessment framework. One part of the framework is emphasized in this paper with the presentation of a list of possible client strengths for consideration by worker and client during the assessment process. The framework and list are understood as generic and can be applied while utilizing any of a variety of theoretical practice models.

THE STRENGTHS PERSPECTIVE
IN SOCIAL WORK

Many examples of appreciating and building on client strengths as important philosophical and theoretical constructs can be found in social work literature. The social work values of promoting human dignity, worth, and self-determination implicitly recognize clients' innate potentialities, capacities, and strengths. Perlman's (1957) casework model and Ripple's (1964) research both emphasized client motivation and capacity. Schwartz's (1971) interactional approach, with an emphasis on the concepts of interdependence and mutuality, was built on a belief in strengths of people and their health rather than their weaknesses and sickness. The "life" model of social work practice, developed by Germain and Gitterman (1980), captures the transaction between people and environments and emphasizes the qualitative human attributes of identity, compe-

Copyright © 1992 by Longman Publishing Group.

tence, and autonomy. Weick's (1986) health model, which highlights healing and the human body as a self-correcting mechanism, emphasizes the capacities and strengths of human beings. Based on his research findings, Maluccio (1979, p. 401) has argued for a shift in social work from "problems or pathology to strengths, resources, and potentialities in human beings and their environments." These illustrations represent only a small portion of the social work literature whereby client strengths are understood or promoted as central to philosophy, theory, and actual social work practice.

Incongruity in Theory and Practice

Hepworth and Larsen (1982) highlighted the incongruity between the social work theoretical perspective and practice when they stated "social workers persist in formulating assessments that focus almost exclusively on the pathology and dysfunction of clients—despite the time honored social work platitude that social workers work with strengths, not weaknesses" (p. 157). There is very little empirical evidence indicating the extent to which practitioners consciously make use of client strengths in their practice. Maluccio (1979) found that social workers underestimated client strengths and had more negative perceptions of clients than clients had of themselves. It is unlikely that client strengths would have an impact on worker activity, considering the preponderance of deficit assessment instruments as opposed to the lack of assessment tools that consider client strengths. A library search for assessment tools that include client strengths is a particularly unrewarding experience, as is reviewing collections of assessment, diagnosis, and measurement instruments in book and monograph form. The various versions of the American Psychiatric Association's DSM have emphasized client pathology. Although DSM-III (1980) Axis V evaluates the individual's highest level of adaptive functioning during the previous year, there is little evidence it is being used in practice and serious questions persist concerning its reliability (Kirk and Kutchins, 1988).

The Importance of Strengths in the Assessment Process

Central to a strengths perspective of social work practice is to have client strengths as a preeminent concern during the assessment process. How the client and the social worker define the client problem situation and how they evaluate and give meaning to the dynamic factors related to that situation sets the context and content for the life of the helping relationship. If a worker focuses on deficits during the assessment phase, it is likely that deficits will be the focus during remaining contacts with that client. Concentrating on deficits may lead to self-fulfilling prophecies. Hepworth and Larsen (1982, p. 157) point out that such a concentration may impair "a social worker's ability to discern clients' potentials for growth," "reinforce self-doubts and feelings of inadequacy," and predispose workers to "believe that clients should continue to receive service longer than is necessary."

While emphasizing deficits has serious implications for, and imposes limitations on, practice, focusing on strengths provides many advantages. Recognizing client strengths is fundamental to the value stance of the profession. It provides for a leveling of the power social workers have over clients and in so doing presents increased potential for the facilitation of a partnership in the working relationship. Focusing on strengths in assessment has the potential for liberating clients from stigmatizing diagnostic classifications that reinforce "sickness" in family and community environments.

THE ASSESSMENT PROCESS

Assessment is used here rather than *diagnosis* because it is more congruent with a strengths perspective. Typically, the idea of diagnosis evolved and is understood in the medical realm of pathology, deviance, and deficits and has not been thought of in the context of discerning strengths. Assessment, on the other hand, is a process and a product (Hepworth and Larsen, 1982, p. 156). As a process, it is a joint activity between worker and client. As a product, it is a mutual agreement between worker and client. As a process, it is ongoing because discovery and understanding is a dynamic process. As a product, it is constantly being revised during the life of the helping relationship.

The importance of assessment as a joint activity between worker and client, and the assessment product as a mutual agreement, cannot be exaggerated. The worker's role is to listen and then to assist clients to discover, clarify, and articulate their concerns, their needs, and their possibilities. The client gives direction to the content of the assessment. The client must feel ownership of the process and the product and can do so only if assessment is open and shared. Workers should not have a secret assessment or agenda. Because assessment is to provide structure for confronting a client's problem situations, any privately held assessment a worker might have makes the client vulnerable to manipulation.

The assessment process suggested here has two components, which are similar to Mary Richmond's (1917) distinction between "study" and "diagnosis." She proposed that the social worker first study the facts of the situation and then diagnose the nature of the problem. Correspondingly, the first component here is a process whereby a worker and a client define the problem situation or clarify why the client has sought assistance. The second component involves evaluating and giving meaning to those factors which impinge on the problem situation.

Component 1: Defining the Problem Situation

Defining the problem situation is only the beginning of the helping process and should not be confused with evaluation and analysis of the problem situation. It is particularly important at this time to assist the client in telling his story. The client owns that story and if the worker respects that ownership, the client will be able to more fully share it. The following list outlines what the worker and client might do to define the problem situation. Items 2, 3, and 4 are based in part on guidelines developed by Brown and Levitt (1979), and later revised by Hepworth and Larsen (1982, p. 164).*

---

* Hepworth and Larsen use items 2, 3, and 4 as "questions" to identify other people and larger systems that are involved in the problem situation and/or interacting with the problem. These questions are given more assessment import in this paper as they are seen as defining the problem rather than simply identifying involvement or interaction with the problem.

Defining the Problem Situation
or
Getting at Why the Client Seeks Assistance

1. *Brief summary of the identified problem situation.* This should be in simple language, straightforward, and mutually agreed upon between worker and client. It can be no more than a brief paragraph.
2. *Who* (persons, groups, or organizations) is involved including the client(s) seeking assistance?
3. *How* or in what way are participants involved? What happens between the participants before, during, and immediately following activity related to the problem situation?
4. What meaning does the client ascribe to the problem situation?
5. What does the client want related to the problem situation?
6. What does the client want/expect by seeking assistance?
7. What would client's life be like if problem was resolved?

This outline assumes clients know why they seek assistance. With a little help from a worker, a client can clarify, or perhaps discover some new insight, and articulate the nature of the problem situation. These questions are based on a model of practice whereby social workers believe their clients, trust their clients' judgment, and reinforce their clients' competency. The orientation also assumes that when dealing with problem situations, what you see is what you get; that hidden, deep-seated, intrapsychic, and/or unconscious phenomena, if real, are irrelevant.

The word *situation* has a particularly important meaning because it affirms that problems always exist in an environmental context. To focus on the problem situation is to avoid a perception and subsequent definition of the person as pathological that may lead, for the client, to a self-fulfilling prophecy and, for the worker, to ascribing blame. However, using the word *problem* does not suggest that one therefore assumes environmental or situational pathology and continues with a pathological model by simply redirecting pathological assessment to the relevant environment. *Problem* here means only that there exists a mismatch or disequilibrium between the client's needs and environmental demands and resources that is causing difficulty, puzzlement, and often pain. Focusing on the individual alone is irrelevant and may hinder problem solution. Problem situations have a life of their own and are generated by combinations of chance happenings, incongruities, and systems disequilibrium. Understanding problem situations in this way allows the worker and client the freedom to capitalize on personal and environmental strengths to resolve the problem.

Component 2: Framework for Assessment

The second assessment component involves analyzing, evaluating, and giving meaning to those factors that influence the problem situation. The model proposed here revolves around two axes. The first axis is an environmental factors versus personal factors continuum, and the second is a strengths versus deficits continuum (see Figure 11.1).

Concerns about emphasizing either end of the deficit–strengths axis have been discussed previously. A new theoretical interest in how environmental factors affect practice has been increasingly evident in the literature since the early 1970s. However, like renewed interest in client strengths, this interest has not been fully realized in actual practice because practice guidelines and specific practice knowledge have lagged behind theoretical development. The lack of knowledge of, or interest in, the relevant environmental factors, in actual practice, is evident when one reviews available assessment instruments.

When the axes in Figure 11.1 are enclosed, each of the four quadrants that result represents important content for assessment (see Figure 11.2). Because assessment instruments themselves have tended to focus on the elements of Quadrant 4, most practice today emphasizes personal deficits. A comprehensive assessment would have data recorded in each quadrant. The version of the assessment axes in Table 2 has been used as a recording tool in teaching, workshops, and agency consultation and has demonstrated that workers and clients can readily identify content for each quadrant. However, Quadrants 1 and 2 are emphasized when practicing from a strengths perspective. Indeed, *deficits* may well be a misnomer and the end of that continuum might be better understood as "obstacles" to problem resolution.

Quadrant 2, Personal Strengths, with an emphasis on psychological factors, is the concern of this paper. The taxonomy of strengths in cognition, emotion, motivation, coping, and interpersonal relationships is used to organize and structure assessment. The categories are quite traditional and are not free of conceptual problems. For example, it is important to note that although these items are designated as "personal" factors, they do not represent intrapersonal attributes devoid of environmental interaction (e.g., motivation is dependent on a unique set of environmental and personal dynamics). Physiological factors are particularly important for some clients, such as the aged

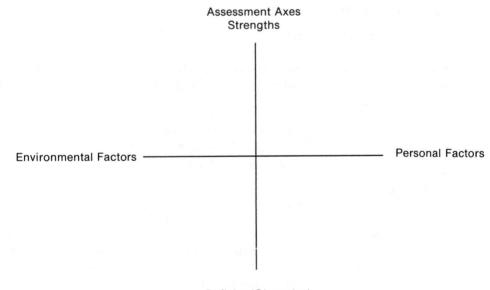

Figure 11.1 Framework for Assessment

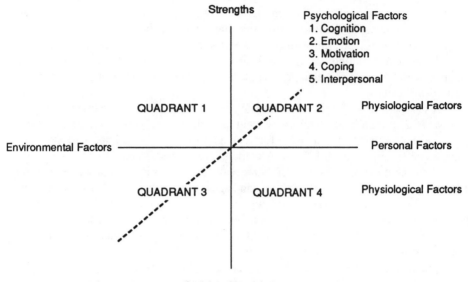

Figure 11.2   Assessment Axes (Quadrants 2 and 4)

or the disabled. However, the physical and environmental assessment components of the assessment axes are beyond the more narrow "personal strength" focus of this paper.

Client Strengths (Quadrant 2)

What might be considered as content for Quadrant 2, "Personal Strengths"? The following list suggests personal strengths workers and clients might consider during the assessment process. These items were arrived at through literature review (e.g., Hepworth and Larsen, 1982; Brown and Levitt, 1979) and workshops with agency practitioners.

ASSESSMENT OF
CLIENT STRENGTHS
(Quadrant 2 of Assessment Axes)

A. Cognition
   1. Sees the world as most other people see it in her culture.
   2. Has an understanding of right and wrong, from her cultural, ethical perspective.
   3. Understands how one's own behavior affects others and how others affect her. Is insightful.
   4. Is open to different ways of thinking about things.
   5. Reasoning is easy to follow.
   6. Considers and weighs alternatives in problem solving.

B. Emotion
1. Is in touch with feelings and is able to express them if encouraged.
2. Expresses love and concern for intimate others.
3. Demonstrates a degree of self-control.
4. Can handle stressful situations reasonably well.
5. Is positive about life. Has hope.
6. Has a range of emotions.
7. Emotions are congruent with situations.

C. Motivation
1. When having problems, doesn't hide from, avoid, or deny them.
2. Willing to seek help and share problem situation with others he can trust.
3. Willing to accept responsibility for her own part or role in problem situations.
4. Wants to improve current and future situations.
5. Does not want to be dependent on others.
6. Seeks to improve self through further knowledge, education, and skills.

D. Coping
1. Persistent in handling family crises.
2. Is well organized.
3. Follows through on decisions.
4. Is resourceful and creative with limited resources.
5. Stands up for self rather than submitting to injustice.
6. Attempts to pay debts despite financial difficulty.
7. Prepares for and handles new situations well.
8. Has dealt successfully with related problems in the past.

E. Interpersonal
1. Has friends.
2. Seeks to understand friends, family members, and others.
3. Makes sacrifices for friends, family members, and others.
4. Performs social roles appropriately (e.g., parental, spouse, son or daughter, community).
5. Is outgoing and friendly.
6. Is truthful.
7. Is cooperative and flexible in relating to family and friends.
8. Is self-confident in relationships with others.
9. Shows warm acceptance of others.
10. Can accept loving and caring feelings from others.
11. Has sense of propriety, good manners.
12. Is a good listener.
13. Expresses self spontaneously.
14. Is patient.
15. Has realistic expectations in relationships with others.
16. Has a sense of humor.
17. Has sense of satisfaction in role performance with others.
18. Has ability to maintain own personal boundaries in relationships with others.

19. Demonstrates comfort in sexual role/identity.
20. Demonstrates ability to forgive.
21. Is generous with time and money.
22. Is verbally fluent.
23. Is ambitious and industrious.
24. Is resourceful.

This outline is proposed as a resource to assist workers and clients in considering those client strengths to be brought to bear on coping with the problem situation. In the initial contact, the worker should be able to begin identifying client strengths. Workers may wish to have a copy of the list readily available during an interview. Other workers may find a review of the list helpful during case reflection, recording, and planning. One worker reported to the author that he has used the list by going through it item by item with the client. Workers may use the list to (1) stimulate thinking about strengths and their importance in the practice process, (2) assist in identifying strengths that otherwise would not be thought of, (3) assist in identifying and selecting positive and supportive content to be shared with clients, (4) provide a foundation for a case plan that is based on client competency and capability rather than inadequacy, and (5) bolster worker confidence and belief in the client. The list is intended to be suggestive and heuristic in nature by illustrating the wide range of strengths that any given client might have. The language in the list is somewhat contaminated with professional and middle class notions of reality and the desirable, and therefore will require either interpretation or revision when the assessment process is shared with clients, especially those from different cultures.

Although this perspective strongly advocates focusing on client strengths, a qualifier needs to be emphasized. Realistically, many clients at risk and those most vulnerable in our society simply are no match for the environmental intrusions and disruptive external impingements on their lives. The use of this list to the exclusion of a thorough assessment of environmental obstacles and strengths (Quadrants 1 and 3, Figure 11.2), provides little advantage over deficit models of practice. Indeed, focusing on individual strengths in the face of overwhelming environmental odds may be no less cruel than a practice model that reinforces client deficits. A comprehensive assessment would include content from all four quadrants. However, a strengths perspective would emphasize Quadrants 1 and 2, elements often missing from assessment.

In summary, social work literature has emphasized philosophy and theory that presents a strengths perspective, but is devoid of practice directives, guidelines, and know-how for incorporating this perspective into practice. Assessment based on a strengths perspective places environmental and individual strengths in a prominent position. Environmental and individual obstacles which hinder a resolution to a problem situation are viewed only as obstacles, and as such, they are not considered the primary content of assessment. An outline of individual client strengths has been presented in an attempt to bridge the gap between philosophy and theory which supports client strengths and practice knowledge which ignores it. Believing in client strengths can generate self-fulfilling prophecy.

REFERENCES

American Psychiatric Association. (1980). *Diagnostic and statistical manual of mental disorders* (3rd ed.). Washington, DC: American Psychiatric Association.

Brown, L. and Levitt, J. (1979). A methodology for problem-system identification. *Social Casework, 60,* 408–415.

Germain, C. and Gitterman, A. (1980). *The life model of social work practice.* New York: Columbia University Press.

Hepworth, D. and Larsen, J. (1982). *Direct social work practice.* Homewood, IL: Dorsey Press.

Kirk, S. and Kutchins, H. J. (1988). Deliberate misdiagnosis in mental health practice. *Social Service Review, 24,* 225–237.

Maluccio, A. (1979). The influence of the agency environment on clinical practice. *Journal of Sociology and Social Welfare, 6,* 734–755.

Perlman, H. (1957). *Social casework: A problem-solving process.* Chicago: University of Chicago Press.

Richmond, M. (1917). *Social diagnosis.* New York: Russell Sage Foundation.

Ripple, L. (1964). *Motivation, capacity and opportunity.* Chicago: University of Chicago Press.

Schwartz, W. (1971). On the use of groups in social work practice. In W. Schwartz and S. Zalba, eds., *The practice of group work.* New York: Columbia University Press.

Weick, A. (1986). The philosophical context of a health model for social work. *Social Casework, 7,* 551–559.

CHAPTER 12

Reconsidering the Environment as a Helping Resource

William Patrick Sullivan

Social work practice has long been guided by the person-in-environment perspective. This perspective recognizes the interdependence of people with objects in the world around them. In daily life, contact with the social environment nurtures, supports, protects, entertains, stresses, and confuses us. An appreciation of the influence of the social environment on individual functioning is particularly crucial for those working in mental health settings. Rarely is a life dilemma, problem, or difficult decision adequately understood without an awareness of the impact of family, work, and the community on an individual, and vice versa. Yet, whether through arriving at a DSM-IIIR diagnosis, completing an individual assessment, or in actual intervention, there appears to be an overemphasis on the deficits or toxic elements in the social environment.

While there are undoubtedly gaps and noxious elements present in the world around us, such a negative view of the social environment is not without its consequences. By narrowing the focus to problems, threats, and lacks in the social environment our view of helping resources becomes unnecessarily constricted. Furthermore, this overemphasis on deficits in both the person and the social environment potentially compromises our time-honored belief in client self-determination, and often results in the exclusion, social and physical, of significant groups of people from various helping and restorative processes.

A strengths perspective of social work practice offers an alternative conception of the environment. This perspective promotes matching the inherent strengths of individuals with naturally occurring resources in the social environment. Such naturally occurring resources are a source of strength in all social environments and available in all social environments. Recognizing, recruiting, and using these strengths can help maximize the potential of our clients and our community. In addition, when the environ-

---

Copyright ©1992 by Longman Publishing Group.

ment is viewed as a source of opportunities for clients, rather than an ecology of obstacles, the sheer number of helping resources we perceive expands dramatically.

While a strengths perspective of social work practice has yet to be fully developed, the importance of recognizing and building from the strengths of people and the environment long has been noted within the profession. In 1958, the Commission on Social Work Practice stated that to "seek out, identify, and strengthen the maximum potential in individuals, groups, and communities" was a primary purpose of social work practice (p. 5). More recently, work by authors such as Hepworth and Larsen (1986) and Germain and Gitterman (1980) expounded again on the importance of recognizing strengths in people and the environment. This chapter will briefly trace historical trends in the conceptualization of the social environment as a contributing factor in the etiology of mental illness, as well as demonstrate how such views have had a pervasive negative impact on dominant views of helping. In addition, it will be argued that the social environment should be reconsidered as a helping resource in social work practice. A case example will be provided to demonstrate the character and potential of this orientation in actual practice.

It is important to acknowledge that adopting a strengths perspective in mental health practice will require new behaviors and adjustments on the practitioner's part. For example, while recognizing and tapping naturally occurring resources appears to be a relatively simple task, in practice it may prove to be problematic to the worker accustomed to relying on a limited set of traditional community resources. In contrast, naturally occurring resources are often nontraditional. To illustrate: in practice with the long-term mentally ill, operationalizing the idea of resources in the environment would require searching for potential employers before relying on vocational rehabilitation services, locating flexible landlords before relying on specialized residential services, and using the YMCA before starting an active recreation group at the mental health center.

Current practice with the long-term mentally ill provides an arena for the development of the strengths model. This group presents a significant challenge to mental health professionals, many of whom find it difficult to focus on the strengths these individuals present in the face of their obvious limitations. Furthermore, the life history of many people in this population is replete with examples of exclusion from social processes both physically, via hospitalization, and socially, through isolation and rootlessness within their communities. Finally, the strengths perspective described in this work has been actually applied to this population with encouraging results (Rapp and Chamberlain, 1985).

HISTORICAL CONSIDERATIONS

Intervention with the mentally ill has been based on such diverse ideologies as social control and humane treatment. Throughout history, persistent ideas about the limitations of the individual and the toxicity of the social environment have shaped dominant modes of helping. In colonial America, helping the mentally ill was viewed as a local responsibility. The mentally ill typically were considered to be poor, and where possible, family members or neighbors assumed responsibility for them. While the care and treatment offered was perhaps less than adequate, the mentally ill usually were allowed to remain in their community. Such benign considerations were not granted to outsiders or vagrants who were either returned to their place of residence, jailed, or placed in asylums (Rothman, 1971).

By the 1830s the popular conception of mental illness had shifted from the idea of moral causation to a sociobiological conception, although the biology was admittedly crude and rudimentary (Rothman, 1971). In short, it was assumed that critical changes in the social order and unhealthy social conditions were at least partially responsible for the onset of mental illness. It was in this period that the prototypical state hospital was developed. These hospitals were removed from the chaos of larger urban areas and were built in idyllic rural areas where patients could be free from the stress of social life and would not contaminate the citizenry. Beyond the purported benefit to the mentally ill was the belief that asylums were model communities that also provided society with direction for future reform (Rothman, 1971). The idealism and optimism of this period had dissipated by the time of the Civil War, but the view that environmental conditions were primary determinants in mental illness continually resurfaced, in both benign and pejorative senses.

The view of the social environment in this country that was dominant from the late 1800s through the first two decades of this century grew out of a tumultuous time. Major urban areas were growing rapidly as industrialization continued and the population was swelled by an influx of immigrants. The deplorable condition of the modern city became the target for reformists of the period, many of whom were social workers. Klein and Kantor (1976) reflect the perceptions of social workers and reformers by suggesting that reform efforts were designed "to cleanse the city of its worst impurities, to make it a better place by scrubbing away the excrescences of evil and disorder . . ." (p. 396).

The profession of social work can trace many of its appreciations of and orientations to the environment to this period. The works of its two most famous theorists, Jane Addams (1910) and Mary Richmond (1917), are particularly illuminating in this regard. These early leaders in the profession of social work paid considerable attention to and expressed deep concern about the impact of the social environment on individuals and their families. Richmond (1922), in developing the idea of "social casework," essentially focused on problems of the adjustment of the individual to the changing and sometimes pernicious social order. From a different perspective, Addams (1910, p. 125) saw the settlement house as ". . . an experimental effort to aid in the solution of the social and industrial problems which are engendered by the modern conditions of life in a great city." Additional reactions during this period, including the public recreation movement, industrial and labor reform, compulsory education laws, and the public health movement, were all strategies of various groups with vested interests to counteract a social environment (particularly urban) that was increasingly perceived as toxic and inimical to the health and moral character of its denizens.

The links between mental illness and the problems as well as the complexities of the modern city were the subject of theories and postulates of the great sociologists of the time: Ernest Burgess (1939), Robert Park (1952), Louis Wirth (1964), Robert Faris and H. Warren Dunham (1939). For example, in the introduction to Faris and Dunham's classic study, *Mental Disorders in Urban Areas* (1939), Singer wrote "that the environmental setting is an important factor in the etiology of these illnesses has long been recognized" (p. vii). Burgess (1939, p. ix), in even stronger language, suggested that the results of Faris and Dunham's study "indicate how definitely and unmistakably the incidence of the chief psychoses are related to the organization of the city." These writings spurred social science's persistent interest in social disorganization.

While theories of the sociocultural basis of mental illness continued to be developed and refined, the influence of Freudian thought began to overshadow these sociological formulations (Robinson, 1934). In the 1930s, '40s, and '50s, the primary causal force hypothesized in the development of mental illness moved from social disorganization to hidden pathological urges, deficits, and dynamic tensions located in the unconscious and conscious dimensions of the personality of the individual. Ironically, no matter how the concept of the etiology of severe mental illness may have changed, the dominant treatment modality remained the same: hospitalization. Whether it was living in the great modern city, or psychodynamic turmoil, or some interaction between the two that produced stresses and strains that caused mental illness, the individual who came to be defined as mentally ill was seen as thoroughly ill-equipped for daily life.

While hospitalization may have continued to be the treatment of choice for major mental illness, the style of hospital treatment underwent some radical changes in the 1940s and 1950s. New concepts, such as the therapeutic community and milieu therapy, gained stature in this period although oppressive physical therapies (such as electroconvulsive therapy and leucotomies) remained widespread (Greenblatt, York, and Brown, 1955; Joint Commission on Mental Health, 1961). Encouraged by the work of Maxwell Jones with adult psychiatric patients and Bruno Bettelheim with children, some hospitals revamped the structure of their organization to reflect more benign and therapeutic approaches. In therapeutic communities, the relationship between staff and patients was reconceived, rules were reconsidered, and meeting the individual needs of patients were reestablished as critical to successful treatment. In such a setting, patients were expected to accept added responsibility not only for their own behavior, but for others as well. It was hoped that by increasing clients' responsibility and participation, they would develop the internal controls and social skills necessary for mastering community living. Therefore, a facsimile of community life was created with hopes that, when released, former patients could handle the everyday demands of modern living.

The expectation and excitement generated by the therapeutic community and open hospital was given an enormous boost by the introduction of psychotropic medications in the 1950s. The combination of these two treatments supported a belief that the severely mentally ill could eventually return to community life. With such a conviction entrenched, and with reports of the scandalous conditions of some state hospitals, there came a general call to close such facilities forever (Foley and Sharfstein, 1983). Herein lie the roots of the community mental health movement.

The Community Mental Health Movement

The idea of community mental health was spawned by the hopes that the mentally ill could be treated in the community, and that primary prevention of mental illness was possible. By emphasizing primary prevention (Hersch, 1972), the community mental health movement followed a public health model wherein the social environment is considered a host that may be hospitable to the fertile eruption of conditions favorable to the development of mental illness. The public health model also commits professionals to the idea of early detection and treatment of incipient difficulties so that more severe mental illness can be preempted. With this broad conceptual underpinning, there were very few social situations, conditions, and institutions that were considered beyond the purview of mental health professionals and unworthy of their efforts (Brown and Cain, 1964).

Coinciding with and in part due to this movement, large numbers of former psychiatric patients were discharged into the community, a phenomenon that later became known as "deinstitutionalization." For a variety of reasons and from a variety of perspectives, it is generally acknowledged that this movement of former patients into the community has been a failure (Foley and Sharfstein, 1983; Klerman, 1977). The support, services, and attention so critical to the reintegration of severely psychiatrically disabled into the community has been lacking. Soon, "psychiatric ghettos" were noted in major metropolitan areas (Aviram and Segal, 1973; Segal, Baumohl, and Johnson, 1977; Reich and Siegel, 1978). More recently, there has been concern expressed over the number of former patients now among the homeless (Lamb, 1984). While the responses to the social problem of individuals with mental illness unintegrated into the community have been diverse, they contain the seeds of the traditional responses traced throughout this analysis. In short, they are based on the perceived deficits of the individual and of the disorganization and fulminating "disease-carriers" in the social environment.

Concern about the lack of adequate care and support of the long-term mentally ill has resulted in a variety of alternative policies. One has been a reconsideration of hospitalization as a viable option. Couched in terms of "the need for asylum," the flaws in the ability of the long-term mentally ill to successfully master community living have been again underscored (see Talbott, 1984). In a similar vein, there has been support for liberalizing the civil commitment laws to allow the involuntary hospitalization of those "obviously ill, and in need of treatment" (Treffert, 1985, p. 259). While these solutions have often been justified on humanitarian grounds, they still emphasize the defects and deficits of these people. Perhaps even more importantly, these solutions lack imagination.

Also in response to the pressing needs of the mentally ill, community support services, including partial hospital programs, skills training, and case management services have proliferated. Joined with these are ancillary services such as residential services, sheltered workshops, job clubs, and various social and recreational programs. These programs are thought to be necessary supports allowing the mentally ill to remain in the community (Talbott, 1981). On closer inspection, they appear to represent an effort to develop services designed to correct and contain the limitations of these individuals and their environments. The expansion of community programs for the mentally ill has followed the blueprint of the state hospital system. By developing segregated housing programs, therapy, and recreational groups, and by relying on sheltered employment opportunities, the state hospital, in effect, has been replicated in the community. As a result, thousands of mentally ill individuals are living in prophylactic environments, systematically and silently excluded from natural community processes. This "hospital in the community" phenomenon is not without its consequences, as the following case vignette will illustrate.

CASE STUDY

Frank S. was forty-three years old when he was referred to the community support program. He had been recently discharged from the state hospital, his second stay in a twenty-year period. Frank has a diagnosis of schizophrenia. Previously, Frank had lived in rural Kansas, where for most of his life he had worked on the family farm.

Frank's recent difficulty followed the death of both of his parents. His increasingly bizarre behavior and inability to care for himself led to his commitment to the hospital.

At the time of his referral, Frank was basically noncommunicative, had poor personal hygiene, and suffered continuously from auditory hallucinations. These factors, plus his nonverbal threats to leave the board and care home, led to a prediction by the staff that he would soon be rehospitalized. Given his current condition, the community support staff did not feel he would be able to benefit from the structured groups offered at the center. Instead, he was placed in a "maintenance group" which was largely devoted to arts and crafts activities. He was subsequently referred to the case management project.

Frank S. was not adjusting or responding to this artificial environment. Among the staff there was an overriding concern about his individual problems and limitations. Frank's interests, aspirations, and strengths were not considered in intervention or case planning. The resources and environments at Frank's disposal were generic. There was no attempt to tailor them to his needs, wants, and desires. These specialized resources were specifically designed to offset the presumed limitations of Frank as an individual and of his constricted environment. Furthermore, these resources were both costly and scarce. And if Frank had only these paltry resources available to him, failure to adjust to this artificial environment could lead to only one end: rehospitalization.

APPLICATION OF THE STRENGTHS PERSPECTIVE

When an assessment of individual and environmental strengths, capabilities, and resources is a regular feature of case planning, the number of strategies and possible benefits available to the clinician and client are boundless. The social environment, rather than being seen as a barrier to clients, is thought to be a vast source of opportunities. The abilities, goals, and dreams of clients guide interventions, but they succeed only as relevant resources in the community are discovered, created, and used to promote individual growth. Continuing the story of Frank Smith can help illustrate this model in practice.

The case manager assigned to work with Frank began the contact by discussing Frank's goals and desires for his life. Not unlike most people, Frank wished to have a job and a place of his own to live. The case manager also completed a strengths assessment: a record of previous and current activities and involvements. (See chapter 6.)

The most striking impression of these early meetings was Frank's consistent expression of a continued interest in farmwork. His history of farmwork and clear expertise in this field suggested this as an area of interest worth pursuing. Together Frank and the case manager began an exploration of area farms and ranches that might accept a volunteer. Soon a rancher was found who was agreeable to the idea. The relationship that developed was so strong that the owner of the ranch made it clear that Frank could come as often as he liked. When transportation became a problem, Frank surprised everyone with news that he owned a truck that was stored in his hometown. Even more surprising was the ease with which he passed a driver's examination.

At the time contact with the Community Support Program was terminated, Frank was working at the ranch regularly, was providing his own transportation, and was beginning discussions about moving into paid employment. In addition, there were a number of spin-off effects, including improved hygiene and increased interaction with those around him.

Reconceptualizing the Environment

The social environment is, among other things, a fund of resources that are crucial to the continued growth of all people. In our daily lives, we rely on family, church, friends, clubs, work, businesses, and recreational opportunities to enrich us. The long-term mentally ill are no different. The application of the strengths perspective in social work practice, in conjunction with a reconsideration of the environment as a helping resource, can lead to many benefits for those we serve. The case of Frank Smith will be used to illustrate several major points.

Using naturally occurring resources promotes the reintegration of the mentally ill into community life. A ranch is not a special program designed only for the long-term mentally ill. Relying solely on specialized programs designed for the mentally ill limits their daily contact to those with similar difficulties and mental health professionals. If the long-term mentally ill are going to be successful at community life, they must have contact and discourse with others in the community. Thus, using naturally occurring resources assures that the mentally ill will not remain segregated from the mainstream of community life. This is a necessary first step toward reintegrating into community life.

The resources used in this example are expandable, reusable, and limitless. The number of sheltered workshops and residential programs available in a given community is limited. In contrast, there is practically no limit to the number of farms, apartments, softball teams, and other life-enhancing resources available in a person's hometown. By locating sympathetic individuals and programs in the community, we identify and expand the number of natural helpers and propitious opportunities available to our clients. When community members enjoy rewarding contacts with clients, their willingness to work with others increases and they may become an enduring resource. The assets available to our clients may only be foreshortened by failures of our creativeness and willingness to work.

When the strengths, aspirations, and needs of the client are considered in planning for helping and amelioration, the resources used can genuinely be tailored to the individual client, thus emphasizing the uniqueness of each individual. Currently, many partial hospital and day programs design groups and exercises based on a generic mentally ill person. Developing programs in this manner turns on discerning the common features and difficulties of clients being served, and subsequently designing interventions to address these common features. Such an orientation does not fully account for individual differences, needs, strengths, or abilities and build treatment around the possibilities therein. Furthermore, this appears to reflect a dominant belief that clients cannot or should not use resources commonly or naturally available in the community. All individuals have the right to avail themselves of community resources, and it may be the practitioner's responsibility to see that opportunities are made known and available to clients. The successful use of naturally occurring environmental resources may be one of the most important keys in demonstrating that people with mental illness can live successfully in our communities. And as they do become functioning members of neighborhoods, families, townships, churches, etc., the communities' expectations of them may become more positive. And we know that the expectations we hold have a powerful shaping effect on those we serve.

When the environment is regarded as a bounty of potential opportunities for clients rather than a barren field, clients have more tools to build on the more positive aspects of their lives. To accent and pursue activities we excel in or enjoy is a commonplace for most, one we hardly think of. Participating in community processes enriches and invigorates our enjoyment of life. But for many mentally ill individuals such pursuits are rare, even forgotten. This opportunity should be available to all people. To feel successful in some aspect of life not only gives us some reflective satisfaction but helps us tackle more difficult and unpleasant tasks. When the social environment is considered as inimical (or parts of it, forbidden) to the mentally ill, the barriers we erect (presumably to protect them) wall them off from what are potentially healing life experiences. Often, too, the emphasis in structured mental health programs is often on those aspects of living where the mentally ill have experienced less success and/or have little interest. The mental health system, in this way, continually loses opportunities to exploit the resources the environment has to offer. Failure to tap naturally occurring resources in the community sends a powerful message to clients: It creates a demoralizing and hopeless atmosphere and continues a policy of sequestration and separation.

When disadvantaged groups are disengaged from continuing community processes and people, a source of opportunity and learning is taken from our society; that is to say, we lose what the mentally ill have to give us. The vitality of our culture can only be abetted by the presence of diverse peoples and groups. In addition, using natural resources in the community provides opportunities and incentives for community members to be helpful to others. For some individuals, the altruistic impulse is a strong one, but it has to be exercised. And, indeed, individuals with mental illness often express a strong desire to be helpful to others as well. We have much to offer the long-term mentally ill, and they have much to offer to others.

Finally, the employment of naturally occurring resources in the community is less costly. In an age of shrinking budgets and decreasing federal and state roles in funding social programs, unless we are ready for revolution, less costly alternatives should be explored. Using resources available in the community does not require allocation of funds for professional staff nor upkeep of specialized facilities.

A SOCIAL WORK FUNCTION

The profession of social work's traditional person-in-environment perspective is hospitable to the application of the model described. Through involvement with families, the workplace, and the community as a whole, social workers long have recognized the importance of a beneficent interaction between certain social influences and more competent and satisfying individual functioning. This interchange is not always a source of difficulty and stress as we sometimes theorize and agonize, but it is also a potential fount of sustenance, opportunity, and growth. Emphasizing the strengths of both the person and the environment (the neighborhood, the family, friends, businesses, churches, interested individuals) can help elicit the capacities and contributions of people with mental illness as well as the community. Building on the goals and aspirations of clients, fundamental social work values are realized and respected.

Social workers are taught at an early stage in their careers to avoid judgmental attitudes toward those with whom they work. A complete and well-rounded perspective on the individual's unique situation and struggles is thought to enhance the ability to understand illogical and even destructive behavior. This holistic perspective should be adopted when assessing features of the social environment. The blocks from which we help fashion individuals' strengths may well be found in the community. For over six years, this model has been successfully used in work with the long-term mentally ill (Rapp and Wintersteen, 1985; see also chapters 5, 6, and 9). Incorporating this orientation more fully in social work practice and education would reap the potential benefit of tapping community possibilities in the amazing variety of settings and situations in which social workers practice, settings that now suffer from a dearth of "official" supports and resources.

REFERENCES

Addams, J. (1910). *Twenty years at Hull House*. New York: Macmillan.

Aviram, U. and Segal, S. (July, 1973). Exclusion of the mentally ill. *Archives of General Psychiatry, 29*, 126–131.

Brown, B. and Cain, H. (October, 1964). The many meanings of "comprehensive." *The American Journal of Orthopsychiatry, 34*(5).

Burgess, E. (1939). Introduction. In R. Faris and H. W. Dunham, eds., *Mental disorders in urban areas*. Chicago: University of Chicago Press.

Commission on Social Work Practice, Subcommittee on the Working Definition of Social Work Practice, National Association of Social Workers. (April, 1958). Working definition of social work practice. In H. Bartlett, Toward clarification and improvement of social work practice. *Social Work, 3*, 5–9.

Faris, R. and Dunham, H. W. (1939). *Mental disorders in urban areas*. Chicago: University of Chicago Press.

Foley, H. and Sharfstein, S. S. (1983). *Madness and government*. Washington, DC: American Psychiatric Press.

Germain, C. and Gitterman, A. (1980). *The life model of social work practice*. New York: Columbia University Press.

Greenblatt, M., York, R., and Brown, E. L. (1955). *From custodial to therapeutic patient care in mental hospitals*. New York: Russell Sage Foundation.

Hepworth, D. and Larsen, J. A. (1986). *Direct social work practice*. Chicago: Dorsey Press.

Hersch, C. (August, 1972). Social history, mental health, and community control. *American Psychologist, 27*, 749–754.

Joint Commission on Mental Health. (1961). *Action for mental health*. New York: Science Editions.

Klein, M. and Kantor, H. (1976). *Prisoners of progress*. New York: Macmillan.

Klerman, G. L. (1977). Better but not well: Social and ethical issues in the deinstitutionalizations of the mentally ill. *Schizophrenia Bulletin, 3,* 617–631.

Lamb, R., ed. (1984). *The homeless mentally ill.* Washington: American Psychiatric Press.

Park, R. (1952). *Human communities.* Glencoe, IL: Free Press.

Rapp, C. and Chamberlain, R. (September–October, 1985). Case management services for the chronically mentally ill. *Social Work, 30,* 417–422.

Rapp, C. and Wintersteen, R. (1985). *Case management with the chronically mentally ill: The results of seven replications* (unpublished monograph). Lawrence: University of Kansas School of Social Welfare.

Reich, R. and Siegel, S. (1978). The emergence of the Bowery as a psychiatric dumping ground. *Psychiatric Quarterly, 50,* 191–201.

Richmond, M. (1917). *Social diagnosis.* New York: Russell Sage Foundation.

Richmond, M. (1922). *What is social casework?* New York: Russell Sage Foundation.

Robinson, V. (1934). *A changing psychology in social casework.* Chapel Hill, NC: University of North Carolina Press.

Rothman, D. (1971). *The discovery of the asylum.* Boston: Little, Brown.

Segal, S., Baumohl, J., and Johnson, E. (1977). Falling through the cracks: Mental disorder and social margin in a young vagrant population. *Social Problems, 24,* 387–400.

Singer, H. D. (1939). Forward. In R. Faris and H. W. Dunham, eds., *Mental disorders in urban areas.* Chicago: University of Chicago Press.

Talbott, J., ed. (1981). *The chronic mentally ill.* New York: Human Services Press.

Talbott, J. (March, 1984). Commentary. *Hospital and Community Psychiatry, 35,* 209.

Treffert, D. (1985). The obviously ill patient in need of treatment: A fourth standard for civil commitment. *Hospital and Community Psychiatry, 36,* 259–267.

Wirth, L. (1964). *On cities and social life,* selected papers edited by A. Reiss. Chicago: University of Chicago Press.

CHAPTER 13

Social Work Research and the Empowerment Paradigm

Gary E. Holmes

The idea of empowerment as the emerging paradigm in social work and other human service fields presents some perplexing challenges and interesting opportunities for researchers. Empowerment requires new thinking about old problems. Empowerment invites us to see the world differently as it abandons the limits and distortions of the pathology model and focuses on human strengths and abilities as the proper starting point for social work practice. Empowerment requires that human service resources be tailored to individuals in such a way that those receiving help have the opportunity to experience personal power leading to change.

The empowerment paradigm demands as well that we reconsider some of the basic notions of how we plan and conduct social work research. The empowerment agenda requires researchers to enter into a new kind of relationship with practitioners and clients, a relationship that fosters and supports individual and collective development. This chapter addresses some of the issues, possibilities, and requirements of conducting social work research to empower people. At the least, an empowerment paradigm signifies that social work chooses to practice its profession in a way that allows humans to be the authors of change in their own lives.

RESEARCH THAT EMPOWERS

The idea that social work research should be empowering is a natural extension of basic social work values. With a genuine shift toward empowering those who are the ultimate consumers of social workers' efforts, these values may be more uniformly and confidently expressed. If research is to contribute something of worth, it, too, must be

Copyright ©1992 by Longman Publishing Group.

guided by an empowerment ideology. The purpose of research is to provide conceptual tools, action guidelines (Rosen, 1978, p. 440), and useful information, not just for professionals, but for their clients. Roszak (1980) observed that there are styles of knowledge as well as bodies of knowledge. He commented that in addition to what we know, there is the issue of how we know it—"how wisely, how gracefully, how life-enhancingly" (p. 309).

Part of the problem of how we know things and what we know is normal or conventional science's general reluctance to allow human participation in inquiry and knowledge-building. Empowerment research not only allows for participation by subjects, but relies upon and solicits it. Giddens (1984) claimed that to describe human behavior in a valid way demands that those doing the describing be able to participate in the forms of life constituted by the behavior. It is important, too, that those being described participate in the development of research questions and designs. Researchers in sociology and anthropology have been similarly cautioned in the past that they must deal with actual humans living in real environments if they hope to understand social phenomena (Girvetz et al., 1966). The same holds true for social work.

How should empowerment research be planned and conducted to avoid the pitfalls of the empiricist-pathology model while exploring "real" environments? More precisely, what is empowerment research, and how do we go about doing it? As a starting point, some basic characteristics can be identified that give empowerment research its flavor. The following statements reflect some of the assumptions and goals of empowerment research:

- Empowerment research is defined as inquiry that contributes to knowledge while empowering people, helping give them voice and tools to pursue and develop their agendas (Rappaport, 1990).
- Methods and designs used to gather data should never subvert the empowerment of people.
- The problems, solutions, needs, and aspirations that research attempts to understand should be framed in terms defined by the group under study.
- The traditional values of social work and the empowerment agenda should guide research design; methods reflect values. Researchers have a greater obligation to client empowerment than to traditional social science values.
- Research questions and designs should be proactive so that information derived from them will be of positive use and benefit to the group under study.
- The population under study should be collaborators and stakeholders in the research project. Research design should encourage those under study to participate in knowing and in knowledge-building.
- Research design should reflect the recognition that those under study have authority over their own lives and possess abilities to express that authority in some way—that they have strengths. Research should focus on eliciting, understanding, and developing these strengths; on how these individuals and groups have surmounted difficulties and coped.

- Research design should accept social phenomena as they are without trying to simplify them.
- Research design should not create artificial encounters and environments from which to gather data.
- Research design should build a body of knowledge of human creativity and wellness; knowledge emerging from the design should foster development and growth.
- Research should be planned and conducted in such a way that those under study can perceive that empowerment is the goal of the research.

Research is a cooperative enterprise toward recognizing and developing individual and community strengths and resources. It does not seek to create new and perhaps invasive technologies with which to intervene in the lives of others. The focus on situation-specific social terrains helps the researcher understand the settings in which strengths and resources exist (or might exist) and how they are defined and used by those under study. This understanding, in turn, gives meaning to how power might be applied constructively for personal or community growth. The focus on situational variety allows us to appreciate more clearly and understand the realities and possibilities in individual choice, responsibility, and strengths. The goal is to understand how those under study might or do express power in their own social world as we help them understand their situations and abilities as strengths instead of as pathologies, as possibilities instead of as limitations.

Science is a model and methodology whose purpose is to enable the user to better handle the complexity of life (Hall, 1981). Yet normal science has not done well in addressing the complexity of interconnectedness in "real worlds" where variables are not so easily quantified (Sutherland, 1974). To conduct social work research in complex social environs, researchers must first accept the fact that the complexities are enduring and cannot be oversimplified. Research, then, is to be conducted in natural settings. (Wicker, 1985).

In the traditional research paradigm, that scientific objectivity itself was a subjective construct was usually ignored. Research dedicated to empowerment views objectivity and detachment as illusory. The researcher goes about the task of exploring and becoming immersed in natural settings of peoples' lives, and does not pretend to be anything other than a human being trying to understand and participate in the human world.

The researcher's interpretation of behavior in the social world can be checked against the interpretations of consumers only if he or she becomes a participant and a collaborator, and ceases to be a mere observer (Schutz, 1967). From the perspective of traditional science, the researcher entering into an actual social encounter as a participant is no longer an impartial, objective observer and, therefore, no longer a scientist. In empowerment research, the "realness" of objectivity is less important than the act of gaining, sharing, and developing information through authentic social encounters. The illusion of objectivity in the past required that researchers observe without any emotion or participation. This produced encounters that, at best, possessed an artificial quality and, at worst, separated the researcher from the real concerns, hopes, and possibilities of those under study. In real life, there is no separation between knowing and action (Goldstein, 1986); empowerment research helps to instigate action in the social world as a way of increasing knowing.

The empowerment paradigm embraces holism. Holistic healing depends on, among other things, human consciousness and will (Otto and Knight, 1979). Medical researchers are beginning to understand the intricate connections between mind, body, and environment (Rossi, 1986), an understanding quite outside the historical acceptance of the dualism of mind and body. Human consciousness is always extant in the social world; authentic and healing encounters among researchers and people being studied begin with an appreciation of how people understand, conceive of, and experience their world. For empowerment research, the social world is forever grounded in human consciousness and the understanding of any particular consciousness is grounded in human participation.

The need to understand people from their own frame of reference (Taylor and Bogdan, 1984), then, is a driving force in social work empowerment research. Usually, much of the dynamic, artful, and concerted quality of everyday life goes unnoticed until it is purposely encountered and made visible (Garfinkel, 1967). The language and discourse of everyday life are composed of feelings, attitudes, beliefs, personal identities, moods, rituals, and stories (Hickerson, 1980). The understanding of such things is of value to social workers and researchers. The focus on natural settings or authentic encounters provides data about the depth of interrelatedness of individuals in the social world. Even when research has to be confined to the study of small groups in their natural environs, the members' experiences may point to patterns that exist in a wider human sphere (Seamon, 1979).

Past research on, and handling of, many social problems has often encouraged researchers and practitioners alike to divide human beings into distinct categories according to their diagnosed life problems so that specialized interventions could be designed; social programs thus depended for continuation on large populations of "deviants" (Watzlawick, Weakland, and Fisch, 1974). Examination of problems in the natural setting of day-to-day life helps counter this empiricist and bureaucratic practice by giving understanding to the nonpathological character of most social existence, and the synergistic character of most problems. Thus, empowerment presupposes that knowledge will be put to good use in day-to-day living by the stakeholders in the research. Because the researcher participates and collaborates, many of the pitfalls of traditional research are avoided.

METHODS OF INQUIRY

Beyond the need for examination of natural settings, empowerment research must also address issues related to methods of inquiry. Researchers need to identify existing tools and develop new ones with which to gain the sort of knowledge needed to help empower people served by social workers. Heineman Pieper (1985) has argued that social work researchers should use any and all methods of research that might shed light on those things that interest the profession. Although empowerment research is more concerned with outcomes than with methodologies, it can make use of a variety of research methods.

Among the methods available are the same quantitative methods used so often in articulating the pathology model. However, empowerment research uses them differently; not as singular preemptive approaches but as appropriate methods for counting and correlating discrete events of certain kinds.

However, qualitative methods may be more useful to empowerment research. Focus groups, for example, may help the researcher understand social phenomena by providing an arena in which firsthand reports of experiences are shared, examined, and understood (Morgan, 1988; Seamon, 1979). Additionally, the in-depth interview can bring into focus the complex experiences of single individuals (McCracken, 1988). Similarly, participant observation puts the researcher directly (and authentically) into the flow of interaction. From this the researcher's questions and concerns develop as they reflect the reality defined by subjects (Taylor and Bogdan, 1984).

These methods require personal interaction between the researcher and those whose lives and experiences are being studied. This interaction helps make the research encounter authentic (open to and reflective of the subjects' orientations) and helps prevent those under study from feeling a sharp separation and inequality between themselves and the "expert" researcher. Thus, research takes on a quality of mutuality in which information and concerns are shared and evaluated among people. Saleebey (1989) suggested that social work abandon the tools of scientific rationalism in favor of helping clients find languages, images, and the faith to reframe problems to enhance the process of dialogue between people and their life situations, and assist in generating real solutions to everyday problems. Each of these can arise from research grounded in everyday experiences, ordinary language, authentic encounters, and genuine collaboration.

Rappaport (1990) has argued that empowerment research tied to a strengths perspective emphasizes description, multiple perspectives, and authentication of voices that are too often ignored. Much traditional research began and ended with preconceived notions about people and their lives. So Rappaport's ignored voices belong to those who were studied as subjects of science, but who had no active way of participating in knowledge-building. Their knowledge was subjugated by that of the research enterprise. Qualitative methods are an attempt to correct this subversion of subjects' reality.

The philosophical connection between phenomenology and qualitative methodology is strong, and is important to empowerment research because the qualitative methods based on phenomenological appreciation allow the researcher to explore people in their social worlds as they are, without first having to reduce the complexity and richness of daily life. As a way of understanding the world, these methods examine the qualities of life which are not accessible through traditional science.

Phenomenology, itself a method of inquiry, is opposed to simplification and reductionism (Spiegelberg, 1982) and trusts description over explanation because the latter always leads to simplification (Ricoeur, 1966). Phenomenology is a critical "science" in that it is skeptical of all "facts" before they are themselves explored (Husserl, 1962). This skepticism includes a distrust for a priori theories because they attempt to organize the empirical context beforehand (Seamon, 1982). Finally, many phenomenologists are suspicious of social science laws because such laws may be nothing more than reflections of the perspective and preferences of the historical epoch in which they were formulated (Schutz, 1967).

Empowerment research, with its link to phenomenology, attempts to dispense with preconceived notions, however difficult that may be. Theory or conclusions follow from the authentic accounts and interactions of the individuals studied, as well as from their concerns and aspirations. Empowerment research takes its understanding of the world from those who live in it. Thus, a major step of empowerment research in social work is to free those under study from preemptive and prior categories, destinies, or limiting hypotheses and theories. Research methods do not interfere with life, but help articulate it and conceive of its possibilities.

Many research questions in the past had meaning only within the context of a particular theoretical approach. Research of this type did not answer the fundamental questions of those being studied (Mahrer, 1978). Empowerment research that is successful in avoiding preconceived notions avoids this epistemological error by asking fundamental questions as voiced by those under study.

THE LANGUAGE OF RESEARCH

There is a strong connection between linguistic taxonomies and world view. The products of research typically create a lexicon that is often adopted as "reality" by those who use it, including social workers and their clients. Language perpetuates world views (Bruner, 1973) in a manner that encourages words, phrases, and metaphors to be understood as reality. Ideas from various social science disciplines have often come to social work in the form of metaphors that shape perceptions about groups of people that may be inimical and negative. If such metaphors go unexamined, they become part of social work lore and, in the end, may actually interfere with the process of empowerment in social work practice.

Many of the terms of the pathology model are based on a metaphor that suggests the somatic conditions treated by physicians (Church, 1961). The language of pathology has reinforced the notion that the cause of the illness must be identified before a solution (cure) can be possible (Weick et al., 1989). Such language may encourage social workers to become preoccupied with finding causality (assessment/diagnosis) at the expense of ignoring the effect of people's life struggles and transitions. The language of pathology may seem benign and even helpful while camouflaging the idea that identifying or labeling causation somehow is the same as or as good as providing a solution. It is research, of course, that is thought to be the method for discerning cause and devising treatment.

Kuhn (1979) suggests that one field borrows discoveries from other fields only to the extent that a discovery applies to the borrower's tasks. Unfortunately, what is borrowed as "fact" from one discipline may be applied in a different field in which it is meaningless because of different contexts, and because the values or assumptions supporting the fact conflict with those of the borrower.

As Haworth (1984) pointed out, social sciences have generally borrowed scientific assumptions naively and have held them tenaciously. When a metaphor is applied as if it were a kind of neutral scientific knowledge, it can hide an agenda for researchers and practitioners so deeply embedded within the language that it is not recognized. A central task of empowerment research is to help clarify the meaning and assumptions of such language so that clients do not suffer from the impact of limiting metaphors and from treatment methods arising from them, or from oppressive research designs meant to articulate the metaphor or theory. It is likewise important for empowerment research to understand and affirm folk wisdom.

Another problem of language that researchers and practitioners must deal with is that communication aimed at helping, derived from research, has often become an instrument of social control. Such communication has been called *discourse technology* and seeks to invade or colonize everyday life through bureaucratic control (Fairclough, 1989, p. 211). This brand of discourse is funded by unexamined metaphoric language that hides bureaucratic goals behind the guise of clinical explanation. Such language places institutional goals above client empowerment by defining "official" client goals and the methods of reaching them independent of the client's immediate life context.

BACK TO THE SOCIAL WORLD

For empowerment research to break with the pathology model and to revise and extend traditional research, it must focus its attention upon the many social worlds where different understandings of life and possibility abound. In the old paradigm, empowerment typically meant power over someone else (Emerson, 1970). Often the power was resident in oppressive technologies or alien languages. In contrast, empowerment in our sense is an orientation to the daily lives of groups of people; Keiffer (1984, p. 31), for example, called such empowerment "participatory competence." This competence allows for personal creativity to spark growth and change in the individual and community's daily round of life as the participants live it. It is also based on individuals coming to understand the sources of their oppression.

Empowerment research in social work attempts to identify sources and varieties of, and the means to extend, participatory competence. Romanyshyn (1982) argued that human psychological life is characterized not by fact but by story. Stories are autobiographical "I" narratives of personal meaning (Goldstein, 1986, p. 355). As Sacks (1987) expressed it, "We have, each of us, a life-story, an inner narrative—whose continuity, whose sense, *is* our lives" (p. 110). Life stories are vital to social work's understanding of how the individual perceives his or her life condition in relation to having or not having power to act. Ideally, the social work encounter and social work research help client groups understand their own strengths and potentials to alter or embellish definitions of life as lived. And as life is lived, we can assist client groups to redefine their experience of the world, to act within it from a position of greater human potential and power.

The potential for change and new directions within personal stories helps create individualized, localized hypotheses about human behavior and strengths. Empowerment research makes use of what Saleebey (in press) borrowing from Gergen (1981) describes as generative theories—theories that are valued to the degree that they provide the means for individual and collective liberation. This liberation can best be understood as opportunities for transformation. Although normal science has not generally recognized it, all of us have transformed ourselves countless times without medicine, therapy, invasive theories, or social services. Giving legitimacy and spark to this power to heal, grow, and change is the essence of the empowerment paradigm. Research in support of empowerment can gather data on these neglected topics to help social workers and clients alike discover new dimensions and potentialities in everyday living, everyday discourse, and everyday striving. The empowerment agenda recognizes the life narrative given by the client, in part, as a self-assessment of strengths, resources, and power. The act of telling the story to the social worker who validates its authenticity may be the first step in refurbishing or refining the story so it can be more generative.

A key source of empowerment in the social world is the social worker–client relationship. Perlman (1979) stated that relationships depend on caring, interest, attention, and concern. This investing of the self by the worker and the client signifies a commitment to one another to explore collaboratively the possibilities of liberation. Researchers should have a great interest in this relationship because it is the moment in which social work empowers or fails to empower. As the social worker and the client come together, each has an opportunity to discover aspects of the self and the situation, and to assist the other in better understanding inherent potential. In the process of sharing, the personal story may be transformed into a mutually crafted narrative of the client and the social worker, one which may hold more promise for empowerment. Research into this process would focus on the ways in which the social worker and the client can create new ways of being, doing, and telling that did not exist prior to the encounter. This kind of relationship might guide researcher–subject interactions as well.

Advocacy through empowerment is not limited to extending political and social power, but, as mentioned earlier, is also aimed at helping the individual understand and appreciate himself or herself in a more holistic sense. Empowerment as advocacy attempts to restore the integration of inner and outer worlds of experience by offering the client the opportunity to develop participatory competencies in every area of life. In this way, empowerment augments the individual's attempt to engender and participate in a human community in which he or she can express, act, and live personal power. The social worker participates in this creation by fostering the search for personal and communal power. Because of the interrelatedness between the client and the social world, the act of searching for power is the first act in producing it.

CONCLUSION

The empowerment paradigm promises to bring social work research and practice back together; their tasks will be similar. In this chapter the social world has been described as complex. That complexity is what researchers must understand so that social workers can offer their clients a more humane opportunity for growth and change.

The empowerment paradigm offers social work the opportunity to put to use its core values without needing to make excuses for their lack of scientific truth. Social work practice requires skill, caring, courage, collaboration, and authenticity (Konle,

1982). So does research. These are not scientific constructs, but human aspirations and qualities. Once practitioners, researchers, and clients understand their common goals, empowerment will be the mainstay of the social work profession—practice, research, and education.

There is, of course, much to be done to bring about that understanding. Each concept, idea, and metaphor currently used by social workers must be examined for its potential to empower clients. When social work first adopted the scientific method, the implications were not examined closely. Such a mistake should not be repeated. Social work now has the opportunity to work from an entirely different perspective and should not forgo the opportunity to scrutinize its own beliefs and methods, and those of any new approach—including the empowerment agenda.

Empowerment researchers should be committed to identifying methods of inquiry that are genuinely consistent with social work values and practice principles. They can also call upon the perspectives of practitioners and clients to examine the intricate workings of the person-in-environment as a creative and ever-changing enterprise. The strength and genuineness of the relationship among researchers, social workers, and clients will determine the fate of a profession dedicated to positive empowerment. As a cooperative effort aimed at transformations in individuals and communities, the relationship figures prominently in helping construct a more humane community at the point of the social work encounter. To again use the words of Roszak (1980), researchers must know what they know "wisely, gracefully, and life-enhancingly," (p. 309) for then others can know it in the same fashion. By empowering people in need, social work will invest itself in the future of human beings, a commitment of professional energies and beliefs that will never become obsolete.

REFERENCES

Bruner, J. S. (1973). *Beyond the information given: Studies in the psychology of knowing.* New York: W. W. Norton. Article by P. M. Greenfield and J. S. Bruner, Culture and cognitive growth. Reprinted from D. A. Goslin, ed., *Handbook of socialization theory and research* (pp. 633–654). Chicago: Rand McNally.

Church, J. (1961). *Language and the discovery of reality.* New York: Random House.

Emerson, R. M. (1970). Power-dependence relations. In M. E. Olsen, ed., *Power in societies,* pp. 44–53. New York: Macmillan.

Fairclough, N. (1989). *Language and power.* New York: Longman.

Garfinkel, H. (1967). *Studies in ethnomethodology.* Englewood Cliffs, NJ: Prentice-Hall.

Giddens, A. (1984). Hermeneutics and social theory. In G. Shapiro and A. Sica, eds., *Hermeneutics: Questions and prospects,* pp. 215–230. Amherst: University of Massachusetts Press. Reprinted from Giddens, A. (1983). *Profiles and critiques.* London: Macmillan.

Girvetz, H., Geiger, G., Hantz, H., and Morris, B. (1966). *Science, folklore, and philosophy.* New York: Harper & Row.

Goldstein, H. (1986). Toward the integration of theory and practice: A humanistic approach. *Social Work, 3,* 352–357.

Hall, E. T. (1981). *Beyond culture.* Garden City, NY: Anchor/Doubleday. Work originally published 1976.

Haworth, G. O. (September, 1984). Social work research, practice, and paradigms. *Social Service Review, 58,* 343–357.

Hickerson, N. P. (1980). *Linguistic anthropology.* New York: Holt, Rinehart and Winston.

Heineman Pieper, M. (1985). The future of social work research. *Social Work Research and Abstracts, 21*(4), 3–11.

Husserl, E. (1962). *Ideas: General introduction to pure phenomenology.* W. R. Boyce Gibson, trans. New York: Collier Macmillan. Originally published in 1931.

Keiffer, C. H. (1984). Citizen empowerment: A developmental perspective. *Prevention in Human Services, 3*(2/3), 9–36.

Konle, C. (1982). *Social work day-to-day.* New York: Longman.

Kuhn, T. S. (1979). The relations between history and history of science. In P. Rabinow and W. M. Sullivan, eds., *Interpretive social science: A reader,* pp. 267–300. Berkeley: University of California Press. Reprinted from *Daedalus, 100*(2), 1971.

McCracken, G. (1988). *The long interview* (Sage University Paper Series on Qualitative Research Methods, vol. 13). Beverly Hills: Sage.

Mahrer, A. R. (1978). *Experiencing: A humanistic theory of psychology and psychiatry.* New York: Brunner/Mazel.

Morgan, D. (1988). *Focus groups as qualitative research* (Sage University Paper Series on Qualitative Research Methods, vol. 16). Beverly Hills: Sage.

Otto, H. A. and Knight, J. W. (1979). Wholistic healing: Basic principles and concepts. In H. A. Otto and J. W. Knight, eds., *Dimensions in wholistic healing: New frontiers in the treatment of the whole person,* pp. 3–27. Chicago: Nelson-Hall.

Perlman, H. H. (1979). *Relationship: The heart of helping people.* Chicago: University of Chicago Press.

Rappaport, J. (1990). Research methods and the empowerment social agenda. In P. Tolan, C. Keys, F. Chertok, and L. Jason, eds., *Researching community psychology.* Washington, DC: American Psychological Association.

Ricouer, P. (1966). *Freedom and nature: The voluntary and the involuntary,* E. V. Kohak, trans. Evanston, IL: Northwestern University Press. Originally published in 1950.

Romanyshyn, R. D. (1982). *Psychological life: From science to metaphor.* Austin: University of Texas Press.

Rosen, A. (1978). Issues in educating for the knowledge-building research doctorate. *Social Service Review, 52,* 437–448.

Rossi, E. L. (1986). *The psychobiology of mind-body healing: New concepts of therapeutic hypnosis.* New York: W. W. Norton.

Roszak, T. (1980). The monster and the titan: Science, knowledge, and gnosis. In E. D. Klemke, R. Hollinger, and A. D. Kline, eds., *Introductory readings in the philosophy of science,* pp. 305–322. Buffalo, NY: Prometheus.

Sacks, O. (1987). *The man who mistook his wife for a hat and other clinical tales.* New York: Harper & Row.

Saleebey, D. (1989). The estrangement of knowing and doing: Professions in crisis. *Social Casework: The Journal of Contemporary Social Work, 70,* 556–563.

Saleebey, D. (in press). Theory and the generation and subversion of knowledge. *Journal of Sociology and Social Welfare.*

Schutz, A. (1967). *The phenomenology of the social world,* G. Walsh and F. Lehnert, trans. Evanston, IL: Northwestern University Press.

Seamon, D. (1979). *A geography of the lifeworld.* London: Croom Helm.

Seamon, D. (1982). The phenomenological contribution to environmental psychology. *Journal of Environmental Psychology, 2,* 119–140.

Seamon, D. and Mugerauer, R. (1985). Dwelling, place and environment: An introduction. In D. Seamon and R. Mugerauer, eds., *Dwelling, place and environment: Towards a phenomenology of person and world,* pp. 1–12. The Hague: Martinus Nijhoff.

Spiegelberg, H. (1982). *The phenomenological movement: A historical introduction* (3rd ed.). The Hague: Martinus Nijhoff.

Sutherland, J. W. (Spring, 1974). Attacking organizational complexity. *Fields Within Fields, 11,* 52–65.

Taylor, S. J. and Bogdan, R. (1984). *Introduction to qualitative research methods: The search for meanings* (2nd ed.). New York: John Wiley & Sons.

Watzlawick, P., Weakland, J., and Fisch, R. (1974). *Change: Principles of problem formation and problem resolution.* New York: W. W. Norton.

Weick, A., Rapp, C., Sullivan, W. P., and Kisthardt, W. (July, 1989). A strengths perspective for social work practice. *Social Work, 34,* 350–354.

Wicker, A. W. (1985). Strategies for expanding conceptual frameworks. *American Psychologist, 40,* 1094–1103.

CHAPTER **14**

Conclusion:
Possibilities of and Problems with the Strengths Perspective

Dennis Saleebey

Focusing and building on client strengths is not only a counterweight to the prevalent deficit model. It is an imperative of the several values that govern our work and the operations of a democratic and pluralistic society including distributive justice, equality, respect for the dignity of the individual, and the search for maximum autonomy within maximum community.

Justice and equality in Walzer's (1983) view are not the quest for the elimination of differences, but rather the elimination of certain kinds of differences—those defined or created by people in power that are the crux of domination of their fellows, whether the differences be couched in the language of race, gender, religion, sexual orientation, or class. As he says,

> It's not the fact that there are rich and poor that generates egalitarian struggle but the fact that the rich grind the faces of the poor. It's always what one group with power does to another group—whether in the name of health, safety, security—it makes no difference. The aim, ultimately, of the fight for equality is always the elimination of subordination . . . no more toadying, scraping and bowing, fearful trembling (p. xiii).

For us, the message is that many models of helping have become pillars of inequality in the sense outlined above. They have evolved into means of domination through identity-stripping, culture-killing, status degradation, base rhetoric, and sequestering. We dominate under the banner of good, welfare, service, helping (or control and socialization). What we finally have done, by emphasizing and giving social status to a person's deficiencies, differences, and defects, is rob individuals of their inherent powers, or at least steal from them the courage, presumption, and opportunity to use those powers. In a sense, we have impoverished, not empowered. If we believe that people (indi-

---

Copyright © 1992 by Longman Publishing Group.

vidually and together) do have an array of personal strengths and powers—cognitive, intentional, behavioral, political—then we might also believe that the root act of oppression is to deny them awareness of these, to subvert them by failing to provide the opportunities to develop them, or to rename them in the language of calumny and aspersion.

Social justice, too, is related to domination; domination of the distribution of social goods—those resources essential for survival, for growth, for development and transformation—whether we talk of welfare, communal support, security, commodities, goods, health, or education. These goods are an important source of identity and being. Walzer (1983) quotes William James, who said that the "line between me and mine is very hard to draw" (p. 8). The pursuit of justice is a march toward systems of definition and distribution of those social goods that underlie the possibility of becoming as human and competent as possible. The social welfare enterprise is obviously the way that we most clearly see the attempt to achieve distributive justice and, therefore, a modicum of equality. A more just distributive system is at the heart of the development and expression of individual powers and strengths. As social workers, we confront the idea of strengths at two very different levels—policy (philosophy) and practice (principles)—but they always find their intersection in, say, the client sitting with us.

In the 1960s we talked of "power to the people," and that had several shadings of meaning, not the least of which seemed to be that a government or a social movement must dedicate itself to returning social, economic, political, and material goods to the people who had been systematically denied them. As people thought about it, this raised nettlesome questions. What, in fact, do we need? What are we entitled to? On what basis shall these goods be distributed? When the ardor of the '60s was stanched in 1973–1974, these questions still had not been answered.

Related to these questions was the suspicion or firm belief that these resources, whether knowledge, health, shelter, money, etc., had some relevance for becoming optimally human. Now an increasing sense that these resources must be provided in the marketplace dominates our collective consciousness. The obvious but often ignored trouble with such a view is that the marketplace can, at best, provide only limited resources, often on a quite selective basis. A related issue is that the marketplace is no venue for the pursuit of justice, equity, or recompense. Unless it might sell beans, philosophic assertions about the roots of democracy are anathema to selling for profit.

One would think, judging by all the books, talk shows, articles, workshops, etc., about developing the self in any number of ways, that the marketplace distribution of social goods has been an enormous success. I think, rather, that the caravan of pop psychology nostrums indicates that we have failed through normal socializing institutions and processes to help many individuals develop a sense of autonomy and personal power; failed to assist neighborhoods, communities, and cultures to retain their sense of uniqueness and value. We have, as Russell Jacoby (1975) says, become seconds in the fire sale of life, homogenized role players performing dutifully but suffering viscerally—an outcome much appreciated by the key players in marketplace stratagems.

So far the aspirations of the '60s, and their current disappointments or manifestations, seem pretty much what we are about. But we have argued in this book for a subtle change in the basic equation between equality, justice, and autonomy, and that is that there is power in the people. No matter how subordinated, no matter how lacking in sufficient social resources, people have found some nourishment for their identity somewhere. It frequently may be suppressed or distorted, but however unspoken, it is there awaiting expression. When we talk of building on client strengths, of respecting people's accounts of their lives, of revering a people's culture, of hearing out an individual's narratives and stories, we are, in a sense, giving testimony that, in spite of injustice and inequity, people do have prospects. People show a kind of resilience and vitality that, even though it may lie dormant or assume other guises, is inward. Not that the quest for the distribution of social resources should end, but that we do not have to wait for the millennium in order to do this work.

SOME QUESTIONS ABOUT THE STRENGTHS PERSPECTIVE

Why is it that people do not look as though they have strengths? Why do they seem beaten, angry, depressed, rebellious? Dominated people are often alienated people; that is, they are separated from their inner resources, their consciousness, their bodies, and their history and traditions. The essential self has been betrayed, and the betrayal has become incorporated in their orientation to the world, a self that has become an artifact of a society grown heavy with dominative relationships. One of the key symptoms of alienation is identifying with the oppressors. It assumes many forms, but is, regrettably, common (Freire, 1973). What the oppressor defines as the reality of that person, that group, is so powerful that "to be," as Freire (1973) says, becomes "to be like" and "to be like" means "to be like the oppressor" or to be what the oppressor says I am.

A second reason that clients, the vulnerable populations we have talked about, look less than strong and no more than deviant is that the building blocks of anyone's identity are ultimately words, images, phrases, symbols that can stunt, thwart, defame, sicken, and enrage or encourage, elevate, inspire, and strengthen. The human service professions generally have extensively developed a language that sickens and does not heal. Joel Kovel (1981), one of the few "radical" psychoanalysts in this country, says that the mental health enterprise turns on the administration of people's minds and the bureaucratization of their health; both depend on the power to define. The more specific the definition, the more the true inner experience and capacities of individuals becomes lost to them—and to the definers. Consider, he says, hyperactivity (ADHD), a disorder manifested by the fact that kids move around too much—too much, that is, for school authorities. The child occupies the wrong kind of space in too little time, and is thus considered to have a disease. Once defined, the system can control and administer. And once defined, the child has the beginnings of a new identity so that ten years later he or she might be known and regard himself or herself as a hyperactive adult. And yet whether hyperactivity is a disease at all is a serious question (Kohn, 1989).

Isn't it terribly naive to assert and focus on client strengths when they clearly have problems? The strengths perspective does not require helper to blithely ignore a client's concerns, problems, illnesses, and conflicts. It demands, instead, that they be understood in a larger context of individual and communal resources and possibilities. At the least, the strengths perspective obligates workers to understand that, however downtrodden or sick, individuals have survived (and in some cases even thrived). They have taken steps, summoned up resources, and coped. We need to know what they have done, how they have done it, what they have learned from doing it, who was involved in doing it, what resources (inner and outer) were available in their struggle to surmount their troubles. People are always working on their situations, even if just deciding to be resigned to them; as helpers we must tap into that work, elucidate it, find and build on its possibilities. Maybe in some contexts, even resignation is a sign of strength. Who is to say until we are with the client in that moment?

More importantly, a perspective on client strengths may compel us to rethink the nature of problems. We make the most elemental semantic error when we mistake, for example, the label for the person: Richard Doe, in all his complexity and with his singular history, becomes a schizophrenic; Bobby Roe becomes a hyperactive child; and Mary Noe, a borderline. The application of such labels, taken to signify the individual, subjugates the individual's own experience of difficulties and obscures other dimensions of the individual. In addition, individuals always learn something and demonstrate capacities, often in a unique fashion, in coping with problems. That knowledge and that experience are essential materials out of which we help clients construct and reconstruct their situation, their efforts, and their systems of meaning. In Alcoholics Anonymous, it is understood that any individual's experience of alcoholism is, in some ways, unique; and telling the story of the particularity of that experience is important to the process of recovery. "Elpenor" (a pseudonym) (1986) says about the importance of talk and talk of the "spirit" in AA:

> . . . the AA stories told in the diction of suffering, the eloquence of shared experience, the rhetoric of hope against hope . . . it was then I began to see that the true spirit of these rooms is the spirit of human life; a thing godlike, perhaps, but not transcendent; not "high"; a thing altogether human. In AA we dry moist souls on the *logos,* the Word (p. 48).

It is well, then, to keep firmly in mind that labels bespeak the reality of an outsider (worker and agency), collectivize and abstract experience, and make the client's own understanding and experience seem alien. We must use labels judiciously if at all, and with a profound respect for their distortions and limitations, and with an equally profound respect for their capacity to "mortify" (Goffman, 1961) individuals, stripping them of their idiosyncratic identity (depersonalizing) and overwhelming them, through various rituals and social processes, with their new and alien identity.

How does practice from a strengths perspective change what professionals do? Both loudly and implicitly, many chapters herein have decried the medical model, the notion of the helper as crafty and cunning expert, the idea of the profession as applied technology. Are we, then, to surrender our status as experts, our esoteric and practical knowledge? While we might well want to reexamine the notion of expert, especially the implicit paternalism that it abets, we do have special knowledge and it would be foolish to deny that. However, it might be very important to critically analyze the assumptions, the consequences of the use of this knowledge, as well as its cultural, racial, class, and gender distortions and biases. It may be that a better characterization of professional knowing and doing can be found in the idea developed by Schön (1983), of the "reflective practitioner (see discussion in the Introduction). Subduing rigor in favor of elevating relevance in professional practice, Schön's description of the reflective practitioner not only highlights the considerable artistry of practice but leads, inevitably, to a different kind of contract between client and professional, one very much in keeping with the strengths orientation.

A reflective contract finds the practitioner with obvious and esoteric knowledge and real skills willing to share those with the client, but with the recognition that the professional is clearly not the only one in the situation with relevant knowledge. The professional also sees the work as a mutual quest in which she joins with the client in a search for solutions and possibilities. Both parties to the contract have control; in a sense, they are independent but mutually involved. The professional asks the client to judge the work that is done and revise its content and course as necessary. In any case, the core of the contract is in the establishment of a real connection to the client. In Schön's (1983) words:

> . . . the reflective practitioner's relation with his client takes the form of a literally reflective conversation. Here the professional recognizes that his technical expertise is embedded in a context of meanings. He attributes to his clients, as well as to himself, a capacity to mean, know, and plan. . . . He recognizes an obligation to make his own understandings accessible to his client, which means that he needs often to reflect anew on what he knows (p. 295).

So the nature of the contractual relationship, implicit and explicit, surely changes as the shift is made to a strengths approach to practice: a major shift is in the direction of power equalization.

How can practitioners work from a strengths vantage point when they are involved in an agency pervaded with the deficit model? We can hardly be at the business of empowering clients if we feel weak, defenseless, and alienated from our own work because of agency policies, philosophies, and prevailing attitudes that may subvert positive notions of client possibilities and aptitudes. Nevertheless, as Walsh (1987) argues, our values and commitments can save us, serve as a protective belt around our work. Clearly, an agency designed to serve social control functions, however subtly, or to ferret out and solve social problems, is likely to develop a negative atmosphere about clients who are apt to be seen as outsiders rife with problems and deficits. Beatrice Wright (1982) contends that:

> . . . preoccupation with the negative tends to lead counselors to underrate the abilities of clients. Clients are then perceived as less able and more dependent than they are or need to be. They will be devaluated, and their role as active, self-determining, or genuine participants in the treatment plan will be diminished (p. 232).

But do you need to succumb to the blandishments and seductions of such a view of clients? We think not. There is always choice. For example, you can choose how you will see, regard, and evaluate your client. You can take the time, make the effort to discover resources within your client and his environment. To do so, however, does require a lively commitment and belief in the possibilities of the client. You can also choose how you will interpret information and impressions you receive as well as deciding what kind of information you will seek. Wright (1982), in that regard, provides the following example:

> Imagine learning that James, an adolescent of fourteen, has spastic cerebral palsy, frequently relates to his siblings and peers aggressively, is two years below grade level in reading and arithmetic, and has parents who are rarely present in the home. Without proceeding further you are asked to form an impression of James. Now consider the difference in impression when one also learns that James does an outstanding job on his paper route, likes to write poetry and fantasy stories, has a close relationship with his uncle and aunt who live nearby, and is making steady progress in physical therapy (p. 233).

Values, then, guide personal choices and we can apply those values in personal and interpersonal circumstances as well as in the conditions of our professional work with clients and colleagues.

How can I and why should I give up the disease or deficit model of the human condition when it is so acceptable and widespread in culture, generally, and the culture of helping, in particular? You can give up the disease (pathology, deficit) model by examining it critically, and examining the consequences of its employment. The disease model has reigned in many fields (mental health, for example) at least since the 1920s and, in many cases, far earlier than that, but it has produced very little in the way of positive results. By almost any measure, the problems we have confronted with the disease model and its various methodologies remain rampant and poorly understood, except at the most general level (Peele, 1989). The disease model has reproduced itself over and over again in many different arenas so that, in spite of failures in treating common human frailties and conditions, more and more human behavior patterns, life transitions, and life dilemmas are regarded as diseases—from extremist thought (right and left) to self-doubt, from persistent sexual activity to adolescence.

Stanton Peele (1989), long an opponent of metaphorically turning complex and often common human behaviors and relationships and experiences into diseases, maintains:

> The pseudomedical inventions and treatments of new diseases increasingly *determine* our feelings, our self-concepts, and our world-views. Our emotional and behavioral diseases define our culture and who we are—this is the diseasing of America . . . the promotion of these new diseases—as well as being ungrounded scientifically and worse than useless therapeutically—holds out the possibility for a totalitarianism similar to but more insidious than the one George Orwell imagined would occur through political means in *1984* (p. 28).

The disease model should be surrendered because, at the least, it discourages two facets of good social work practice:

- Searching the environment for forces that enhance or oppress human possibilities and life chances,

- Emphasizing client self-determination, responsibility, and possibility so cherished in the rhetoric of social work practice.

And certainly we would argue that the disease model obliterates the nascent and emerging emphasis on client strengths.

The disease model, in the end, undercuts in the broadest and deepest way the possibility of personal autonomy and community responsibility by sparing no human behavior from the lash of disease, no group of human beings from the rack of illness (frequently hidden or unknown to the "victim"). Adult Children of Alcoholics and its progeny, the co-dependence movement, are examples. Not to belittle the pain and confusion that children growing up with an alcoholic parent must contend with, but to extend this to all adult children of alcoholics and adult children of parents with other problems is unwarranted and in the end may obscure the idea that people do gain knowledge and develop resilience and strength in coping with difficult and traumatizing situations. The first things I want to know about someone going through or having gone through this maelstrom of betrayal, pain, and unpredictability are how they did it, what they learned, what worked for them and why, how they used that knowledge, what they thought they demonstrated about their own resourcefulness as they tried to cope, where they found succor in the environment, and what they learned from, and appreciated about, their alcoholic parents.

There are diseases, to be sure, and we may find others as our internal and external environments change. But not every departure from a narrow conception of acceptable or "healthy" human behaviors is a disease, nor must it be treated. And, even if we do concede the reality of an illness, that does not absolve us from finding the resources within that person, her environment, and relationships, and assisting her in capitalizing on those in living through the disease and improving the quality of her life.

There must be many more questions about the strengths perspective as it has unfolded in this book, but we think these are the central ones.

THE FUTURE OF THE STRENGTHS PERSPECTIVE

This is a perspective aborning. Much remains to be done to fill out, correct, revise, and evaluate it. More than just another untested "theory of intervention," the strengths approach is a patchwork of value commitments, philosophical obligations, practice principles, and critiques of the conventional wisdom about the nature of professional knowing and doing generally and social work helping specifically. This perspective encourages us to reexamine and reshape the way we do research, the way we teach our students, the way we relate to colleagues, the way we define our roles and responsibilities in social service agencies and bureaucracies, and the way we help our clients.

It took decades for the disease/deficit model to take hold and its ultimate supremacy was as much a political, social, and economic phenomenon as it was a result of scientific demonstrations of its utility. There is a sense among people from a variety of disciplines and professions that we are undergoing something like a fundamental shift in the way we understand and relate to our world (Rifkin, 1985; Capra, 1983; Dossey, 1989; Ornstein and Sobel, 1987; Berman, 1981). These changes are not uniform, nor are they spawned from a single source or from a single place. But there do seem to be some themes that span all of these urges and shifts, themes which seem to have some consonance with elements of the strengths perspective. To put it another way, the strengths perspective (or something like it) is unlikely to become stronger unless it does so in league with other perspectives, and within the context of larger cultural changes.

Themes for the Future

The strengths orientation, as we have emphasized, is not a unitary approach. But it does have some consistent themes inherent in its agenda, and, to an extent, shares these with stirrings in other segments of society. What follows is a brief speculation on some of the themes.

Holism and Healing.   In medicine, barely begun, but promising of a revolution, is a recasting of the medical model along more holistic lines. That is, the health or wellness of the body is understood as depending on the interaction of a number of factors, perhaps different for different individuals. These factors include (and all interacting in some way together) emotions, thinking and beliefs, relationships, elements of the physical environment, sociocultural factors, and spiritual orientations. There simply is no single factor that causes (or cures) any disease (Cousins, 1989; Capra, 1983). Any individual is embedded in a complex and elegant web of relationships and objects and can only be understood as a part of the dynamics of the relationships between these factors, internal and external.

It is also clearer now that our beliefs, our stories and myths, our interpretations of our situation influence how we respond. Evidence is mounting that positive expectations and beliefs in one's resilience and strength can, if not alter the course of a disease, definitely improve the quality of life during the illness (Cousins, 1989; Ornstein and Sobel, 1987). A strong will to live, the maintenance of control, and positive emotions can alter, for example, the functioning of the immune system.

So it is with the strengths perspective. We understand that the individual response is a product of the interaction of many events, people, experiences, symbols, and institutions. If we are to appreciate the individual, we must develop as clear an understanding of that as we can manage. As Pieper (1989) has suggested, where we draw the line between system (those things of interest) and environment (those things in the background) makes all the difference in the world in how we understand and assess a situation. We know now that drawing the line between the individual as system and everything else as environment or background leads, usually, to misunderstanding (or misdiagnosis) and, not infrequently, victim blaming (Sampson, 1983). The strengths perspective also subscribes to the belief that people have credible, though often untapped or unknown, resources for transformation and development. Knowing this (or believing it) allows us to help the individual (or neighborhood) create positive, realistic expectations about outcome.

Participation.   In realms as different as physics and medicine, the importance and effect of participation is becoming well known, if not completely understood (Capra, 1983). The eminent physicist John Wheeler (1973) describes the effect of the researcher of the subatomic world as participant in this way:

Nothing is more important to the quantum principle than this, that it destroys the concept of the world as "sitting out there," with the observer safely separated from it by a 20-centimeter slab of glass. Even to observe so minuscule an object as an electron, he must shatter the glass. He must reach in. He must install his chosen measuring equipment. It is up to him to decide whether he shall measure position or momentum. . . . The measurement changes the state of the electron. The universe will never afterward be the same. To describe what has happened, one has to cross out that old word "observe" and put in its place the new word "participator" (p. 244).

In medicine, more physicians are coming to understand that in any effective treatment regimen the patient must be an active agent. The cure ultimately comes from within as the mind activates a variety of defense mobilizing hormones and other agents of the immune system. These are facilitated by events and people in the environment as well. But such an outcome is considerably less likely if the medical treatment is preemptive and paternalistic, involving the patient only as passive recipient (Dossey, 1989). In a sense, the individual is primary author of the cure or recovery; the medical staff are collaborators.

The strengths perspective is likewise respectful of the powers of participation in at least two ways. First, practice done from the standpoint of client strengths begins with the idea that, like the physicist, we become a part of the system of our interest (the client, family, group, neighborhood) and thus make it different. We must be very careful with that trust, if it is offered us. We cannot, however, be of help, or understand the system, unless we are in some visible way a part of it. Second, just as the physician can only mobilize the transformative powers within and only if the patient is in control, the social work practitioner can help only if the individual is an active participant in the helping process.

Process.   The idea of process is complicated and does have something of an honored place in some of the writing on social work practice (especially the idea of the helping relationship as process), but we mean here to contrast it with more static notions of change. Sometimes, we conceive of change in the old billiard-ball analogy: we do something and something happens or changes: A → B → C. But when we immerse ourselves in a complex situation with other individuals, we become part of an old dynamic and begin to set in motion a new one, one whose shapes and colors we will never completely know from moment to moment. That is, we cannot in any thorough way predict what it will be like as it unfolds. So it is with clients. When we involve ourselves with them—truly engage them and be a part of their world—we become a part of a process that requires of us continuing adjustments, responsiveness, and alertness. We might be able to impose on the process—especially as we reflect on it—some sense of order. And while that might be useful, it is not the process itself, but only our interpretation of it.

One way of highlighting these themes is to examine Rappaport's (1990) vision of the empowerment agenda as it applies to social science and social work research. The idea of empowerment, as discussed in this volume, is to help people gain (and regain) control and influence over the course of their daily lives, to tap into the inherent resources, knowledge, and interests they have, and to help them enhance those and develop other resources. In empowerment research, as in holistic healing, we understand that people do know things, have solved problems, and have survived difficult, even catastrophic events, and we want to know how they did it and with what supports so that those do not remain hidden and can be extended. The researcher seeks the abilities and skills inherent in the individuals, and seeks to clarify the contexts in which they can become even stronger. People, as we have said many times, often do not know the strengths they have (or do not define them as such). The empowerment research agenda suggests that we help authenticate the resources and transformative capacities that individuals and groups have—"give voice to the voiceless" (Rappaport, 1990).

But as important is the idea that those who are the concern of our research are active collaborators, participants, and stakeholders in the inquiry. As collaborators they have a say over the direction, methods, design, and use of the research. They are not passive subjects but active partners in the research that is done, and they should expect to derive real benefit, in everyday terms, from that research.

Finally, empowerment research recognizes that the contexts of experience are unique and constantly changing; that they are a product of social forces, institutions, and ideologies, but more importantly of the day-to-day perspectives, interpretations, and exchanges of the individuals in that context. For the empowerment researcher to genuinely understand the life and possibilities of the people, he or she must be "in process" with them, open to their perspectives and orientations, understanding how they construct and construe their daily round of life. So the researcher is obligated, for a time, to be immersed in that round of life.

CONCLUSION

The contributors to this volume—all of whom are practitioners as well as scholars and educators—hope that you find something of value here that can be translated for use with the individuals, families, and groups that you help. We all believe that the initiatory act in employing a strengths perspective is a commitment to its principles and underlying philosophy, a credo that, at many points, is at serious odds with the point of view we have labeled variously as the deficit, problem-focused, or pathology orientation. We firmly believe that, once committed, you will be surprised at the array of talents, skills, knowledge, and resources that you discover in your clients—even those whose prospects seem bleak—some of which they either were not aware of or did not define as a strength. That, in a nutshell, is the best rationale for embracing an orientation that appreciates and fosters the powers within and around clients.

REFERENCES

Berman, M. (1981). *The re-enchantment of the world.* Ithaca, NY: Cornell University Press.
Capra, F. (1983). *The turning point.* New York: Bantam Books.
Cousins, N. (1989). *Head first: The biology of hope.* New York: E. P. Dutton.
Dossey, L. (1989). *Recovering the soul: A scientific and spiritual search.* New York: Bantam Books.
"Elpenor." (October, 1986). A drunkard's progress: AA and the sobering strength of myth. *Harpers, 272,* 42–48.

Freire, P. (1973). *Pedagogy of the oppressed*. New York: Seabury.

Goffman, E. (1961). *Asylums*. New York: Doubleday/Anchor.

Jacoby, R. (1975). *Social amnesia: A critique of conformist psychology from Adler to Laing.* Boston: Beacon Press.

Kohn, A. (November, 1989). Suffer the restless children. *The Atlantic, 264,* 90–100.

Kovel, J. (1981). *The age of desire: Reflections of a radical psychoanalyst.* New York: Pantheon.

Ornstein, R. and Sobel, D. (1987). *The healing brain.* New York: Simon and Schuster/ Touchstone.

Peele, S. (1989). *The diseasing of America: Addiction treatment out of control.* Lexington, MA: Lexington/D. C. Heath.

Pieper, M. (November, 1989). The heuristic paradigm: A unifying and comprehensive approach to social work research. *Smith College Studies in Social Work, 60,* 9–33.

Rappaport, J. (1990). Research methods and the empowerment agenda. In P. Tolan, C. Keys, F. Chertak, and L. Jason, eds., *Researching community psychology*. Washington, DC: American Psychological Association.

Rifkin, J. (1985). *Declaration of a heretic.* London: Routledge and Kegan Paul.

Sampson, E. E. (1983). *Justice and the critique of pure psychology.* New York: Plenum.

Schön, D. (1983). *The reflective practitioner.* New York: Basic Books.

Walsh, J. A. (May, 1987). Burnout and values in the social service profession. *Social Casework, 68,* 279–283.

Walzer, M. (1983). *Spheres of justice.* New York: Basic Books.

Wheeler, J. (1973). Cited in J. Mehra, ed., *The physicists' conception of nature*, p. 244. Holland: D. Reidel.

Wright, B. and Fletcher, B. (April, 1982). Uncovering hidden resources: A challenge in assessment. *Professional Psychology, 13,* 229–235.

Bibliography

Abels, P. and Murphy, M. (1981). *Administration in the human services: A normative systems approach.* Englewood Cliffs, NJ: Prentice Hall.

Addams, J. (1909). *The spirit of youth and the city streets.* New York: Macmillan.

———— (1910). *Twenty years at Hull House.* New York: Macmillan.

———— (1954). *Twenty years at Hull House,* 16th ed. New York: Macmillan.

Alderfer, C. P. (1969). An empirical test of a new theory of human needs. *Organizational Behavior and Human Performance, 4,* 142–175.

Alinsky, S. (1972). *Rules for radicals.* New York: Vintage.

Allport, G. W. (1955). *Becoming.* New Haven: Yale University Press.

American Psychiatric Association. (1980). *Diagnostic and statistical manual of mental disorders* (3rd ed.). Washington, DC: American Psychiatric Association.

Aviram, U. and Segal, S. (July, 1973). Exclusion of the mentally ill. *Archives of General Psychiatry, 29,* 126–131.

Bandura, A. (1977). Self-efficacy: Toward a unifying theory of behavioral change. *Psychological Review, 84,* 191–215.

Barker, R. G. (1960). Ecology and motivation. In M. R. Jones, ed., *Nebraska symposium on motivation.* Lincoln: University of Nebraska Press.

Becker, E. (1964). *The revolution in psychiatry.* New York: Free Press.

———— (1968). *The structure of evil.* New York: George Braziller.

Becker, H. (1963). *Outsiders: Studies in the sociology of deviance.* New York: Free Press.

Beisser, A. (1990). *Flying without wings: Personal reflections on loss, disability, and healing.* New York: Bantam.

Berger, P. L. and Luckmann, T. (1967). *The social construction of reality.* Garden City, NY: Anchor/Doubleday.

Berman, M. (1981). *The re-enchantment of the world.* Ithaca, NY: Cornell University Press.

Bisno, H. (1956). How social will social work be? *Social Work, 1*(2), 12–18.

Bledstein, B. (1978). *The culture of professionalism.* New York: W. W. Norton.

Bond, G. R., Miller, L. D., Krumwied, R. D., and Ward, R. S. Assertive case management in three CMHCs: A controlled study. (1988). *Hospital and Community Psychiatry, 39,* 411–417.

Brandt, A. (1975). *Reality police: The experience of insanity in America*. New York: William Morrow.

Brown, B. and Cain, H. (1964). The many meanings of comprehensive. *American Journal of Orthopsychiatry, 34*(5).

Brown, L. and Levitt, J. (1979). A methodology for problem-system identification. *Social Casework, 60*, 408–415.

Bruner, J. S. (1973). Beyond the information given: Studies in the psychology of knowing. New York: W. W. Norton. Article by P. M. Greenfield and J. S. Bruner, Culture and cognitive growth. Reprinted from D. A. Goslin, ed., *Handbook of socialization theory and research*, 633–654. Chicago: Rand-McNally.

Bruno, F. J. (1957). *Trends in social work 1874–1956*. New York: Columbia University Press.

Buber, M. (1955). *Between man and man*. Boston: Beacon Press.

Burgess, E. (1939). Introduction. In R. Faris and H. W. Dunham, eds., *Mental disorders in urban areas*. Chicago: University of Chicago Press.

Burtt, E. A. (1931). *The metaphysical foundation of modern science*. London: Routledge and Kegan Paul.

Buss, A. R. (1979). *A dialectical psychology*. New York: Irvington Publishers.

Butle, R. N. (1975). *Why survive? Being old in America*. New York: Harper and Row.

Capra, F. (1983). *The turning point*. New York: Bantam Books.

Carkhuff, R. R. (1969). *Helping and human relations* (Vol. 1: Selection and training; Vol. 2: Practice and research). New York: Holt, Rinehart and Winston.

Carkhuff, R. R. and Anthony, W. A. (1979). *The skills of helping: An introduction to counseling*. Amherst, MA: Human Resource Development Press.

Center for Research and Advanced Study. (1982). *Improving protective services for older Americans*. Portland: University of Southern Maine.

Chambers, C. A. (1962). An historical perspective on political action vs. individualized treatment. In *Current issues in social work seen in historical perspective*, pp. 51–64. New York: Council on Social Work Education.

Church, J. (1961). *Language and the discovery of reality*. New York: Random House.

Clark, A. N. G., Mankikar, G. D., and Gray, I. (1975). Diogenes syndrome: A clinical study of gross neglect. *Lancet, 1*, 366–368.

Clark, F. W. and Arkava, M., eds. (1979). *The pursuit of competence in social work*. San Francisco: Jossey-Bass.

Claus, K. E. and Bailey, J. T. (1977). *Power and influence in health care: A new approach to leadership*. St. Louis: C. V. Mosby.

Cole, T. R. (1986). Putting off the old. In D. Van Tassel and P. N. Sterns, eds., *Old age in a bureaucratic society*, pp. 49–65. Westport, CT: Greenwood.

Commission on Social Work Practice, Subcommittee on the Working Definition of Social Work Practice, National Association of Social Workers (April, 1958). Working definition of social work practice. In H. Bartlett, Toward clarification and improvement of social work practice. *Social Work, 3*, 5–9.

Compton, B. and Galaway, B. (1989). *Social work processes* (4th ed.). Chicago: Dorsey Press.

Cornell University Empowerment Group (October, 1989). *Networking Bulletin, 1*(2).

Cousins, N. (1989). *Anatomy of an illness*. New York: W. W. Norton.

——— (1989). *Head first: The biology of hope*. New York: E. P. Dutton.

Davidson, W. and Rapp, C. (1976). Child advocacy in the justice system. *Social Work, 21*(3), 225–232.

Deitchman, W. W. (1980). How many case managers does it take to screw in a light bulb? *Hospital and Community Psychiatry, 31*(11), 788–789.

de Shazer, S., Berg, I. K., Lipchik, E., Nunnally, E., Molnar, A., Gingerich, W., Weiner-Davis, M. (1986). Brief therapy: Focused solution development. *Family Process, 25,* 207–221.

de Shazer, S. (Summer, 1988). A requiem for power. *Contemporary Family Therapy, 10,* 69–76.

Dossey, L. (1989). *Recovering the soul: A scientific and spiritual search.* New York: Bantam Books.

Dowd, J. J. (1984). Mental illness and the aged stranger. In M. Minkler and C. L. Estes, eds., *Readings in the political economy of aging,* pp. 94–113. Farmingdale: Baywood.

Dubos, R. (1965). *Man adapting.* New Haven: Yale University Press.

Dunst, C. J., Trivette, C. M., and Thompson, R. B. (1990). Supporting and strengthening family functioning: Toward a congruence between principles and practice. *Prevention in Human Services, 9,* 19–43.

Egan, G. (1986). *The skilled helper: A systematic approach to effective helping* (3rd ed.). Monterey, CA: Brooks/Cole.

Ellenberger, H. (1970). *The discovery of the unconscious.* New York: Basic Books.

"Elpenor." (October, 1986). A drunkard's progress: AA and the sobering strength of myth. *Harpers, 272,* 42–48.

Emerson, R. M. (1970). Power–dependence relations. In M. E. Olsen, ed., *Power in societies,* pp. 44–53. New York: Macmillan.

Epstein, L. (1988). *Helping people: The task-centered approach* (2nd ed.). Columbus, OH: Merrill.

Etzioni, A. (1970). Power as a societal force. In M. Olsen, ed., *Power in societies.* New York: Macmillan.

Ewalt, P. L. and Honeyfield, R. M. (1981). Needs of persons in long term care. *Social Work, 26,* 223–231.

Fairclough, N. (1989). *Language and power.* New York: Longman.

Faris, R. and Dunham, H. W. (1939). *Mental disorders in urban areas.* Chicago: University of Chicago Press.

Fisher, G., Landis, D., and Clark, K. (1988). Case management service provision and client change. *Community Mental Health Journal, 24,* 124–142.

Flexner, A. (1915). Is social work a profession? *Proceedings of the National Conference on Charities and Corrections,* pp. 576–590. Chicago.

Florin, P. and Wandersman, A., eds. (1990). Citizen participation, voluntary organizations and community development: Insights for empowerment through research. *American Journal of Community Psychology, 18,* 41–54.

Foley, H. and Sharfstein, S. S. (1983). *Madness and government.* Washington, DC: American Psychiatric Press.

Ford, C. V. and Sbordone, R. J. (1980). Attitudes of psychiatrists toward elderly patients. *American Journal of Psychiatry, 137,* 571–575.

Foucault, M. (1980). *Power/knowledge.* New York: Pantheon.

Fox, R. W. (1978). *So are disordered in mind: Insanity in California 1870–1930.* Berkeley: University of California Press.

Franklin, J., Solovitz, B., Mason, M., Clemmons, J., and Mitler, D. (1987). An evaluation of case management. *American Journal of Public Health, 77*(6), 674–678.

French, J. R. P. and Raven, B. (1960). The bases of social power. In D. Cartwright and A. F. Zander, eds., *Group dynamics.* Evanston, IL: Row Patterson.

Friedman, M. (1985). *The healing dialogue in psychotherapy.* Northvale, NJ: Jason Aronson.

Freire, P. (1973). *Pedagogy of the oppressed.* New York: Seabury.

Gallant, R. V., Cohen, C., and Wolff, T. (1985). Change of older persons' image, impact on public policy result from Highland Valley Empowerment Plan. *Perspective on Aging, 14,* 9–13.

Gambrill, E. (1983). *Casework: A competency-based approach*. Englewood Cliffs, NJ: Prentice-Hall.

Garber, J. and Seligman, M. E. P., eds. (1980). *Human helplessness: Theory and applications*. New York: Academic Press.

Garfinkel, H. (1967). *Studies in ethnomethodology*. Englewood Cliffs, NJ: Prentice-Hall.

Gazzaniga, M. S. (1988). *Mind matters*. Boston: Houghton Mifflin.

Geertz, C. (1973). *The interpretation of cultures*. New York: Basic Books.

Gergen, K. (1981). *Towards transformation in social knowledge*. New York: Springer-Verlag.

Gergen, K. J. (1985). The Social Constructionist Movement in modern psychology. *American Psychologist, 40*, 266–275.

Germain, C. B. and Gitterman, A. (1980). *The life model of social work practice*. New York: Columbia University Press.

Giddens, A. (1984). Hermeneutics and social theory. In G. Shapiro and A. Sica, eds., *Hermeneutics: Questions and prospects,* pp. 215–230. Amherst: University of Massachusetts Press. Reprinted from Giddens, A. (1983). *Profiles and critiques*. London: Macmillan.

Girvetz, H., Geiger, G., Hantz, H., and Morris, B. (1966). *Science, folklore and philosophy*. New York: Harper & Row.

Glaser, B. G. (1978). *Theoretical sensitivity: Advances in the methodology of grounded theory*. Mill Valley, CA: The Sociology Press.

Glaser, B. G. and Strauss, A. (1967). *The discovery of grounded theory*. New York: Aldine.

Gleick, J. (1987). *Chaos: Making a new science*. New York: Viking Press.

Goering, P. N., Wasylenki, D. A., Farkas, M., Lancee, W. J., and Ballantyne, R. (1988). What difference does case management make? *Hospital and Community Psychiatry, 39*(3), 272–276.

Goffman, E. (1959). *The presentation of self in everyday life*. Garden City, NY: Anchor/Doubleday.

——— (1961). *Asylums: Essays on the situation of mental patients and other inmates*. Garden City, NY: Anchor/Doubleday.

Goldman, H. H., Adams, H. H., and Taube, C. A. (1983). Deinstitutionalization: The data demythologized. *Hospital and Community Psychiatry, 34*(2), 129–134.

Goldstein, H. (September-October, 1986). Toward the integration of theory and practice: A humanistic approach. *Social Work, 31*, 352–357.

Gordon, C., ed. (1980). *Michel Foucault—Power/knowledge*. New York: Pantheon.

Gordon, W. E. (1969). Basic constructs for an integrative and generative conception of social work. In Gordon Hearn, ed., *The general systems approach: Contributions toward an holistic conception of social work*. New York: Council on Social Work Education.

Gouldner, A. W. (1970). *The coming crisis of Western sociology*. New York: Basic Books.

Gowdy, E. and Rapp, C. A. (1988). *Managerial behavior: The common denominators of successful community based programs*. Unpublished manuscript. Lawrence: University of Kansas, School of Social Welfare.

Gowdy, E., Rapp, C. A., and Poertner, J. (1987). *Managing for performance: Using information to enhance community integration of the chronically mentally ill*. Unpublished manuscript. Lawrence: University of Kansas, School of Social Welfare.

Gratton, B. (1986). The new history of the aged: A critique. In D. Van Tassel and P. N. Sterns, eds., *Old age in a bureaucratic society,* pp. 3–29. Westport, CT: Greenwood.

Greenblatt, M., York, R., and Brown, E. L. (1955). *From custodial to therapeutic patient care in mental hospitals*. New York: Russell Sage Foundation.

Gutride, M. E., Goldstein, G. P., and Hunter, G. F. (1973). The use of modeling and role playing to increase social interaction among social psychiatric patients. *Journal of Consulting and Clinical Psychology, 40*, 408–415.

Haber, C. (1986). Geriatrics: A specialty in search of specialists. In D. Van Tassel and P. N. Sterns, eds., *Old age in a bureaucratic society*, pp. 66–84. Westport, CT: Greenwood.

Hall, E. T. (1981). *Beyond culture*. Garden City, NY: Anchor/Doubleday. Originally published in 1976.

Harding, C. M., Brooks, G. W., Takamaru, A., Strauss, J. S., and Breier, A. (June, 1987a). The Vermont longitudinal study of persons with severe mental illness II: Long-term outcome of subjects who retrospectively met DSM-III criteria for schizophrenia. *American Journal of Psychiatry, 144*(6), 727–735.

Harding, C. M., Zubin, J., and Strauss, J. S. (May, 1987). Chronicity in schizophrenia: Fact, partial fact or artifact? *Hospital and Community Psychiatry, 38*(5), 477–486.

Hashimi, J. (1988). United States elders with chronic mental disorders. In E. Rathbone-McCuan and B. Havens, eds., *North America elders*, pp. 123–138. Westport, CT: Greenwood.

Haworth, G. O. (September, 1984). Social work research, practice, and paradigms. *Social Service Review, 58*, 343–357.

Heineman, M. B. (1981). The obsolete scientific imperative in social work research. *Social Service Review, 55*, 371–397.

Heineman Pieper, M. (1985). The future of social work research. *Social Work Research and Abstracts, 21*(4), 3–11.

——— (November, 1989). The heuristic paradigm: A unifying and comprehensive approach to social work research. *Smith College Studies in Social Work, 60*, 8–33.

Heisenberg, W. (1958). *Physics and philosophy: The revolution in modern science*. New York: Harper & Brothers.

Hepworth, D. and Larsen, J. (1982). *Direct social work practice*. Homewood, IL: Dorsey Press.

——— (1986). *Direct social work practice*. Chicago: Dorsey Press.

——— (1990). *Direct social work practice: Theory and skills* (3rd ed.). Chicago: Dorsey Press.

Hersch, C. (August, 1972). Social history, mental health, and community control. *American Psychologist, 27*, 749–754.

Hickerson, N. P. (1980). *Linguistic anthropology*. New York: Holt, Rinehart and Winston.

Hobbs, N. (1982). *The troubled and troubling child*. San Francisco: Jossey-Bass.

Houts, P. S. and Scott, R. A. (1975). Goal planning in mental health rehabilitation. *Goal Attainment Review, 2*, 33–51.

Husserl, E. (1962). *Ideas: General introduction to pure phenomenology*, W. R. Boyce Gibson, trans. New York: Collier Macmillan. Originally published in 1931.

Illich, I. (1976). *Medical nemesis: The expropriation of health*. New York: Pantheon.

Jacoby, R. (1975). *Social amnesia: A critique of conformist psychology from Adler to Laing*. Boston: Beacon Press.

Jaffe, P. G. and Carlson, P. M. (1976). Relative efficacy of modeling and instructions in eliciting social behavior from chronic psychiatric patients. *Journal of Consulting and Clinical Psychology, 44*, 200–207.

Johnson, J. H. and Sarason, I. G. (1978). Life stress, depression and anxiety: Internal-external control as a moderator variable. *Journal of Psychosomatic Research, 22*, 205–208.

Joint Commission on Mental Health. (1961). *Action for mental health*. New York: Science Editions.

Katz, R. (1984). Empowerment and synergy: Expanding the community's healing resources. In J. Rappaport, C. Swift, and R. Hess, eds., *Studies in empowerment: Steps toward understanding and action*. New York: Haworth Press.

Kieffer, C. H. (1984). Citizen empowerment: A developmental perspective. *Prevention in Human Services, 3*(2/3), 9–36.

——— (1984). Citizen empowerment: A developmental perspective. In J. Rappaport, C. Swift, and R. Hess, eds., *Studies in empowerment: Steps toward understanding and action*. New York: Haworth Press.

Kirk, S. and Kutchins, H. J. (1988). Deliberate misdiagnosis in mental health practice. *Social Service Review, 24,* 225–237.

Kisthardt, W. E. (1990). *The impact of the strengths model of case management from the consumer perspective.* Unpublished doctoral dissertation. Lawrence: University of Kansas School of Social Welfare.

Kisthardt, W. E. and Rapp, C. A. (1989). *Bridging the gap between principles and practice: Implementing a strengths perspective in case management.* Lawrence: University of Kansas School of Social Welfare.

Klein, M. and Kantor, H. (1976). *Prisoners of progress.* New York: Macmillan.

Klerman, G. L. (1977). Better but not well. *Schizophrenia Bulletin, 3,* 617–631.

Knitzer, J. (1982). *Unclaimed children.* Washington, DC: Children's Defense Fund.

Kobasa, S. C. (1979). Stressful life events, personality, and health: An inquiry into hardiness. *Journal of Personality and Social Psychology, 37,* 1–11.

Kohn, A. (November, 1989). Suffer the restless children. *The Atlantic, 264,* 90–100.

Konle, C. (1982). *Social work day-to-day.* New York: Longman.

Kosberg, J. and Harris, A. (1978). Attitudes toward elderly clients. *Health and Social Work, 3,* 68–90.

Kovel, J. (1981). *The age of desire: Reflections of a radical psychoanalyst.* New York: Pantheon.

Kuhn, T. S. (1979). The relations between history and history of science. In P. Rabinow and W. M. Sullivan, eds., *Interpretive social science: A reader,* pp. 267–300. Berkeley: University of California Press. Reprinted from *Daedalus* (1971), *100*(2).

Laing, R. (1971). *Self and others.* New York: Penguin Books.

Lamb, R., ed. (1984). *The homeless mentally ill.* Washington, DC: American Psychiatric Press.

Lamb, R. H. (1980). Therapist-case managers: More than brokers of service. *Hospital and Community Psychiatry, 31*(11), 762–764.

Lee, P. R. (1929). Social work: Cause and function. *Proceedings of the National Conference of Social Work,* pp. 3–20.

Leiby, J. (1978). *A history of social welfare and social work.* New York: Columbia University Press.

Levinson, D. J., Darrow, C. N., Klein, E. B., Levinson, M. H., and McKee, B. (1978). *The seasons of a man's life.* New York: Alfred Knopf.

Liberman, P., Massel, H. K., Mosk, M. D., and Wong, S. E. (1985). Social skills training for chronic mental patients. *Hospital and Community Psychiatry, 36*(4), 396–403.

Lourie, I. S., and Katz-Leavy, J. (1986). *Severely emotionally disturbed children and adolescents (Report).* Washington, DC: National Institute of Mental Health.

Lowry, L. (1985). *Social work with the aging.* New York: Longman.

Magura, S. (1982). Clients view outcomes of child protective services. *Social Casework, 63,* 522–531.

Mahrer, A. R. (1978). *Experiencing: A humanistic theory of psychology and psychiatry.* New York: Brunner/Mazel.

Maluccio, A. (1979). The influence of the agency environment on clinical practice. *Journal of Sociology and Social Welfare, 6,* 734–755.

——— (1979). *Learning from clients: Interpersonal helping as viewed by clients and social workers.* New York: Free Press.

——— (1981). *Promoting competence in clients.* New York: Free Press.

Marks, J. (1987). Services for children returning to school after brief psychiatric hospitalization. *Social Work in Education, 9*(3), 169–179.

Martin, P. Y. (1980). Multiple constituencies, dominant societal values, and human service administrators. *Administration in Social Work, 4,* 15–27.

McClelland, D. (1987). *Human motivation.* Cambridge: Cambridge University Press.

McCracken, G. (1988). *The long interview* (Sage University Paper Series on Qualitative Research Methods, vol. 13). Beverly Hills: Sage.

Minkler, M. (1984). Introduction. In M. Minkler and C. L. Estes, eds., *Readings in the political economy of aging*, pp. 10–22. Farmingdale: Baywood.

Modrcin, M., Rapp, C. A., and Chamberlain, R. (1985). *Case management with psychiatrically disabled individuals: Curriculum and training program*. Unpublished manuscript. Lawrence: University of Kansas, School of Social Welfare.

Modrcin, M., Rapp, C. A., and Poertner, J. (1988). The evaluation of case management services with the chronically mentally ill. *Evaluation and Program Planning, 11*(4).

Morgan, D. (1988). *Focus groups as qualitative research* (Sage University Paper Series on Qualitative Research Methods, vol. 16). Beverly Hills: Sage.

Mumma, E. W. (1989). Reform at the local level: Virginia Beach empowers both clients and workers. *Public Welfare, 47*(2), 15–24.

National Child Welfare Resource Center for Management and Administration. (Summer, 1988). *Training Newsletter, 1*(2).

Navarro, N. (1984). The political economy of government cuts for the elderly. In M. Minkler and C. L. Estes, eds., *Readings in the political economy of the aging*, pp. 37–46. Farmingdale, Baywood.

Norman, L., ed. (1987). *Taking charge: A handbook for parents whose children have emotional handicaps*. Portland, OR: Portland State University.

Ornstein, R. and Sobel, D. (1987). *The healing brain*. New York: Simon and Schuster/Touchstone.

Otto, H. A. and Knight, J. W. (1979). Wholistic healing: Basic principles and concepts. In H. A. Otto and J. W. Knight, eds., *Dimensions in wholistic healing: New frontiers in the treatment of the whole person*, pp. 3–27. Chicago: Nelson-Hall.

Palmer, P. J. (1974). *Action research: A new style of politics in education*. Boston: Institute for Responsive Education.

——— (September–October, 1987). Community, conflict and ways of knowing: Ways to deepen our educational agenda. *Change, 19*, 20–25.

Park, R. (1952). *Human communities*. Glencoe, IL: Free Press.

Peele, S. (1989). *The diseasing of America: Addiction treatment out of control*. Lexington, MA: Lexington/D. C. Heath.

Perlman, H. H. (1957). *Social casework: A problem-solving process*. Chicago: University of Chicago Press.

——— (1979). *Relationship: The heart of helping people*. Chicago: University of Chicago Press.

Petr, C. and Spano, R. (1990). Services for emotionally disturbed children: Historical perspectives and contemporary opportunities for social work. *Social Work, 35*, 228–234.

Pieper, M. (November, 1989). The heuristic paradigm: A unifying and comprehensive approach to social work research. *Smith College Studies in Social Work, 60*, 9–33.

Poertner, J. (1986). The use of client feedback to improve practice: Defining the supervisor's role. *The Clinical Supervisor, 4*, 57–67.

Polansky, N., Borgman, R. D., and DeSaix, C. (1972). *Roots of futility*. San Francisco: Jossey-Bass.

Polansky, N., Chalmers, M., Buttenweiser, E., and Williams, D. (1981). *Damaged parents: An anatomy of child neglect*. Chicago: University of Chicago Press.

Powell, D. R. (March, 1986). Parent education and support programs. *Young Children, 41*, 47–52.

Randall, J. H., Jr. (1926). *The making of the modern mind*. New York: Columbia University Press.

Rapp, C. A. and Chamberlain, R. (September-October, 1985). Case management services for the chronically mentally ill. *Social Work, 30*(5), 417–422.

Rapp, C. A., Gowdy, E., Sullivan, W. P., and Wintersteen, R. (1988). Client outcome reporting: The status method. *Community Mental Health Journal, 24*(2), 118–133.

Rapp, C. A. and Wintersteen, R. (1985). *Case management with the chronically mentally ill: The results of seven replications.* Unpublished monograph. Lawrence: University of Kansas School of Social Welfare.

———— (1986a). *Client outcome monitoring and evaluation systems.* Unpublished manuscript. Lawrence: University of Kansas School of Social Welfare.

———— (1986b). *Case management with the chronically mentally ill: The results of seven replications.* Unpublished manuscript. Lawrence: University of Kansas School of Social Welfare.

———— (July, 1989). The strengths model of case management: Results for twelve demonstrations. *Journal of Psychosocial Rehabilitation, 13*(1), 23–32.

Rappaport, J. (1977). *Community psychology: Values, research, and action.* New York: Holt, Rinehart and Winston.

———— (1981). In praise of paradox: A social policy of empowerment over prevention. *American Journal of Community Psychology, 9,* 1–25.

———— (1985). The power of empowerment language. *Social Policy, 16,* 15–21.

———— (1987). Terms of empowerment/exemplars of prevention: Toward a theory for community psychology. *American Journal of Community Psychology, 15,* 117–148.

———— (1990). Research methods and the empowerment social agenda. In P. Tolan, C. Keys, F. Chertak, and L. Jason, eds., *Researching community psychology.* Washington, DC: American Psychological Association.

Rappaport, J., Seidman, E., Toro, P. A., McFadden, L. S., Reischl, T. M., Roberts, L. J., Salem, D. A., Stein, C. H., and Zimmerman, M. A. (1985). Collaborative research with a mutual help organization. *Social Policy, 15,* 12–24.

Rappaport, J., Swift, C., and Hess, R., eds. (1984). *Studies in empowerment: Steps toward understanding and action.* New York: Haworth Press.

Rathbone-McCuan, E. and Bricker-Jenkins, M. (1989). Self-neglect and adult protective services. In M. Bricker-Jenkins, ed., *Resource handbook assessment,* pp. 297–341. Knoxville: University of Tennessee College of Social Work, Office of Research and Public Service.

Reich, R. and Siegel, S. (1978). The emergence of the Bowery as a psychiatric dumping ground. *Psychiatric Quarterly, 50,* 191–201.

Reissman, F. (1965). The "helper" therapy principle. *Social Work, 10,* 27–32.

Report of the research meeting on community support and rehabilitation service. (May 3–5, 1988). Bethesda, MD: National Institute of Mental Health Community Support Program and National Institute on Disability and Rehabilitation Research.

Reynolds, B. C. (1951). *Social work and social living: Explorations in philosophy and practice.* Silver Spring, MD: National Association of Social Workers.

———— (1964). The social casework of an uncharted journey. *Social Work, 9,* 13–17.

Rhodes, M. (1986). *Ethical dilemmas in social work practice.* Boston: Routledge and Kegan Paul.

Richmond, M. (1917). *Social diagnosis.* New York: Russell Sage Foundation.

———— (1922). *What is social casework?* New York: Russell Sage Foundation.

Rickman, H. P. (1979). *Wilhelm Dilthey: Pioneer of the human studies.* Berkeley: University of California Press.

Ricouer, P. (1966). *Freedom and nature: The voluntary and the involuntary,* E. V. Kohak, trans. Evanston, IL: Northwestern University Press. Originally published in 1950.

Rifkin, J. (1985). *Declaration of a heretic.* London: Routledge & Kegan Paul.

Ripple, L. (1964). *Motivation, capacity and opportunity.* Chicago: University of Chicago Press.

Roberts, L. J. (1989). Giving and receiving help: Behavioral predictors of outcomes for members of a mutual help organization. PhD dissertation. Psychology, University of Illinois, Urbana-Champaign.

Roberts-DeGennaro, M. (1987). Developing case management as a practice model. *Social Casework, 68,* 466–470.

Robinson, V. (1934). *A changing psychology in social casework.* Chapel Hill: University of North Carolina Press.

Romanyshyn, R. D. (1989). *Psychological life: From science to metaphor.* Austin: University of Texas Press.

Rooney, R. (March, 1988). Socialization strategies for involuntary clients. *Social Casework, 69,* 131–140.

Rose, S. (1985). *Advocacy and empowerment: Mental health care in the community.* Boston: Routledge and Kegan Paul.

Rosen, A. (1978). Issues in educating for the knowledge-building research doctorate. *Social Service Review, 52,* 437–448.

Rosenhan, D. L. (January, 1973). On being sane in insane places. *Science, 179,* 250–258.

Rossi, E. L. (1986). *The psychobiology of mind-body healing: New concepts of therapeutic hypnosis.* New York: W. W. Norton.

Rothman, D. (1971). *The discovery of the asylum.* Boston: Little, Brown.

Roszak, T. (1980). The monster and the titan: Science, knowledge, and gnosis. In E. D. Klemke, R. Hollinger, and A. D. Kline, eds., *Introductory readings in the philosophy of science,* pp. 305–322. Buffalo, NY: Prometheus.

Rowles, G. D. and Reinharz, S. (1988). Qualitative gerontology: Themes and challenges. In S. Reinharz and G. D. Rowles, eds., *Qualitative gerontology,* pp. 3–33. New York: Springer.

Ryan, W. (1971). *Blaming the victim.* New York: Vintage Books.

——— (1976). *Blaming the victim* (revised). New York: Vintage Books.

Sacks, O. (1987). *The man who mistook his wife for a hat and other clinical tales.* New York: Harper & Row.

Saleebey, D. (1989). Professions in crisis: The estrangement of knowing and doing. *Social Casework, 70,* 556–563.

——— (in press). Theory and the generation and subversion of knowledge. *Journal of Sociology and Social Welfare.*

Saleebey, D. and Larson, S. (1980). Resource development networks: Theory and practice. Unpublished manuscript. Fort Worth, TX: Bridge Association.

Salem, D. A., Seidman, E., and Rappaport, J. (1988). Community treatment of the mentally ill: The promise of mutual help organizations. *Social Work, 33,* 403–408.

Sampson, E. E. (1983). *Justice and the critique of pure psychology.* New York: Plenum.

Sandler, I. N. and Lakey, B. (1982). Locus of control as a stress moderator: The role of control perceptions and social support. *American Journal of Community Psychology, 10,* 65–80.

Scheff, T. (1966). *Being mentally ill.* Chicago: Aldine.

——— (1984). *Being mentally ill: A sociological theory* (2nd ed.). New York: Aldine.

Schön, D. A. (1983). *The reflective practitioner.* New York: Basic Books.

Schutz, A. (1967). *The phenomenology of the social world,* G. Walsh and F. Lehnert, trans. Evanston, IL: Northwestern University Press.

Schwartz, S. R., Goldman, H. H., and Churgin, S. (1982). Case management for the chronically mentally ill: Models and dimensions. *Hospital and Community Psychiatry, 33*(12), 1006–1009.

Schwartz, W. (1971). On the use of groups in social work practice. In W. Schwartz and S. Zalba, eds., *The practice of group work.* New York: Columbia University Press.

Scott, B. and Miller, H. (1971). *Problems and issues in social casework.* New York: Columbia University Press.

Seamon, D. (1979). *A geography of the lifeworld*. London: Croom Helm.

———— (1982). The phenomenological contribution to environmental psychology. *Journal of Environmental Psychology, 2*, 119–140.

Seamon, D. and Mugerauer, R. (1985). Dwelling, place and environment: An introduction. In D. Seamon and R. Mugerauer, eds., *Dwelling place and environment: Towards a phenomenology of person and world*, pp. 1–12. The Hague: Martinus Nijhoff.

Segal, S., Baumohl, J., and Johnson, E. (1977). Falling through the cracks: Mental disorder and social margin in a young vagrant population. *Social Problems, 24*, 387–400.

Shore, J. H. (1983). The epidemiology of chronic mental illness. In D. Cutler, ed., *Effective aftercare for the 1980s*, pp. 5–12. San Francisco: Jossey-Bass.

Singer, H. D. (1939). Forward. In R. Faris and H. W. Dunham, eds., *Mental disorders in urban areas*. Chicago: University of Chicago Press.

Smalley, R. (1965). *Theory for social work*. New York: Columbia University Press.

———— (1967). *Theory for social work practice*. New York: Columbia University Press.

Spiegelberg, H. (1982). *The phenomenological movement: A historical introduction* (3rd ed.). The Hague: Martinus Nijhoff.

Stein, L. I. and Test, M. (1980). Alternatives to mental hospital treatment. *Archives of General Psychiatry, 37*, 392–397.

Strauss, A. L. (1986). *Qualitative analysis*. Cambridge, England: Cambridge University Press.

Strauss, J. S., Downey, T. W., and Sledge, W. H. (1979). Intensive psychiatric care for adolescents and young adults. *Hospital and Community Psychiatry, 30*(2), 122–125.

Sutherland, J. W. (Spring, 1974). Attacking organizational complexity. *Fields Within Fields, 11*, 52–65.

Swift, C. (1984). Empowerment: An antidote for folly. In J. Rappaport, C. Swift, and R. Hess, eds., *Studies in empowerment: Steps toward understanding and action*. New York: Haworth Press.

Szasz, T. B. (1970). *The manufacture of madness*. New York: Harper & Row.

———— (1978). *The myth of psychotherapy*. Garden City, NY: Anchor/Doubleday.

Taber, M. (1987). A theory of accountability for human service and the implications for program design. *Administration in Social Work, 11*(3/4), 115–126.

Talbott, J., ed. (1981). *The chronic mentally ill*. New York: Human Services Press.

———— (March, 1984). Commentary. *Hospital and Community Psychiatry, 35*, 209.

Taylor, S. J. and Bogdan, R. (1984). *Introduction to qualitative research methods: The search for meanings* (2nd ed.). New York: John Wiley & Sons.

Teare, R. J. (1979). A task analysis of public welfare and educational implications. In F. W. Clark and M. L. Arkava, eds., *The pursuit of competence in social work*, pp. 131–145. San Francisco: Jossey-Bass.

———— (1981). *Social work practice in a public welfare setting: An empirical analysis*. New York: Praeger.

Thoits, P. A. (1985). Self-labeling processes in mental illness: The role of emotional deviance. *American Journal of Sociology, 91*, 221–249.

Treffert, D. (1985). The obviously ill patient in need of treatment: A fourth standard for civil commitment. *Hospital and Community Psychiatry, 36*, 259–267.

Turner, J. E. and Shifren, I. (1979). Community support system: How comprehensive? *New Directions for Mental Health Services, 2*, 1–13.

Turner, J. E. and Ten Hoor, W. J. (1978). The NIMH community support program: Pilot approach to a needed social reform. *Schizophrenia Bulletin, 4*(3), 319–348.

U.S. Department of Education. (1986). Program update—case management. *Update, 2*(2), 10–12.

Vaillant, G. (1977). *Adaptation to life*. Boston: Little, Brown.

van Uchelen, C. (1989). *Healing and cognitive control in cross-cultural perspective*. Champaign: University of Illinois. Paper presented at the second Biennial Community Psychology Research and Action Conference, East Lansing, MI.

Walsh, J. A. (May, 1987). Burnout and values in the social service profession. *Social Casework, 68,* 279–283.

Walzer, M. (1983). *Spheres of justice.* New York: Basic Books.

Watzlawick, P., Weakland, J., and Fisch, R. (1974). *Change: Principles of problem formation and problem resolution.* New York: W. W. Norton.

Weick, A. (March, 1983). A growth-task model of human development. *Social Casework, 64*(3).

——— (November-December, 1983). Issues in overturning a medical model of social work practice. *Social Work, 28,* 467–471.

——— (November, 1986). The philosophical context of a health model for social work. *Social Casework, 67,* 551–559.

——— (1987). Reconceptualizing the philosophical perspective of social work. *Social Service Review, 61,* 218–230.

Weick, A., Rapp, C., Sullivan, W. P., and Kisthardt, S. (July, 1989). A strengths perspective for social work practice. *Social Work, 34,* 350–354.

Wheeler, J. (1973). Cited in J. Mehra, ed., *The physicists' conception of nature,* p. 244. Holland: D. Reidel.

White, R. W. (1963). *Ego and reality in psychoanalytic theory.* New York: International Universities Press.

Wicker, A. W. (1979). *An introduction to ecological psychology.* Monterey, CA: Brooks/Cole.

——— (1985). Strategies for expanding conceptual frameworks. *American Psychologist, 40,* 1094–1103.

Wirth, L. (1964). *On cities and social life.* Selected papers edited by A. Reiss. Chicago: University of Chicago Press.

Wright, B. and Fletcher, B. (April, 1982). Uncovering hidden resources: A challenge in assessment. *Professional Psychology, 13,* 229–235.

Zimmerman, M. A. (1990a). Toward a theory of learned hopefulness: A structure model analysis of participation and empowerment. *Journal of Research in Personality, 24,* 71–86.

——— (1990b). Taking aim on empowerment research: On the distinction between individual and psychological conceptions. *American Journal of Community Psychology, 18,* 169–177.

Zimmerman, M. A. and Rappaport, J. (1988). Citizen participation, perceived control, and psychological empowerment. *American Journal of Community Psychology, 16,* 725–750.

Zimmerman, M. A., Reischl, T. M., Rappaport, J., Seidman, E., Toro, P. A., and Salem, D. A. (1991). Expansion strategies of a mutual help organization. *American Journal of Community Psychology, 19,* 251–278.

Index